Has Political Correctness Gone Mad?

Has Political Correctness Gone Mad?

Interrogating a Right-wing Conspiracy Theory

Tony McKenna

BLOOMSBURY ACADEMIC
LONDON • NEW YORK • OXFORD • NEW DELHI • SYDNEY

BLOOMSBURY ACADEMIC
Bloomsbury Publishing Plc
50 Bedford Square, London, WC1B 3DP, UK
1385 Broadway, New York, NY 10018, USA
29 Earlsfort Terrace, Dublin 2, Ireland

BLOOMSBURY, BLOOMSBURY ACADEMIC and the Diana logo are
trademarks of Bloomsbury Publishing Plc

First published in Great Britain 2024

Copyright © Tony McKenna, 2024

Tony McKenna has asserted her right under the Copyright,
Designs and Patents Act, 1988, to be identified as Author of this work.

Cover design: Ben Anslow

Bloomsbury Publishing Plc does not have any control over, or responsibility for,
any third-party websites referred to or in this book. All internet addresses given
in this book were correct at the time of going to press. The author and publisher
regret any inconvenience caused if addresses have changed or sites have ceased
to exist, but can accept no responsibility for any such changes.

A catalogue record for this book is available from the British Library.

A catalog record for this book is available from the Library of Congress.

ISBN: HB: 978-1-3504-2956-7
          PB: 978-1-3504-2957-4
        ePDF: 978-1-3504-2958-1
       eBook: 978-1-3504-2959-8

Typeset by Integra Software Services Pvt. Ltd.
Printed and bound in Great Britain

To find out more about our authors and books visit www.bloomsbury.com
and sign up for our newsletters.

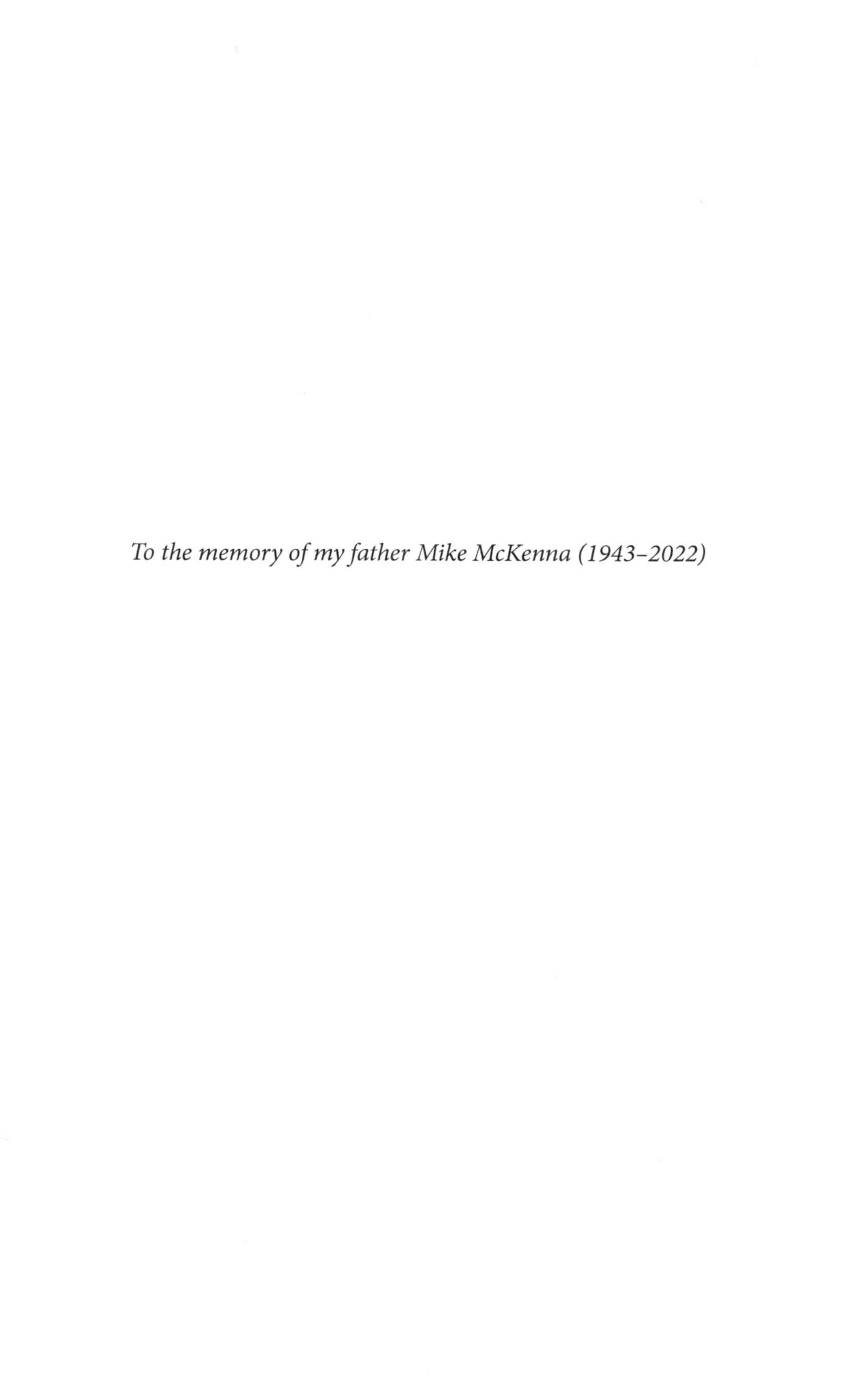

To the memory of my father Mike McKenna (1943–2022)

Contents

1

Muslims murdering Christmas

Cultural coverage

In the run-up to Christmas 2008, one story began to garner a great deal of coverage in the media. It involved a small and unassuming primary school – that happened to be in Nottingham – but could just as easily have been the one round the corner from you, the place where your children or grandchildren go. A quaint school but a rather ordinary one, a place as familiar to the residents of the area as the local fish-and-chip shop, the park or the old pub down the lane. For all intents and purposes Greenwood School was a bastion of normality, and it did all the things you might expect it to do. Lessons were lively, but playtimes livelier still, the children went on school trips once in a while, and every year they put on a nativity play for their stressed teachers and smiley-eyed parents.

But behind the facade of normality and quaintness, something was beginning to stir. There was a group within the school who did not have its best interests at heart. Rather they aimed to subvert its values and impose their own strange and sinister ethos. The core of what the school stood for was being undermined from within, and in 2008, such subversion reached a head. The school was forced to cancel its Christmas nativity play so as to placate that element which was more and more exerting its influence, suppressing an event both traditional and beloved by pushing its own mirthless agenda. The school was forced to cancel the nativity play in order to pacify a Muslim element that was hostile to any Christmas celebrations, and wished to prioritize its own festival of Eid. *Or at least – that's how the story went!*

In the press furore which followed, this would be described as an example of 'the way "political correctness" is transforming British education',[1] – reports of 'infuriated parents', watching powerless, as the play was cancelled in order 'to make way for the Muslim festival of Eid' were rife.[2] Outside the mainstream, far-right groups also picked up the story, bringing the invective to its bitter climax with the flaming 'j'accuse' they hurled at a school that 'cancels Christmas to make way for Islam'.[3]

And yet, the official narrative – shared by much of the mainstream media and the far right – wasn't as clear-cut as it seemed. When looking into the case in more detail, several aspects emerge that contradict the ideological picture of 'political correctness' and sinister subversion the press had painted. It was true that the school had a sizable constituent of Muslim students and that, as one might expect, these were keen on celebrating Eid. But none of the parents or the students had brought to bear any kind of pressure on the school to favour that celebration over Christmas. In fact, the reason the school had stopped the production of the play was because they felt – due to the large number of Muslim students who would be staying home during Eid – the numbers available to perform would be hampered: 'This is due to the Eid celebrations that take place next week and its effect on our performers.'[4] In other words, the decision to stop the play was a result of logistics rather than lobbying. In addition, the information soon emerged that the play had not been cancelled indefinitely but merely postponed for a later date.

These details tended to get lost amidst the furore and the indignance of the media conflagration, but they are vitally important. They show how, in this case, there was no appetite on the part of the Muslim community in the area to impose their own religious agenda on the school – it just didn't exist. Concomitantly, there was no 'politically correct' element in the school's governing bureaucracy which had succumbed to such pressure. These things were simply chimeras in a fantasy narrative that was being made to accord to a very particular vision of society; one in which religious fanatics of a darker hue – in terms of both skin colour and motivation – could be counterposed to 'wholesome', 'British' (read white) children; that the 'traditions' and 'culture' of the latter were being sabotaged by the former; that a group of liberal and painfully naive 'politically-correct' worthies, high up in the school administration, were facilitating such a process in and through their own woolly notions of multiculturalism. This was the narrative the papers were determined to carry, even at the expense of the facts.

Indeed children seem to be a particular focal point of these kinds of stories. Two years after the Christmas story, another hue-and-cry arose, this time centred on a child's toy set. The narrative followed the same essential plotline: children had, since time immemorial, enjoyed playing with toy animals, and this particular set featured those animals living together on a farm. Cow, horse, donkey, hen – everything was in place as it should be when ... shock, horror ... one eagle-eyed mum noticed the set was missing a pig. Again, the organs of the right-wing press honed in on this: it was relayed in shrieking, scandalized tones how 'Early Learning Centre bans toy pig from farmyard set for fear of offending Muslims',[5] while horrified parents decried the spectacle of 'political correctness gone loopy'.[6] Along with the sense of scandalized shock, the invocation of a set of 'politically correct' middle managers prepared to actively threaten the traditional joys of a hallowed English childhood with their bureaucratic dictates provided the fundamental ideological motif. But once again, however, it wasn't as clear-cut as it was presented.

In this case it was true that the makers of the toy set had removed the pig partly in deference to the sensibilities of Jewish and Muslim families. Specifically, however, the decision to do this was a result of the fact that the company was operating on an international scale; that is, it was selling to a number of countries with majority Muslim or Jewish populations. The removal of the pig hadn't been achieved by some kind of 'Muslim lobbying group' in combination with 'politically correct' liberals back in the UK. In fact, the decision had nothing to do with the UK whatsoever – as the makers of the toy-set would go on to state: 'The decision to remove the pig from our Goosefeather Farm set was taken in reaction to customer feedback in some parts of the world'.[7] The company had removed the pig because it believed that so doing would stimulate customer demand on an international scale in accordance with customer preference. The company had not bothered to consider each country on a case-by-case basis, an approach which surely would have proved more costly and time-consuming for the company itself.

But it hadn't anticipated the outraged honking from those British parents who had decided that the removal of the pig was nothing short of a sinister attempt to ruin their offspring's childhood all in the name of a totalitarian multiculturalism. When the company became aware of the controversy, the pig was at once reinstated. By which point, however, the journalistic furore had served its purpose: another piece of the puzzle had fallen into place, another fragment of a much bigger ideological picture – one in which a Muslim minority could be shown to be shaping the cultural and political landscape of the UK subversively and from behind-the-scenes.

The crucible of children's education is a particular favourite for the conspiracy theorists of 'political correctness gone mad', because, so the suggestion goes, not only is the Muslim element able to phase out the traditions and heritage of truly 'British' (read 'white' again) students, but also it is able to replace these aspects with its own cultural enforcements. So, for example, *The Daily Mail* decried the fact of a new syllabus in British schools, averring that it would 'make every lesson politically correct'.[8] What did 'political correctness' consist of in this case? To the same paper's slack-jawed sense of astonishment and horror, it involved teaching '[i]n maths and science, key Muslim contributions such as algebra and the number zero' and studying 'experiences of migration – such as Zadie Smith's novel *White Teeth*, or *Brick Lane*, by Monica Ali'.

Of course, if you begin from fundamentally racist assumptions, as these commentators often do; if you begin from the notion that 'Britishness' corresponds to a narrow ethnicity expressed in a specific set of racial and religious terms (white, protestant) then, *ipso facto*, the endeavour of any curriculum to encompass experiences and peoples which extend beyond those rigid parameters must inevitably read as in some way undermining an 'authentic' sense of Britishness. Black children, Asian children, children of first-generation immigrants, Muslims, and whoever else, of necessity, appear as threats to an authentic Britishness in this kind of narrative; in the words of the ex-Tory MP Douglas Carswell – writing on the new curriculum in question – schools very quickly come to resemble 'vehicles for multicultural propaganda and classrooms turned into "laboratories" for politically-correct thought'.[9]

But for those teachers working on the ground, and who are not employing some pre-ordained and fetishized notion of white-Britishness, there is nothing strange or sinister about examining experiences of immigration (for instance) in the classroom. Not just because immigration is such a part and parcel of a modern world whose social forms are perpetually in flux; a situation where more of us than ever before will relocate in our lifetimes – passing through the barriers of city, state or country in order to respond to new opportunities or escape desperate circumstances. Not just because the experience of immigration speaks directly to the lives of a good number of the pupils in the class, especially if they are the children of first-generation immigrants.

But beyond the practical concerns which any teacher must take into account in order to mediate the lives of the students with the content of the curriculum, there is a more general consideration of the nature of knowledge to be had. Why not teach Zadie Smith alongside William Shakespeare? The novelist Nicole Krauss once described an ideal childhood as being that 'where everything was discovered, and everything was possible'.[10] A lofty ideal and something unrealizable in reality perhaps – and yet something worth aspiring to, for it does speak to one of the fundamental characteristics – perhaps the most fundamental – of childhood itself, that is, that of curiosity. The thrill of entering into the broader world. The excitement of discovery for discovery's sake.

And it seems to me that it is not those who teach a curriculum that is chock-full of the colourful and diverse experiences the modern world provides who are problematic. Rather it is those dull, dismal hacks – mostly middle-aged white men with rather red faces – who fill column after column arguing against the expansion of knowledge and experience in the classroom in favour of some cauterized conception of 'Britishness' that acts as a barrier to curiosity. It seems to me it is *these people* who are sinister, endeavouring to straightjacket children in accordance with some narrow template of ethnicity in the way they seek to do.

But, if the anti-political correctness brigade provides us with a version of Islam which is constantly undermining the cultural and educational lives of our children, destroying 'British identity' in the process, the same people are often prepared to go further. Islam, they aver, represents a serious threat to the physical well-being of children as well. A well-worn narrative follows the same depressing lines. Asian Muslims, often Pakistanis, form gangs which target vulnerable white girls in particular, grooming them for sexual exploitation. In Rotherham and Rochdale, both in northern England, hundreds of such cases were recorded, the crimes being committed by a disproportionately large number of Asian men. And this quickly became a flashpoint for anti-Islamic sentiment.

In an article in *The Sun* newspaper, the Labour MP for Rotherham, Sarah Champion, wrote with typical anti-PC bluster: 'Britain has a problem with British Pakistani men raping and exploiting white girls. There. I said it. Does that make me a racist? Or am I just prepared to call out this horrifying problem for what it is?'[11] Across the pond, an article was published in *Forbes* magazine by one of the leading 'respectable' Islamophobes and cod-philosopher *par excellence* Roger Scruton who described how 'the gangs are for the most part Asian young men who see English society not as the community to which they belong, but as a sexual hunting ground',[12] before adding, 'Pakistani Muslims are more likely than indigenous Englishmen to commit sexual crimes.'[13]

Here the same caveats are in place: firstly, Islam is depicted as antithetical to traditional 'Britishness' or British society – 'not as the community to which they belong'. Once this has been established, once 'Islam' has been demarcated as something 'other', we then come to realize that the offences in question are generated by this 'otherness'. These men's identity as 'Islamic' becomes key to the crimes they go on to commit – 'Pakistani Muslims are more likely than indigenous Englishmen to commit sexual crimes.'[14] Finally, the same question is posed and answered. How were such awful attacks on children allowed to go on for so long unchecked? The answer is 'political correctness'. '[P]olice forces lean over backwards to avoid the accusation of racism, while social workers will hesitate to intervene in any case in which they could be accused of discriminating against ethnic minorities. Matters are made worse by the rise of militant Islam, which has added to the old crime of racism the new crime of "Islamophobia".'[15]

In erecting this particular ideological edifice, Scruton has only succeeded in building a house of cards. A 2012 report for the children's commissioner found that of some 1,514 grooming-gang perpetrators, some 545 were white, 415 were Asian and 244 were Black, with the ethnicity of 21 per cent of the perpetrators not actually accounted for.[16] Superficially, this would seem to support Scruton's claims; the Asian tally registers as a little more than a quarter of the offenders, whereas Asians themselves only form around 7 per cent of the UK's overall population. But, at once, the situation becomes more complex. Only thirty-five of the 415 Asians reported here were recorded as being of Pakistani origin while five came from a Bangladeshi background. In other words, the correlation between race and religion which Scruton postulates – 'Pakistani Muslims are more likely … to commit sexual crimes' – at once begins to break down, because the majority of these suspects – while Asian – were unlikely to have been Muslim.

Of course, if you proceed from essentially racist premises you remain, of necessity, oblivious to these kinds of qualifications – the distinctions between nationality, ethnicity and religion – for you sense on a more protean and emotive level that you are dealing with a singular entity with malevolent and monolithic intentions; that you are on the verge of being overwhelmed by a homogeneous, hive-like mass, a 'Muslim horde'. A synonym for racism has always been the word 'discrimination' and yet, ironically, it is the *inability* to discriminate which informs the racist mindset whereby the real differences between a set of diverse individuals are obliterated and subsumed under the single abstract and inflammatory category – be it 'the yellow peril', to quote the Victorian imperialists of yesteryear, or the immigrant 'invasion' which a more recent bigot[17] used to describe those arriving to his country from Latin America. As the late Christopher Hitchens would note, 'a racist is a racist precisely because he can't distinguish'.[18]

More important still – and this is relevant to the spate of cases in Rochdale and Rotherham – there are more credible reasons than race to account for the higher proportion of Asian perpetrators in these instances. A senior police source suggests that '[i]t is better to focus on the professions of offenders, not their race or religion' and in these cases 'vulnerable girls migrate to the night-time economy, where they come across taxi drivers and people working in takeaways, who are more likely to be Asian'.[19] In other words, these neglected children were drifting into a night-time *demi-monde* in which the adults they encountered were more likely to be Asian men because of the way the division of labour had come to be structured in those places at that period of time.

Most tellingly of all, however, studies have shown that, in the UK, cases of victims of sex abuse in all age groups (including children) 'a large majority of those convicted of sexual offences … are white'.[20] In addition, the most recent report on child grooming gangs – a report commissioned by the Home Office which covered England, Scotland and Wales – revealed that '[t]he majority of child sexual abuse gangs are made up of white men under the age of 30'.[21] These facts are unlikely to deter dyed-in-the-wool racists and Islamophobes precisely because they don't deal in facts but in feelings. More than this, however, the mechanisms of the media which relay the information are themselves problematic. It isn't as though white paedophiles are never featured in their pages – for of course they are. When the Jimmy Savile story finally broke (having been suppressed for some years) the coverage of the extraordinary extent and duration of his crimes was splashed over every major newspaper, and shown on all the main TV stations.

But the issue is not that white paedophiles are never revealed in the press; more specifically, it is that their 'whiteness' as an ethnicity is not seen as a corollary of the crimes they have committed. Jimmy Savile was a white Roman-Catholic, but none of the newspapers led with the headline 'White Roman Catholic man Jimmy Savile commits multiple offences against …' Even when we take something as vast and systematic as the large numbers of Catholic priests implicated in child abuse scandals and the subsequent cover-ups on the part of the higher echelons of the Church itself – few people were tempted to argue that there was something inherent to the nature of Christianity which predisposed worshipers to commit this type of crime. The Church was seen as self-interested and corrupt, for sure; the priests who had committed these atrocities were considered to be the appalling and gruesome predators they were – but no one thought of generalizing such characteristics to the broader religious or racial group.

All of which leads us to the final element in the puzzle; that of 'political correctness'. Having 'established' that 'Muslims' or 'Muslim-Pakistanis' or some riff on the same racist theme – are more inclined to hurt children, commentators like Scruton insist that the true, authentic indigenous (white) community cannot be protected from these alien and external predators because the forces of the state have themselves been emasculated by 'political correctness'.

'In Rotherham', Scruton wrote, 'a social worker would be mad, and a police officer barely less so, to set out to investigate cases of suspected sexual abuse, when the perpetrators are Asian Muslims and the victims ethnically English. Best to sweep it under the carpet'.[22] Indeed those investigating these cases have made repeated nods to their own fear of being branded 'politically incorrect' as when a senior police officer told a victim's father that his daughter had not received protection or justice because the police were so afraid of increasing 'racial tensions'.[23] Even the Prime Minister at the time, Theresa May, blamed 'institutionalized political correctness'[24] for the fact that the police had chosen to turn a blind eye to the abuse of children in Rotherham on a mass scale.

'Political correctness', then, becomes not only the means by which a fundamentally racist vision is facilitated, but it also becomes a crucial alibi for the failures of the police and state more broadly. It helps overlay a more fundamental and insidious problem: that is, the number of men who are successfully prosecuted for rape is incredibly low; indeed a recent report which covered England and Wales suggested that 'the alleged perpetrators of more than 98 per cent of rapes reported to the police are allowed to go free'.[25] On top of this, the girls in Rotherham were, in the main, from the poorest and most deprived backgrounds; they were working-class children, and this had a powerful bearing on the way the authorities were inclined to treat them. When one looks into this in any detail, a sad and harrowing picture emerges: the very people who were tasked with guarding the childhoods of these girls were the same people who were inclined to see them as 'prostitutes',[26] 'rubbish'[27] and 'undesirables'[28] alongside numerous other charming epithets police officials and local counsellors chose to bestow. The police told one desperate mother that what was happening to her daughter was the result of a 'lifestyle choice',[29] a 'lifestyle choice' on the part of a vulnerable twelve-year-old child who was being trafficked and raped by multiple men. In an extensive and independent report into the Rotherham abuse scandal delivered by Professor Alexis Jay, it was confirmed that the police simply hadn't bothered to prioritize child sex abuse and indeed regarded many of the victims of it 'with contempt'[30] while failing to act on their allegations.

Were there any members of the police or the social services who were reluctant to act because they were fearful of heightening racial tensions or because they were frightened of looking 'politically incorrect'? It would be difficult to claim that no one whatsoever was motivated by these types of concerns. But the most effective lies, of necessity, always contain a sliver of truth. The more pertinent point is that the neglect shown towards these children by the authorities was not shaped *fundamentally* by a deference to 'politically correct' attitudes and a sensitivity to the racial aspects of the cases.

It was shaped by a society in which social services are overstretched and underfunded, where teachers are underpaid in classrooms which are oversubscribed, keeping the kind of hours that are conducive to stress and bleary-eyed exhaustion. The type of society where the parents of working-class children are often working all hours, with two or more jobs, the type of society where, inevitably, the poorest children fall through the gaps, disappearing into the night. Such vulnerability is then enforced by the attitude of many of the police and council employees, an attitude which is underpinned by misogyny and class contempt, and which allows working-class girls not to be seen as children at all, but to be perceived as devious, knowing, manipulative and fundamentally adult in their intentions. In this way, their childhood is stolen from them for a second time; not only by the men who have abused and raped them, but by a world which refuses to acknowledge that childhood in the first place.

The ideological framework of 'political correctness' vanquishes all this. It allows the themes of class and gender prejudice to recede into the background, to allow the responsibility for what happened to these children to fall squarely on the shoulders of the 'politically correct worthies' who 'prevented' a police force and social services from acting in good faith and working on behalf of the victims. Not for the first time do we see how the sinister and fantastical depiction of a society that is run according to the totalitarian determinations of a 'politically correct liberal elite' not only helps bolster racist claims about oppressed minorities such as Muslims, but also absolves actually existing power – both of its responsibilities and its crimes.

The press stories examined thus far run the gamut from the absurd (banning of toy pig) to the horrific (physical and sexual abuse of children) but they all share a single thread: the suggestion that 'British' politics, 'British' culture and 'British' lives are being inexorably swamped by the force and flow of an alien contagion – that of 'Islam'. The final set of press stories I want to look at represents the culmination of the concept of the Muslim 'outsider' driven to its logical and most extreme conclusions; that is, not simply content with infiltrating 'our' political system, 'our' media, 'our' laws, 'our' schools and 'our' supermarkets and restaurants (through the imposition of Halal only products) – the Muslim horde is now conquering in a militaristic fashion large swathes of the physical geography of the country itself.

In a 2018 YouGov survey of over 10,000 British respondents, almost a third of people believed there are large pockets within England – so-called 'no-go zones' – where white people cannot venture, and that these places are Muslim-only, run according to the dictates of Sharia law.[31] That a large number of people are susceptible to these kinds of beliefs is not surprising, precisely because of the tenor and content of the articles that have been pumped out on an industrial scale by the mainstream press for the best part of the previous two decades. All that fear, ignorance and race-hate were eventually condensed and concentrated in the beleaguered fantasy of a war-torn landscape, large parts of which were now seen to have fallen to the foreign invaders.

In 2011 *The Daily Mail* quoted favourably a senior politician Baroness Cox who said 'the Muslim population has grown, and the state-sponsored creed of multiculturalism has become ever more powerful, so Sharia law has strengthened its grip on our society' in an article whose headline warned: 'As Islamic extremists declare Britain's first Sharia law zone, the worrying social and moral implications.'[32] In the years that followed, other headlines were run with the same motif; prominent mainstream journalists such as Melanie Phillips bewailed 'the threatening implications of self-declared "Muslim areas" … [which] … are spreading into the heart of our democracy' while the capital city itself was rebranded as 'Londonistan'.[33]

The blogosphere was flooded with maps that purported to show areas Muslims had colonized and which excluded white-British people. In London, the boroughs of Tower Hamlets, Newham and Waltham Forest were particular favourites for this treatment, but even though they are home to some of the highest numbers of Muslim residents in the country, the three boroughs combined still contained an overarching majority (70 per cent) of non-Muslims.[34] And on Fox News, an American commentator on terrorism declared of the UK that '[t]here are actually cities like Birmingham that are totally Muslim, where non-Muslims just simply don't go in,'[35] apparently oblivious to the existence of the 250,000 non-Muslims who happened to reside in Birmingham in 2015, the year in which he made those comments.

Political representation

Such claims are the ultimate excrescence of a racist logic amped up to the point where it starts to demonstrate all the signs of fevered paranoia, and yet the same claims are easily debunked by reference to the clear and obvious facts. But beyond the facts of the actual examples highlighted here, there is a more general means to gauge the validity or non-validity of the 'Muslim horde' thesis. Such a thesis is underpinned by the assumption that the increasing power of Muslims – buttressed by a 'politically correct liberal elite' – is more and more able to reshape the political and cultural landscape of the UK (or France, or the United States etc.) in its own image. In line with this, one would anticipate a higher number of Muslims being boosted into the corridors of power, the upper echelons of the state, the highest positions in the civil service and private enterprise – courtesy of their 'politically-correct' allies. So how many Muslim politicians are active in UK politics for instance?

In 2019, eighteen Muslims were elected to serve in the English Parliament and this was an all-time high, a number which formed 8 per cent of the overall pool of MPs serving in parliament. And yet, this figure would need to have been doubled in order to be brought into line with the Muslim population of the country as a whole.[36] So, in terms of numbers, Muslims are underrepresented in parliament; the presence of Muslims in the higher echelons of politics reflecting around half the level you would expect to see, given the number of Muslims in the population more broadly.

In terms of the specific parties themselves, it is estimated that the Labour Party is home to around 21,100 Muslim members.[37] Based on a recent statistic from 2020, the Labour Party itself has 495,961 members,[38] which means the proportion of Muslims in that overall number is approximately 4.3 per cent.

A 2018 governmental survey estimated the population of Muslims in the UK to be 3,372,966 out of an overall population of 65,288,422,[39] meaning Muslims formed 5.2 per cent of the population that year. This shows us that the percentage of Muslims as members of the Labour Party is significantly (almost a fifth) less than the percentage of Muslims in relation to the general population. Again, the same inevitable conclusion: Muslims are considerably underrepresented, politically speaking.

In addition, a recent and extensive survey found that more than one in four Muslim members of the Labour Party had experienced Islamophobia within the party, often being branded in terms of the stereotypes of 'grooming gang' members, 'terrorists' and 'foreigners' who were machinating 'planned takeovers',[40] while in the same moment 48 per cent of those Muslim members interviewed believed that the party didn't take the issue of Islamophobia seriously, and almost half had no faith that complaints of anti-Islamic racism would be dealt with effectively.

When we turn to the Conservative Party the situation is even starker. In 2019, a research project revealed that a whopping 97 per cent of the Conservative Party membership is white,[41] whereas the overall 'white count' in the UK population for that year was 86 per cent. From all accounts, the Conservative Party provides a toxic environment for Muslims. In 2019, one of the tiny minority of Muslims who managed to attain a high-profile position in the Conservative Party, Baroness Warsi, described the party as being 'institutionally racist' and went on to say she could not 'hand on heart tell young Muslims that this party is a welcoming place for them, and that they will have equal worth and equal value here'.[42]

On top of which almost half of all Conservative Party members believe – according to a 2020 survey – that Islam itself represents 'a threat to the British way of life'.[43] This might go some way to explaining the 300 individuals including '16 MPs, one MEP, nine Prospective Parliamentary Candidates, 103 councillors, former councillors and former mayors, 183 party members and five advisers to the Conservative Party or Government' who had exhibited Islamophobic behaviours, including describing Muslims 'as brutes who beat, kill and maim young women' or calling 'for Muslims to be thrown from bridges'.[44] But as shocking as all this is, perhaps it is not so surprising, especially when one considers that the leader of that same party at the time – the ex-Prime Minister Boris Johnson – is himself a notorious Islamophobe renowned for his off-the-cuff slurs including, in 2018, comparing veiled Muslim women to 'letterboxes'; a comment that, incidentally, precipitated a spike in Islamophobic hate crime of some 375 per cent in the week that followed.[45]

When we examine the objective evidence, it is apparent that Muslims as an ethnic group are marginalized in the political arena, and the possibilities available to them are significantly reduced and curtailed due to prejudice, lack of representation and the fact of being from a more impoverished social group. But explanations of society being run according to the logic of 'political correctness gone mad' – are able to generate the topsy-turvy image of an inverted world: those who are underrepresented politically, those who suffer intense forms of discrimination and find themselves alienated from the corridors of political power – are now recast, reimagined and re-presented as the prime movers of political strategy, the shadowy and subversive puppet-masters who are pulling the strings behind-the-scenes.

Those who believe that the political process has been hijacked by 'political correctness' and the creeping shadow of Islam seem immune to each and every fact, and tend to exhibit the bunker mentality of conspiracy theorists more generally: *they know what they know*, and any counterevidence or factual refutation of their position is itself the work of a 'politically correct' intellectual elite which, lacking in common sense, is blind to what is really going on behind the curtain.

Of course, this inveigles them in deeper and deeper contradictions. One of the favoured claims of those who argue that society is run on the basis of a 'politically correct' elite who force their perspective on everyone else – is this results in a loss of free speech. We've all heard this kind of line. Apparently, there are just certain things you can't say anymore. Venture a negative opinion of the behaviour of a minority person or a minority group, offer up a hesitant criticism of the prevailing 'PC orthodoxy', share any of your concerns about the Black Lives Matter movement, or your horror at a suicide bombing undertaken by an Islamic terrorist, or question the nature of what it means to be 'trans' – then at once you will feel the full wrath of the 'politically-correct' powers-that-be; you will be cancelled, shamed, no-platformed, morally berated and browbeaten into silence by a 'call-out culture' which will brook no challenge to its iron-like dictates of what can and can't be said.

The mainstream media

In the case of Islam, this is thought to be particularly true, especially in terms of its reportage. Those who work for the newspapers, the media, the TV channels are all – according to the 'political correctness gone mad' thesis – straight jacketed by the paralyzing fear of saying anything that might be construed as being 'Islamophobic'. For example, in a 2006 article, *The Daily Mail* claimed that the BBC was anti-Christian and pro-Islam because broadcasting executives claimed 'they would happily broadcast the image of a Bible being thrown away – but would not do the same for the Koran'.[46] The 'journalist' Richard Littlejohn opined in the pages of that same paper how extremism 'is a hallmark of Islam … there is a voluble and intolerant strand of Islam … that proselytizes separatism … a particular problem with Islam which doesn't exist with any other religion in this country' and furthermore, that such a problem is exacerbated by the way criticism towards Islam 'is howled down as 'Islamophobia' – not just by self-appointed 'community leaders' but by brain-dead, white, middle-class Leftists'[47] (note here how two central facets of the 'politically correct' conspiracy theory are slotted into place: Islam is 'separate', refuses to integrate with the 'authentic' 'indigenous' culture, and such implacable 'foreignness' is then nurtured by the 'politically correct' elite – 'brain-dead, white, middle-class Leftists').

In the same moment, celebrity-has-beens such as John Cleese are able to hawk their latest books and revive flagging careers by appearing on HBO talk shows, broadcast to global audiences of millions, talking about how there are certain, unnameable groups you simply can't make jokes about because of a condescending 'politically correct' environment. At which point the talk show host in question (Bill Maher) responds to Cleese with a smug complicit smile and mouths the single word, 'Muslims'.[48] *The Daily Express*, combining two of their favourite themes (hostility towards Muslims and hostility towards the EU) informed us in 2007 how dictates from the EU had been released which allegedly prohibited British politicians from using the words 'jihad', 'Islamic' or 'fundamentalist' to describe terrorist attacks, even those which had quite clearly been committed by Islamic extremists.[49]

There is a glaring irony inherent in all of this. All the journalists, politicians, talk show hosts, cultural commentators and political pundits who proclaim it is quite impossible to make negative mention of Islam in today's political climate are, of course, refuting such an argument in the act of making it before audiences and readerships of millions. They are invariably locating themselves as free-speech martyrs, determined to say unutterable, unrepeatable truths in the context of the sinister, protean forces that are at work behind-the-scenes. They present themselves as beleaguered and moral individuals driven to take a stand against a consensus that is smothering any kind of dissent but the reality is that theirs is, by far and away, the orthodoxy; that is, it is difficult not to find on a daily basis some establishment blowhard belching out banal and bigoted statements towards Muslim people they have never met and whose lives they have no knowledge of.

To elaborate, the MP Sarah Champion's inflammatory article decrying Pakistani men as inherently more likely to sexually abuse children because of their race was published in *The Sun*, the same paper which, from 2019–20, was estimated to have the biggest overall circulation in the UK reaching on average just over 38 million readers per month.[50] The newspaper in second place with over 33 million readers per month[51] happened to be *The Daily Mail/The Mail on Sunday* and was one of the subjects of a 2018 study which discovered that, of all its stories featuring Muslims, 78 per cent of them carried negative themes and implications.[52]

The same major study examined 11,000 articles across the mainstream UK media in a three-month period, and revealed how – of all the articles which focused on Muslims and which were published across the whole spectrum – 59 per cent of these would again carry negative themes.[53] The BBC, the state broadcaster which is so shackled by 'political correctness gone mad', still somehow manages to avoid censure and destruction when broadcasting comedy shows like 'Real Housewives of Isis' which further blurs the distinction 'between harmless symbols of Islam and things that stand for Islamism or

Islamist-inspired terrorism' and ridicules women whose real-life counterparts experience on a regular basis 'physical violence, rape, even death'.[54]

Or to take yet another instance, the BBC's flagship political programme 'Question Time' has allowed the far-right commentator Nigel Farage to be featured more frequently than any other guest in the twenty-first century. Farage has made a career of harnessing anti-immigrant feeling along with racial prejudice; someone who has, unsurprisingly, done a good deal to help popularize the notion that the UK was being overwhelmed by the Muslim hordes, as when he argued that London was blighted by 'wholly Muslim areas'.[55] The only man to equal Farage's number of appearances on the programme in the last two decades is the Conservative politician and MP Ken Clarke who, in turn, has described the Muslim veil as a 'peculiar costume', a 'kind of bag', and called for the banning of them in courts.[56]

This, then, is the special kind of alchemy the 'political correctness gone mad' thesis is able to achieve; it transforms public school, investment bankers and bastions of the establishment such as Nigel Farage into anti-establishment, free-speech rebels who provide our last line of defence against the spectral 'other', the phantom foreigner lurking in the shadows, always on the verge of stamping democratic society with its medieval template of rigid fanaticism. Such a vision is realized through the toxic potion racism always provides, its heady combination of ignorance and fear. But, when you pass through that miasma of fear and suspicion, you realize that the people it stigmatizes are simply people, with the hopes, dreams and aspirations all people have. A group that is a mix of good and bad and every layer in between, who want the most for their children, and are trying, like anyone else, to survive the best they can.

We have seen that there is simply no basis on which to conclude that 'Islam' – aided by a cult of 'political correctness gone mad' – is able to dictate in its own favour the laws politicians make or the things people say on TV or in the papers in the UK. In fact, everything confirms the opposite prognosis; that is, Muslims tend to be portrayed negatively by the mainstream media, often demonized through explicit racial stereotyping, and they remain largely under-represented in the political realm.

But what about on the ground? One of the key arguments of the 'political correctness gone mad' narrative is that – as claimed in the cases of the child abuse scandals in Rotherham and Rochdale – police and local authorities are so hampered by 'political correctness' that Muslim or Asian perpetrators are able to act with impunity. But just as with the commentators who are constantly bewailing the fact that it is impossible to say anything critical in the public sphere about Islam (while constantly saying critical things about Islam) – the advocates of the idea that police cannot act against Muslims because of the need to appear 'politically correct', also run up against a similar set of hard and insoluble contradictions.

The realities of Islamophobia

In London in 2014, for instance, government figures revealed that an 'astonishing' 27 per cent of the prison population is Muslim, 'astonishing' for the reason that the figure is more than double the percentage of London's Muslim population more broadly, which stood at 12 per cent that same year.[57] In 2017 another governmental review discovered that Muslims account for 15 per cent of all Britain's prisoners – despite Muslims only forming around 5 per cent of Britain's overall population.[58] According to the human rights group Cage in a 2019 report, the detentions of Muslims at ports and airports by police employing 'controversial counter-terrorism powers' have become so systematic that 'the practice has become Islamophobic'.[59] In addition, a study from the *British Journal of Criminology* published in 2018 revealed that when police stop a person on foot, if that person is Muslim, they are eight times more likely to be searched, a figure which is higher than that of any other religious or ethnic group.[60] What we see on the part of law enforcement and in terms of patterns of arrest and incarceration is a clear and visible bias against Muslims rather than an inherent tendency to facilitate and favour any type of Islamic agenda.

Again, this demonstrates that the 'political correctness gone mad' thesis has no real correspondence with the reality; rather it operates in accordance with the narrative of the conspiracy theory, providing a fantasy frisson, often powered by a deeply racist inclination, which is completely impervious to the facts – but nevertheless gives its advocate the feeling of being someone supremely important, a lone warrior challenging the 'metropolitan elite', armed only with a sense of 'traditional values', heroically manning a lonely and vanishing outcrop of 'Britishness' in the face of the encroaching darkness of the forces of Islam and multiculturalism.

Perhaps the most pernicious stereotype of all is that of the Muslim as terrorist. The stereotype has been aided by the appalling attacks that took place on 11 September 2001 against the Twin Towers in the United States, attacks that were carried out by Muslim fundamentalists of the most murderous and atavistic stripe. The terror of the men, women and children who were in planes which had been converted into missiles is well-documented, yet never ceases to overwhelm you when you consider what their last moments must have felt like. Likewise, the fleeting and smoky footage of figures leaping from the buildings in order to escape the flames. It was, by far and away, the most deadly example of domestic terrorism in US history and surely the most horrifying.

But it is not the whole story. What is more surprising, perhaps, is the fact that while the September 11 crimes loom so large in the American psyche (understandably so), nevertheless, the majority of terrorist attacks committed on US soil have not been conducted by Islamic extremists. In fact, according to an FBI report, in the period from 1980 to 2006, only 6 per cent of all homeland attacks were carried out by Muslims.[61] Closer to today, *The Washington Post* reports that in the period from 2015 to the start of 2021, there was intensification of domestic terrorism, but this had arisen from a preponderance of attacks on the part of the extreme right, often driven by the logic of white supremacy.

So, for instance, in the period in question, 'at least 15 attacks or plots involved predominantly Black churches' while '16 mosques and 13 synagogues also were attacked or threatened by extremists on the far right'.[62] The rise in far-right terrorism and the politics of white supremacy is partially a response to the election of America's first Black president, strong anti-racist campaigns like the Black Lives Matter movement, and the racist fears of immigration which have been stoked up by demagogues like Donald Trump. For the same reason, the vast majority of victims have tended to be 'Blacks, Jews, immigrants, LGBTQ individuals, Asians and other people of color'.[63]

As a Muslim, therefore, you are far more likely to be a victim of terrorism than a perpetrator of it. And yet, despite this, the portrayal of the Muslim as a deranged and fanatical terrorist is ubiquitous in contemporary Western culture. In the United States, for example, a 2018 study conducted by the University of Alabama, revealed that in the period 2006–15, terrorist attacks committed by Muslims had received '357 per cent more US press coverage than those committed by non-Muslims', despite the fact that in roughly the same timeframe (2008–16) white and right-wing terrorists carried out almost twice as many attacks as their Islamic counterparts.[64]

And it is not just the out-and-out media bias which helps purvey the stereotype of the Muslim as terrorist. There is also the question of the language and tone in which the reportage is couched. In an enlightening piece which examines the 'vocabulary' of terror reporting, the journalist Annalisa Merelli focused on several major terrorist atrocities. In the cases of the San Bernardino mass shooting and attempted bombing of 2015 and the Orlando shootings the year following – Merelli notes how these atrocities were at once described by the authorities as being acts of 'terrorism'.[65] Bombings and shootings committed by white people, however, were often treated with a different type of rhetoric. For instance, a bombing against a mosque that occurred the year after the Orlando shootings and was carried out by a white-supremacist – was initially described by *The New York Times* as an 'early-morning explosion'.[66] In a similar vein, when a white assailant committed a mass shooting, killing more than fifty-eight people in Las Vegas, the head of police there refrained from using the label 'terrorist' and instead talked of someone who was 'a distraught person' and also a 'sole actor, a lone-wolf-type actor'.[67]

Merelli's examples vividly reveal the ideology at play; when a white, non-Muslim suspect is presented by the media he is much more likely to be depoliticized, his actions resulting from individual mental illness, a 'lonewolf' who acts in abstraction from some broader political ideology; whereas the Islamic suspect is much more likely to be described as a terrorist from the get-go. More significantly still, the terrorism in these latter cases is inexorably linked with religion and ethnicity: 'an Islamic terrorist'. We are so familiar with this kind of formulation that it attains a type of invisibility; but when we are presented with a corollary – 'a Roman Catholic terrorist', for example – we realize how absurd that formulation sounds. We almost never hear about white supremacists, who don the mantle of Christ and the Christian religion, being described in ethno-religious terms. In other words, whether consciously or unconsciously, there is a bias in much media reporting on terrorist attacks that works to suggest there is something 'inherent' to Muslims which causes them to commit these kinds of crimes.

But the narrative of 'political correctness gone mad' suggests that, rather than cease linking Muslims as a whole to terrorism on the basis of religion and ethnicity – instead we should do it all the more frequently. In 2013, the Trumpophile and former Mayor of New York City Rudy Giuliani argued that the US political bureaucracy needed to use the phrase 'Islamic extremist terrorists' because you 'can't fight an enemy you don't acknowledge'.[68] The assertion that Muslims being problematized this way is a racist endeavour – is categorized by Giuliani and his ilk on the right wing as simply another example of 'political correctness gone mad', even if that means they have to leapfrog over all the statistical data on the ground which reveals that Muslims are not the most frequent perpetrators of these types of crimes.

All of this begs the overriding question: Why has the 'political correctness gone mad' thesis with a particularly anti-Islamic bent become so popularized in recent times? Why has what is a vulgar almost orientalist fantasy grown so virulent in the twenty-first-century imagination?

The Imperial legacy

In the 1890s, Kipling wrote what is perhaps his most famous poem, 'The White Man's Burden'. In many ways the period of time in which he was writing wasn't so different from our own. After all, the people of Europe had just passed through an economic crisis that had hit globally, and triggered years of depression. The world was fissured by political tensions, particularly those which were opening up between an older and more decadent imperial power (Britain) whose tendrils stretched around the world, and an up-and-coming nation (Germany), with a much more efficient economic engine, desperate to carve out a bigger slice of the pie (one can't help but call to mind the situation today with the United States and China). Britain had recently prosecuted its latest war in Afghanistan. All the European powers were taking part in the 'scramble for Africa' whereby 90 per cent of that continent would be brought under European colonial control.

The economic crisis – along with all these wars and invasions – had set the basis for mass shifts in populations, great waves of people fleeing hearth and home in search of better, brighter horizons. The United States was the focus of many of these peregrinations and in certain sections of its society these great shifts and changes generated fundamental anxieties that were funnelled into notions of 'nativism' and anti-immigration sentiment. Senators such as Henry Cabot Lodge campaigned to introduce 'literacy tests' which would serve to bar poor, illiterate immigrants flooding in from Europe and elsewhere. Alongside this, a passion for 'eugenics' had been discovered in the more powerful of the world's nations which – according to the caveats of a crass pseudo-Darwinism – purported to establish a hierarchy in terms of various racial subsections, something that spoke to the capacities and capabilities of the particular races in question. Inevitably, the 'white race' was declared to have the highest degree of intelligence and humanity.

Prominent figures such as Sir Francis Galton in Britain (who coined the word 'eugenics' in 1883) hoped to create a 'science' that was both intellectual and practical – 'the science of improving stock' – which would allow 'the more suitable races or strains of blood a better chance of prevailing speedily over the less suitable'.[69] Such ideology was, of course, highly conducive to the project of rich white Europeans carving up the territories of Africa, grabbing great swathes of land, exploiting its resources, cultivating vast networks of forced labour from sections of the indigenous Black populations that often bordered on slavery.

In 1906, the crack-pot purveyor of flaked cereal John H. Kellogg founded The Race Betterment Foundation in Michigan USA to combat the issue of 'race degeneracy' (the way the 'superior races' are interbred with the 'inferior' ones, thus losing their special capacities and place in the hierarchy). This tessellated with the Jim Crow laws that had been enacted in the South towards the end of the nineteenth century, and which segregated Blacks on a society-wide basis, thereby enshrining their economic exploitation along with their educational and social disadvantages.

Kipling's poem 'The White Man's Burden' was ostensibly addressed to the United States, exhorting it to assume colonial control over the Philippines. More generally, however, it is imbued with the spirit of the times, offering a peon to colonialism and white supremacy that was bound up with the idea of providing civilization and stability to a world experiencing the most seismic tremors – setting the basis for waves of displaced peoples and the collapse of more venerable and traditional forms of existence. The poem is a rather fulsome entreaty to the Western powers, couched in the wearied refrain of great self-sacrifice, appealing to them to continue their imperial conquests and adventures, so that those who are by nature primitive and barbaric – 'sullen peoples, Half devil and half child' – might be raised up by the benevolent and civilizing qualities of the 'white race'. It is a vision which shares a good deal in common with the Islamophobia of today in as much as there is imagined an ethnic 'other', something classified and delimited by its 'foreignness'.

The 'politically-correct gone mad' thesis so prevalent in the contemporary political landscape allows the Islamophobe to imagine that oppressed Muslims are secretly the ones with all the power, the ones that the police and the press must kowtow to, the ones who are clandestinely shaping politics in line with their own sinister demands while gradually but inevitably overwhelming 'indigenous' culture.

In a similar fashion, the 'white man's burden' thesis also accomplished an inversion of power relations. Those Black people in Africa or the United States who were forcibly conscripted into the colonial project to provide cheap labour in the mines or on the cotton plantations, the Chinese immigrants who were building American railways and dams for a pittance, the half-starved peasants who worked their fingers to the bone in the East Indies, coerced into producing the cash-crops like sugar, coffee or rubber that powered the economy of the imperial heartlands; the 'white's man's burden' – in and through its 'noble', 'wistful' refrain – managed to transfigure such figures in the popular imagination from the remnants of societies and groups that had been brutalized and shattered by imperial force into the childlike but fortunate beneficiaries who would be lifted to the fullest level of wisdom, culture and civilization on the shoulders of their colonial benefactors. In such a rose-tinted vision, the rapacious and murderous imperial conquerors were recast as the reluctant but dutiful moral emissaries charged with raising the world in the beneficent glow of their own resplendent civilization – hence the eponymous 'white man's burden'.[70]

And that sense of the 'other' as 'Half devil and half child' – has also been employed as a rationale for the colonial projects of the twenty-first century. The appalling terrorist atrocity committed by Islamic fanatics on 11 September 2001 provided an impetus for an intensification of war and imperial conquest in the Middle East which burns on, even at the time of writing. More generally, the justification for these programmes of looting and military mass murder is provided by an ideological picture that suggests those societies bearing the full brunt of imperial power are themselves inherently incapable of rising to the level of 'civilization' and 'democracy' because their denizens are in some way innately primitive ('half child') or automatically inclined to the most medieval and vicious forms of religious fundamentalism ('Half devil').

In response to the 2011 uprising in Egypt, part of a series of pro-democratic revolutionary upsurges that occurred across the Levant and North Africa (the Arab Spring), *The Daily Mail* informed its readers that '[q]uestions of democracy, liberty, and freedom of expression were of little interest to the majority of the population'.[71] Another article, in the same paper, averred that: 'We thought the people of Iraq and Afghanistan would be delighted at the prospect of democracy … But many in the region are not, for the simple reason that they think they have a superior system – the rule and power of tribal elders.'[72] *The Telegraph* has devoted many an article to explaining 'Why Western democracy can never work in the Middle East'. The answer – '[t]he Arab states are governed less by the rule of law than by the rule of favour'[73] – again a result of the backward and tribal nature of the societies in question.

In his searing and splendid novel *A Thousand Splendid Suns,* Khaled Hosseini presents us with two Afghanistans. The first one is a place where girls go to school, where people dress freely (or at least as freely as in any other place), where they choose with whom they wish to have sex, where books on the most diverse themes are readily available and where music forms a natural, if unremarked upon, background to everyday life. Hippies from all over Europe come here to smoke pot. In contrast to this, the second Afghanistan is a place of fear, where the relationships between people are overseen by the guns and knives of soldiers attired in black, where books are burnt and girls are forbidden from attending school. Execution by stoning is a common public event. There is, of course, no music in this place.

But what is interesting about these starkly different portrayals of Afghanistan – the first the Afghanistan of the mid-seventies, the second Afghanistan at the turn of the millennium – is that both have a Muslim government which presides over a predominantly Muslim population. To say the same, the horror that is such a sustained part of the latter Afghanistan is not the result of a generic form of Islam. Instead it is the expression of a historical transformation: the arming of Mujahedeen fighters by the US government in the late 1970s in order to repel Soviet influence, the Soviet invasion of 1979 and the decade-long occupation, the civil war which followed between the remnants of the Soviet inspired government of Najibullah and the Taliban. It was under the pressure of these events that the cohesion and infrastructure of Afghani society seized and fragmented, and the possibility of a military fundamentalist dictatorship, which might restore order, developed.

In other words, democratic developments in the Middle East are often thwarted by the historical relations that open up between imperial powers and their subaltern territories, whether that means the decimation of the latter through the out-and-out struggle for domination that opens up between competing global powers (as was the case in Afghanistan), or perhaps more insidious forms of control – such as the sponsoring of military dictatorships like that of Egypt under Mubarak, whereby the toad-like dictator was funded to the tune of 1.3 billion per year by the United States in order to maintain the crumbling charnel house to which Egypt under his tyranny had been reduced (a regime favourable to American economic investment, of course). Or consider the case of the radical and secular social reformer Mohammad Mosaddegh, who was democratically elected in Iran in 1950 and who proceeded to nationalize the Iranian oil industry before his government was overthrown in 1953 in a military coup orchestrated by the CIA.

But the idea that Arabs and other darker-skinned peoples of the Middle East are tinged by primitivism and inherently incapable of rising to the level of 'civilization' and 'democracy' demanded by the West, not only obscures those cases where more democratic social forms have been thwarted by the process in which the Middle East is carved up according to powerful external interests – but also provides the rationale for the invasion and decimation of the region in the first instance. In this respect, there is an ideological thread which runs through the imperialism of yesteryear to the modern-day variant, and it works by subsuming a whole group under the generic categories of 'primitivism' and 'backwardness'.

And yet, there is as well a great gulf of time which separates us from Kipling's epoch. Kipling could mainstream imperialist sentiment through an explicitly racial rhetoric – 'the white man's burden' – in a way which would prove much more problematic today. The racialist pseudo-science that was key to establishing the 'biological supremacy' of the 'white race' has been thoroughly and systematically debunked by scientists across the board. More significantly, the consequences of such theories reached their ghastly fruition with what Victor Serge described as 'the midnight in the century' when Nazi eugenicists erected death camps on an industrial scale facilitating the murder of millions. It is the dark shadow of historical memory which inoculates many people today against the perverted and sinister Utopia the eugenicists seek to hawk. I do not say, of course, that racism – grounded in explicitly biological categories, carried by notions of superior bloodline or the like – no longer exists in today's world, but it is something which has been, in the main, exiled to the far-right fringes of the political realm, not only because of the horror of the Holocaust, but also because of the incredible protests that have opened up across the globe in our own times, from the Civil Rights movements to Black Lives Matter.

And yet, racism is like a virus. It evolves like a virus. It mutates like one. Any contemporary discourse or ideology which seeks to justify the use of imperial power and promote the subjugation of minorities or colonized peoples can no longer resort to archaic notions of race and bloodline, if it wants to be politically persuasive. So we experience a change, a shift; the people, the victims of imperial power and discrimination are still conceived of as being inherently primitive and sinister – 'Half devil and half child' – but their 'otherness' does not stem from a set of racial characteristics but rather a series of 'cultural' ones. 'Culture', not biological 'race', becomes the central determinate which informs prejudice and discrimination, and it becomes the most pressing rationale for prosecuting war and conquest in lands faraway. The natives are primitive and belligerent, not simply because of the colour of their skin, but because of the character of their religion.

Islam, as a cultural form, prevents them from ever realizing 'democracy' or 'civilization' through their own efforts; it condemns them to societies that must languish in conditions of tribal barbarism, where women can attain no rights cr status. And so it provides the rationale by which those same societies have to be subdued and civilized, pulverized by the application of the most tremendous military force, into the shape and set which is most conducive to the conquerors – the politicians, the military, the oil barons, the arms contractors and producers, private capital and state sponsored enterprise. All these underlying interests are cloaked by the need to protect 'civilization' and spread 'democracy', and thus force back the barbaric, Islamic hordes. This is, of course, racism gone to ground; racism appearing in a new and rejuvenated guise in the arena of twenty-first-century politics, 'the white man's burden' now reimagined as the forces of a new secular Enlightenment set against the darkness of religious medievalism in its snarling 'Islamofacist' guise.

But if Islamophobia provides an updated version of the old 'white man's burden' imperial ideology, then it also has a key bearing in rationalizing and enshrining domestic and local exploitation. In October 2008, as part of the global economic crisis more broadly, the UK government announced a bailout of the banks which would amount to £500 billion[74] and which was to be funded by sweeping austerity reforms that would target the poor majority in what was the biggest transfer of wealth from the bottom to the top in all of UK history. It was, one astute commentator quipped, 'socialism for the rich'.[75] In the years to follow, along with the austerity measures themselves, there developed a toxic ideological climate that was laced with both fear and contempt for the poorest and most vulnerable.

A toxic culture

TV series such as 'Benefits Street' were aired whereby moneyed, upper-middle-class producers and directors driven by ambition and aspiration sought to make a name for themselves by creating 'edgy' shows that depicted poor, out-of-work people almost as animals in a cage for the voyeuristic delight of their sneering 'betters', thereby fuelling 'the pervasive sense that people on benefits are feckless scroungers'.[76] Programmes like 'The Jeremy Kyle Show'[77] wheeled out bewildered, belligerent poverty-stricken figures, often addicted to drugs or alcohol, so as to inculcate the image of a boozy, vomitus underclass that was at the same time prepared to suck the benefits system dry in order to ensure the next can of cheap cider or the next hit of illegal drugs. The print media followed suit, article after article demonizing single mothers or immigrants on benefits, living the life of Riley, all at the decent hardworking tax payer's expense.

All this was an inevitable consequence of austerity politics and the need to shift the responsibility for the economic crisis from the rapacious and profligate sections of high finance that had helped facilitate it, to the most downtrodden and desperate who were forced to bear the brunt of it. And in this period, the categories of Victorian ideology were once again revived; the poor were split into two sections – deserving and undeserving. The 'deserving' were those loyal, patriotic British people who had lived in the country for generations, were the repositories of a 'traditional' British culture that emphasized civil duty and hard work (and whiteness). The undeserving were the undesirables; the single mothers whose sexual profligacy was undermining the traditional British family, the ignorant and feckless abusers of drugs and alcohol, but more than anything else the undeserving 'poor' were those who interjected that element of foreignness, that 'otherness' into the 'British' landscape, filching precious social resources from under the noses of those who most needed them.

Stories were carried about all the foreigners who had come to this country in order to abuse the benefits system, the NHS 'tourists' who arrive on 'holiday' to take advantage of free health benefits, the immigrants who had managed to secure cheap housing and places for their children at local schools while good hardworking people and their families were left out in the cold by that same liberal elite whose 'politically correct' mantras inclined them to betray over and over the 'true' 'authentic' 'British' (white) people they had been tasked to represent. Naturally Islamophobia formed a component part of this narrative; newspaper reports were rife with Islamophobic scare stories, from Muslim men using multiple wives to better game the benefit system – 'The truth about polygamy: A special investigation into how Muslim men can exploit the benefits system'[78] – to 'Millionaire Muslims' who were claiming free flats despite owning multiple homes – 'Millionaire Muslim woman Rebecca Khodragha posed as "battling single mother".'[79]

In this way, we can see that Islamophobia becomes the modern-day equivalent of the 'white man's burden' by shifting (ostensibly) the focus from race to religion, and thereby producing a more effective and potent strain of contemporary racism that works to justify the economic and political projects of the powerful. In terms of imperial interventions in the oil-rich countries of the Middle East, but also in terms of decimating the wages, benefits and economic rights of the domestic UK workforce and the poor majority of the population in and through the ongoing strategies of austerity that expropriate wealth from the bottom in order to benefit those at the top.

In all this, we can see how the notion of 'political correctness' is vital to the deployment of Islamophobia in the interests of the powerful. 'Political correctness' manages to invert the essential power relation: that is, hostility to Muslims becomes something that expresses the interests of the poor majority rather than the wealthy elite. For Muslims are seen as having developed an almost preternatural ability to insinuate themselves into the political and economic bloodstream of the country to the detriment of the 'indigenous' population – such a process being facilitated by a liberal and, above all, *'politically correct'* elite. The racism and smears which are then spread by papers controlled by billionaire press barons can be recast as the 'common sense' wisdom of the average man or woman on the ground fighting against a 'politically correct' establishment and the existential threat 'Islam' provides to their 'culture' and economic opportunities.

But the revolution against 'political correctness gone mad', however, will always be reactionary rather than radical. Ultimately, it is the product of a brown-shirt mentality. One in which the fundamental social groups and classes and the historical relations of power and exploitation which spring up between them is replaced by a national chauvinism that has been melded to the fretful and dark intimations of the conspiracy theory; an indurate world view in which racial fears and anxieties are materialized in the aspect of a sinister and fantastical chimera, the darkness which is forever on the edge of one's vision, the spectral shadow of the inhuman 'other'.

2

Me Too and the rise of the Feminazi

The Weinstein crimes

Harvey Weinstein is the name which will be forever intertwined with the Me Too movement. It is difficult to describe Weinstein or the extent of his crimes. If you were to feature him as a villain in a Hollywood movie, you would perhaps be charged by critics as having written someone too monstrous to be credible.

A film producer who came from relatively modest beginnings, but formed the incredibly successful Miramax production company with his brother and was catapulted into the very highest level of the Hollywood elite – Weinstein's behaviour seems to have grown systematically more grotesque, the more accustomed to power he became. He developed a reputation for bullying those who worked for him. He became high-handed and abusive with virtually anyone of a junior position according to many who were unfortunate enough to be in his employ and witness his behaviour first-hand.

One such individual recalls how difficult it was to get 'through the day without being screamed at, or without him publicly abusing someone else – a waiter, a colleague, a director, a driver'.[1] Weinstein became adept at intimidation, and yet, like so many men whose destiny consists in the accumulation of money and power rather than talent and ability – his rage was driven by a deep-seated anxiety and inadequacy. He was suspicious and distrustful of talent, tending to promote lickspittles and lackeys rather than independent-minded creatives – '[p]lenty of stupid people could rise through the ranks, and plenty of great people were lost to the company'.[2]

At the same time, he was possessed of an unbearably thin-skin; painfully aware of his own grotesqueness and lack, he was automatically antagonistic to those whose talent or good looks might overshadow the prestige of his own jealously guarded power: 'There was the odd male assistant. They were always quite tall and good-looking, and they were resented and envied by Harvey. His insecurities were close to the surface, and his awareness that he was not an attractive man was quite evident.'[3]

Sometimes the bullying would graduate into out-and-out violence. One of Weinstein's assistants, Mark Lipsky, reported how a colleague had come running into the office before exclaiming 'Call the police, Harvey just attacked me!'[4] In another incident, the journalist Rebecca Traister describes how she had angered Weinstein and so 'he called me a cunt and declared that he was glad he was the "fucking sheriff of this fucking lawless piece-of-shit town." When my colleague Andrew (who was also then my boyfriend) intervened, first calming him down and then trying to extract an apology, Weinstein went nuclear, pushing Andrew down a set of steps inside the Tribeca Grand – knocking him over with such force that his tape recorder hit a woman, who suffered long-term injury – and dragging Andrew, in a headlock, onto Sixth Avenue.'[5]

The remarkable thing about this blatant assault was that it was captured on camera by several paparazzi and yet, because of Weinstein's power and influence – being the 'fucking sheriff of this fucking lawless piece-of-shit town' – those pictures never saw the light of day. A culture of complicity and silence arose around the kind of warped power relations which Weinstein enacted: 'Sometimes he'd scream at you in front of someone you respected or had worked with, and that bothers me to this day – that they would let it pass. Everyone wanted to get their movie made, and I understand that; but I feel sick that his bullying was allowed to flourish in public and no one ever said, "This isn't acceptable." If you raised it, you were laughed off as naive; there was the underlying feeling that maybe you just weren't good enough to really impress him.'[6]

Perhaps one of the most telling descriptions of Weinstein was to come from the actor Jennifer Aniston. She details a small piece of his behaviour, almost insignificant – in the context of the many horrific incidents he perpetrated – but something that speaks to the kind of entitlement and indifference to others his position allowed him to cultivate. Aniston was sitting with a friend at a dinner to celebrate the new film she had been working on, when Weinstein arrived at their table 'and said to my friend: "Get up!" And I was like, "Oh my gosh." And so my friend got up and moved and Harvey sat down.'[7] One receives the sense of a man acting with the same kind of impunity as a feudal lord imposing his will on the serfs of his fiefdom, his economic and cultural power all the time buttressing the grotesqueness of his actions.

Without a doubt, the most sickening element of the Weinstein case is the sexual crimes. One of the first known victims of Harvey Weinstein was the actor Katherine Kendall. As a young actor, aged twenty-three, she was pressured to go to the movie mogul's hotel room, where he stripped naked, blocked the exit and tried to compel her into sexual acts. She was terrified and humiliated. And yet, she wouldn't make public what had happened to her for another quarter of a century. As a working actor, low down in the Hollywood pecking order, she correctly inferred that a man with Weinstein's economic power and connections could end her career – 'You make yourself a target in a way – I was awful scared that I would be judged, even blackballed. They could make it so you don't work.'[8]

Weinstein's crimes against women were legion. In 2020, Weinstein was convicted of raping an aspiring actor in 2013, forcibly performing oral sex on a production assistant, and the third-degree rape of another woman. The woman who was assaulted by Weinstein in 2013 said that his propensity for abuse was well-known, but for raping her, he only got 'slaps on the wrist'. She went on to describe the effects of that trauma in a soft but harrowing fashion: 'The impact of rape is profound. I live in a body that feels unsafe … I am forced to carry that experience until I die.'[9]

For these crimes, Weinstein was given a twenty-three-year prison sentence. But they were just the tip of the iceberg. At the time of writing, more than ninety women have come forward to accuse Weinstein of crimes which range from 'misconduct, including harassment, inappropriate touching and sexual assault'.[10] These alleged crimes go back decades, the first allegation coming from an employee who said he had raped her in 1978 on a business trip.

There is a particularly humiliating aspect to this type of abuse. A sense of being made vulnerable, rendered powerless, but in an obscenely intimate way. Something that is conducive to shame even though you, yourself, have done nothing wrong. As Kendall comments, 'I think that when people perpetrate against you, you are the one that feels the shame … You think that it's just you.'[11] That, more than anything, seems apparent. These crimes can create in the victim a sense of utter isolation. The feeling that you are alone and you won't be believed. Better just try to choke down the indignity and pain of what has happened. Put it behind you. And try to live the rest of your life, as best you can.

The Me Too movement

The 'Me Too' concept was originally formulated by the activist Tarana Burke in 2006 to raise awareness of the pervasiveness of sexual abuse and assault in society. In 1997, Burke had been working at a youth camp when a thirteen-year-old girl told her she was being sexually abused by her mother's boyfriend. Later Burke wished she had responded differently to that conversation, that she had told the girl 'me too' with regard to her own experiences of childhood sexual abuse, thus preventing her from going 'back into the world like she was all alone'.[12]

The phrase was re-coined more than ten years later. After the deluge of accusations against Harvey Weinstein in late 2017, the actor Alyssa Milano encouraged survivors of sexual harassment and abuse to use the hashtag #metoo on the social media forum Twitter as a way of drawing attention to just how widespread the phenomenon was. Her call was taken up by a long list of celebrity women, including Lady Gaga, Viola Davis and Evan Rachel Wood, but women (and some men) 'who were not household names also spoke out: nurses, teachers, engineers, florists, waitresses and students – mothers and daughters, sisters and wives'.[13]

What is apparent in these often heart-breaking accounts is not just the ubiquity of the phenomenon but also the way in which broader forms of social organization, especially those centred around the workplace, had evolved to facilitate it. There were umpteen accounts of women working in low-wage customer services jobs, often dependent on tips, suffering the depredations of male customers or bosses – but what became clear is that those who did complain were, more often than not, met with a wall of hostility or simple indifference.

In the case of the Arizona waitress Amanda Yennie – she recalls standing up to a male customer who tried to grope her, and then being told by her boss that letting 'them grab you' was part of the job description. When she refused to acquiesce, she was fired. Later, she worked in a nightclub where she was routinely harassed by male customers, including being twice followed out to her car after work by men who attempted to rape her. But by this stage, it didn't even occur to her to report these incidents. There didn't seem any point: 'It's not the culture … We're conditioned to be thankful that they decided not to hurt you.'[14]

For her part, Nora Yolles Young was sexually assaulted while she was studying at university, but when she was finally able to build up the courage to tell a professor about what had happened, he dismissed the incident with that hideous phrase 'boys will be boys'.[15] The Me Too movement called into being millions of such stories, indeed in the first twenty-four hours of its inception the Me Too hashtag was used by 4.7 million people who created over 12 million posts.[16]

The vast number of these accounts speak to the systematic nature of the crimes: women were rendered voiceless and invisible, precisely because they were faced by the modes and mechanisms of a vast economic and cultural bureaucracy that was calibrated to isolate them, to make them feel as though they were being ridiculous or trouble-makers, giving them the sense that their experience was invalid, that they had brought it upon themselves. And because the shame was theirs and theirs alone, because they were so fundamentally isolated, nothing could come of creating a fuss except for further sanctions in terms of demotion or loss of job, or having to endure a hostile and incriminating work environment.

If one had to distil the importance of Me Too into a single phrase, it might simply be the overcoming of such isolation. If before, a victim had felt walled in, unvoiced, trapped in a place of silence – Me Too connected the victim with millions of others, amplifying a single voice into that of a whole movement, such that it shattered those walls and barriers and put an end to such unremitting silence: 'By saying "me too", an individual woman makes herself a part of a broader group, and chooses to stand with others who have been harassed, assaulted or raped. This solidarity is powerful. It is still rare to see such a large group of women identifying their suffering as women's suffering, claiming that they have all been harmed by the same forces of sexism, and together demanding that those forces be defeated.'[17]

And although the movement was born in America, it has had a truly international resonance. Beyond the English-speaking world, equivalent Me Too hashtags were employed: #YoTambien in Spain and Latin America, #BalanceTonPorc in France, #quellavoltache in Italy. In China, where the Me Too hashtag was censored, users circumvented the problem by using the alternate #ricebunny – which, in Mandarin Chinese, echoes the phonetics of 'me too'. Despite the level of repression against the movement, high-profile cases have arisen whereby victims endeavour to call powerful men to account. So, for instance, in China, the billionaire executive Liu Qiangdong was sued for an alleged rape while the state media anchor Zhu Jun was sued for alleged sexual harassment and assault. The case against the former was dismissed; the case against the latter is ongoing at the time of writing. In India the Federal Minister M. J. Akbar was forced to resign after multiple allegations of sexual assault while 1000 professors were 'named and shamed' by students who provided first-hand testimonies of alleged sexual harassment and assault in a list which went viral.

In Japan, the journalist Shiori Ito became the face of the Me Too movement there, when she courageously spoke out against a powerful television chief who had allegedly raped her. The movement also targeted outmoded and old-fashioned patriarchal dress codes that forced women to wear high heels in a campaign which garnered the support of the Prime Minister – and when, recently, the head of the Tokyo Olympics organizing committee Yoshiro Mori made sexist comments he was forced to stand down. In Argentina, feminist movements were already highly organized and they used the event of Me Too 'to push for the legalization of abortion'[18] which was achieved in 2020 to rapturous and moving scenes of millions of pro-choice crowds celebrating, while similar pro-abortion protests swept across Latin America. One year after the inauguration of the movement, the Me Too hashtag was being used on average 55,319 times daily in at least eighty-five countries.[19] One cannot but call to mind the words of the great French novelist Victor Hugo – 'There is nothing more powerful than an idea whose time has come!'

The backlash against Me Too

And yet, when any great political movement shakes the foundations of society to its core, it also unleashes all those social elements who are made terrified and frenzied by the prospect of fundamental change, from the most powerful financial barons to the smallest of clerks or shopkeepers, blinking out through terrified angry eyes, harkening back in their minds to a more venerable time of tradition and stability, when men were men and women were women, when young people were less vocal and those of colour and other minorities knew their place. The various strategies which were used to delegitimize the Me Too movement were, in this way, both inevitable and inevitably banal.

The usual suspects, the various edgy libertarians who are nearly always from wealthy, privileged backgrounds took to the media *en masse* in order to decry the Me Too movement as the plaything of rich debutante actresses who had too much time on their hands and were consistently craving the attention and prestige of the media spotlight. Constipated public-school boy Brendan O'Neill – in order to bolster his reputation of writing controversial things for money and fame – took aim at one of the first actors to accuse Weinstein of rape, saying of Rose McGowan that she 'has effectively built a second career on having allegedly been a victim of Weinstein's' and describing how her 'narcissistic performances capture the extent to which #MeToo has become bound up with self-promotion, a means for influential women to gain even greater influence via the politics of victimhood'.[20]

The inversion which O'Neill performs is illuminating; the actors who are Weinstein's victims are transformed into the perpetrators – those who found themselves in humiliating situations of powerlessness and exploitation are reimagined as the ones wielding the power. The issue of their abuse now becomes the means by which they are seen to assert their own privilege, through 'narcissistic performances' and the entitlement of 'influential women'. It is not difficult to surmise that behind O'Neill's edgy libertarian rants, behind the shock jock's sensationalized idiom, there is, in fact, a rather fusty conservatism; O'Neill is disgusted by the presence of the 'influential women' who set the Me Too campaign into motion, and rather wishes they had a little less influence, would make a little less noise.

An article written in much the same vein bemoans how focussing on 'white, financially secure women' tends to promote 'trivial' issues – 'news that Kate Maltby's knee may or may not have been touched by Damian Green or that Michael Fallon attempted to kiss Jane Merrick' – while ignoring the plight of impoverished working-class victims: 'The lack of comment on the Telford abuse scandal exposes the hypocrisy at the heart of the #MeToo movement … why have there been no outpourings of sympathy or expressions of outrage for the girls of Telford? Perhaps the women of Telford are simply the wrong kind of victim. #MeToo prefers its victims to be posh.'[21]

This is slippery and disingenuous in the extreme. It is true that the disregard of the children in Telford was a travesty, but the invisibility of the victims was generated by a system in which working-class girls were not seen as children – but as manipulative, knowing, cynical and grasping, and not worthy of any human consideration. To link the Me Too movement with this is obscene, especially considering that the *raison d'être* of Me Too has been the collective endeavour of victims around the world sharing their stories and overcoming the type of invisibility in which the Telford children were mired.

But more than this, because of its scope, the Me Too movement isn't a uniform entity which can be made to comment on this or that particular issue with a single voice. It provides an amplification of millions of voices raised in tandem. The fact that it isn't possible to issue a statement from a non-existent central office on every instance of sexual abuse taking place in the world at any given moment cannot be made to 'speak' to the 'fact' that Me Too is indifferent to the suffering of this or that particular group. It is itself the conglomeration of an infinite variety of social elements and shades.

The endeavour to portray a movement as governed fundamentally by the whims and ambitions of rich and narcissistic Hollywood women at the expense of the everyday and ordinary women whose voices were drowned out – was always going to be a classical and cynical exercise in the divide-and-rule stratagems which establishment power deploys in a crisis. The opposition between one section of the movement and the other was, in many ways, an artificial one in as much as the prominence of some of Weinstein's victims helped to amplify the nature and ubiquity of these kinds of crimes in society more broadly. The Me Too movement was like a rock dropped into the water, its ripples echoing outward, expanding to encompass more and more social groups. This was reflected in many of the legal changes made in politics, businesses and civil society more generally, changes which did indeed impact the lives of ordinary women and girls for the better.

For example, in November 2017, the month after the Me Too movement hit, mass demonstrations took place in Los Angeles as hundreds of ordinary women took to the streets in order to protest their experiences of sexual harassment and intimidation at work in what became dubbed 'The Take Back the Work-Place' march. In addition, Latina farmworkers, some 700,000 strong, got their regional organization to issue a statement in support of Me Too and the Los Angeles women – choosing to emphasize the commonality that bound them together rather than the differences in their social or economic status: 'Even though we work in very different environments, we share a common experience of being preyed upon by individuals who have the power to hire, fire, blacklist and otherwise threaten our economic, physical and emotional security.'[22]

These types of convergences between women of different places and different backgrounds in the context of political protest and struggle have affected important political and legal changes. In 2018, New York expanded its sexual harassment laws to include independent contractors (who often employ particularly vulnerable and low paid female staff) while in 2019 that same state improved protections for domestic workers. In 2018, the state of California enacted similar regulations, including legislation that overrides non-disclosure clauses, the expansion of sexual harassment training in the workplace and the mandatory requirement for a certain number of female directors on the boards of a number of companies.[23]

None of this means that wealthier, white women won't have access to forms of economic redress and cultural representation which their poorer black counterparts, for instance, won't. None of this means that the Me Too movement doesn't have a social complexion that is tinged with class implications, and the privileges and disadvantages to the different layers that these bring. But in their endeavour to neuter the movement, elements of the right-wing press are going much further; they are making the claim that Me Too is *enhancing* the privilege and power of the women at the top to the detriment of those at the bottom. It is perhaps the only time such commentators will ever show such ardent 'concern' for those at the bottom, for it allows them to impose an artificial opposition that severs the movement in two, thereby curtailing its sweep, its organic unity.

Such dissembling, such vulgar tactics are transparent and crude, but patriarchal power sought to defend its privileges in other ways too. During his trial, Weinstein decried the Me Too movement by comparing it to the McCarthyism which reached its height in the 1950s and involved the persecution of those suspected of having radical left or 'unpatriotic' sympathies. Weinstein likened his position to that of the writer Dalton Trumbo who was blacklisted and jailed for being a communist sympathizer, before describing himself as one man among many being subject to a form of collective persecution.[24] The kind of logic on display here – mawkish self-pity and victimhood married to the paranoid and fevered mindset of the conspiracy theorist – was deployed in the defence of other 'important' Hollywood men whose sex crimes were rationalized or effaced by those sections in the press and society with slavish instincts and an unerring need to genuflect before power.

In the late 1970s, paedophile auteur Roman Polanksi brutalized and sodomized a thirteen-year-old child whom he had first plied with drugs and alcohol. He did not deny raping this child. He acknowledged it. One would think that if any crime might put the perpetrator beyond the ken of sympathy or justification, it would have been this one. But members of the Hollywood elite, including Sigourney Weaver, Harrison Ford, Johnny Depp,

Ewan McGregor, Pierce Brosnan and Kate Winslet,[25] all signed up to work with Polanski in the decades following. One Harvey Weinstein even penned an open letter which demanded forgiveness for his fellow rapist and hoped to prevent Polanski being extradited to the United States to serve the prison sentence he (Polanski) had jumped bail to avoid. Perhaps most shockingly, Weinstein would go on to question whether the horrific act Polanski had committed was even a crime at all – 'Whatever you think about the so-called crime …'[26]

One receives the impression of an insidious network of celebrity power. A realm where many of the same actors, directors and producers who use the podium to burnish their progressive credentials, speaking out about environmentalism and world hunger before glittering, tuxedoed members of the audience who have paid thousands to mingle with stars – are also the same individuals who, for the sake of their own careers, remain quietly indifferent to the exploitation and suffering of many of those who have fallen foul of a Weinstein or a Polanski. But the Me Too movement has helped shatter this kind of complicity. It has helped reveal the furtive connections and sullied hypocrisy that underlies the kind of corrosive, neurotic ambition which powers celebrity and its compulsive yearning for the spotlight.

For the movement has caused the mask of celebrity to slip; behind the charisma and the glamour, it has revealed something inhuman and grotesque, something dead. And yet, the mechanics of power continue to grind away. Celebrities such as Kate Winslet who worked with and defended sexual predators like Roman Polanski – garlanding him with laurels of praise while deftly avoiding the rather distasteful subject of child-rape[27] – since the Me Too movement has shone its spotlight, they have had to recalibrate their Hollywood personas in order not to seem the cold, callous, ambition-driven creatures they are. After the Me Too movement broke, Winslet took to the podium to give a tearful speech outlining her 'bitter regrets' at having worked with directors like Polanski and Woody Allen, and affirming her incredible, heartfelt solidarity with the victims of 'harassment, exploitation and abuse'.[28] After all, she is nothing if not a consummate actor.

Some, it must be said, felt a genuine sense of horror at what had been revealed, and stood in solidarity with the victims of Weinstein, Polanski and others, not simply in order to protect their careers at the last moment. Others have actually gone on the offensive by trying to burnish the reputations of those predators who have been so unceremoniously unmasked. Isabelle Hupert – an actor known for her portrayals of cold and disdainful characters devoid of humanity – likened the campaign to bring Polanski to justice (the director is currently facing six allegations of sexual abuse) to a 'lynching'.[29] I mention Hupert in particular, because the way she has framed her defence of Polanski is similar to how Weinstein would cultivate his own defence; both of them, by way of analogy, refer to forms of persecution enacted by vested right-wing interests. Weinstein talks about the persecution and imprisonment of suspected communists by a powerful and rabid right-wing senator, while Hupert talks about 'lynching' – a form of murder against disempowered, disenfranchised Black people on the part of a powerful and entrenched system of white supremacy.

In a sane world, the idea that the multi-millionaire Hollywood baron Weinstein or the rich, world famous Oscar winning director Polanski had anything in common with victims of McCarthyism or a poverty-stricken and oppressed Black man living under the tyranny of apartheid in the Mississippi Delta – would seem out-and-out laughable. The notion that a convicted multiple-rapist, or a child-rapist who has acknowledged his crime but is accused of many more – the *very notion* that these figures achieve some kind of parity with the innocent men and women who had committed no crime, and were assailed, imprisoned or murdered merely for the colour of their skin or the content of their opinions – should be something to be greeted with cold contempt. And yet, it is precisely this kind of topsy-turvy vision of the world that the *modus operandi* of the 'political correctness gone mad' thesis seeks to call into being.

Me Too as witch hunt

Other powerful men such as Woody Allen, also accused of sexual abuse, crawled out of the woodwork to respond to the Me Too movement by casting dark ominous warnings about the possibility of a 'witch hunt'.[30] The 'witch hunt' metaphor was particularly favoured by extremely wealthy and privileged older men in the Hollywood elite who had no doubts spent much of a lifetime enjoying all the privileges and perks their power bestowed upon them. When confronted by the voices of those whose subjugation was supposed to be an invisible and inevitable part of Hollywood business as usual, such men began to get more and more uncomfortable – experiencing the rising tide of protest against oppression as a personal and oppressive attack on themselves and the freedoms they had always enjoyed.

Geriatric ramblers like the high-profile film director Terry Gilliam – who, to be fair, was less than coherent even in his prime – wandered into the media pulpit before launching bile-saturated rants that averred the most devastating and ubiquitous forms of oppression were not experienced by women enduring sexual assault in the workplace, or the victims of racial or homophobic prejudice – but rather the trials and tribulations of millionaire white males such as himself. Gilliam was 'tired, as a white male, of being blamed for everything that is wrong with the world'.[31] Of Weinstein's victims, he remarked 'Hollywood is full of very ambitious people who are adults and they make choices'.[32] With the reluctant stoicism of the worldly-wise, Gilliam went on to explain how the use and abuse of power was an inevitable and unchangeable feature of Hollywood, and indeed of all human life: 'When you have power, you don't take responsibility for abusing others. You enjoy the power. That's the way it works in reality'.[33]

He made one crucial exception, however. If the victims began to take matters into their own hands, if they began to raise their voices and assert their own power against the conditions of their exploitation – for Gilliam that was beyond the pale, that was something which must be stopped, for that was .... *a witch hunt*: '#MeToo is a witch-hunt. I really feel there were a lot of people, decent people, or mildly irritating people, who were getting hammered. That's wrong. I don't like mob mentality'.[34]

From the very outset of the Me Too movement this type of counter narrative was fulminated. The same inversion in which the powerful were depicted as the powerless, the perpetrators as the victims. The result of a rising tide of 'political correctness', so we were told, had unleashed a totalitarian 'witch hunt', sucking more and more innocent men under, destroying careers on a whim, sinking people in prison without due process, substituting moral hysteria for hard evidence, and creating frigid work environments where the 'natural' relationships that develop between men and women have all the joy and spontaneity choked out of them by bureaucratic diktat.

Fugitive from justice and child rapist Roman Polanski waded in to decry the movement as 'collective hysteria' and much of the mainstream press dutifully followed in shaping the narrative in this direction; headlines proliferating like fungi in warm rain. *The Los Angeles Times*, for instance, offered up a rhetorical question uttered in fretful tones – 'Is 'Weinsteining' getting out of hand?[35] – while *USA Today* declared emphatically that '[it] now takes only one accusation to destroy a man's life' and that we are 'on a sexual harassment warlock hunt'[36] while for its part *The Washington Post* – echoing Weinstein's own sentiments – informed its readers how 'McCarthyism is back, but this time it's woke'.[37]

The methodological basis for these kinds of claims rested on two central tenets. First, that a woman – any woman – could accuse a man of a sexually related crime and that he was automatically assured to lose position, social standing and even liberty. Second – and related to the first condition – there was no due process; the need to 'believe' and 'validate' the word of the victim had removed any standard of material evidence or burden of proof. In this way, the image of a 'McCarthyite witch-hunt' could be cultivated; the vision of a series of hysterical denunciations spreading in a wave, washing away all the legal measures and protections which are designed to guarantee that most famous of liberties in any civilized society – *innocent until proven guilty*.

One would have to pause to note that this kind of rhetoric is not just mobilized against the Me Too movement. It is deployed whenever there is any concerted political effort to improve the laws and culture that surround sexual assault in favour of the victims who are subject to it. The same arguments are used. The fear that innocent men will be the victims of vindictive women; that the latter – wielding their own self-righteous sense of 'victimhood' – will be able to inflict totalitarian punishments on the former as a way of taking revenge for even the smallest perceived slight. It is, in many ways, an effective argument; it puts the person who is making it in the position of someone who seems determined to protect the rational and hard-fought-for rights that pertain to the legal sphere, the sphere of justice, and which have developed in the context of a post-Enlightenment world.

And nobody could deny that there are women who accuse men of sexual assault or harassment on an entirely false basis, motived by a petty spite, financial considerations or by the type of delusions that are wrought from trauma and mental health issues. Such cases occur – and they have been documented. In the UK, for instance, there was the case of the actor Michael Le Vell who was falsely accused of raping a child. The evidence from the prosecution was not so much based on solid witness testimony and a systematic reconstruction of the alleged events leading up to the 'crime' – but more on airing the 'dirty little secrets' of the private life of the accused who was an alcoholic, a serial adulterer and someone who could be painted in terms of 'a seedy, washed-up actor who had considered quitting Britain's longest-running soap'.[38] In the event, Le Vell was rightfully and thankfully cleared of all charges – but that doesn't negate the two years of hell that he was put through by the trial, the violation of his privacy or the damage his reputation would sustain for the future.

The realities of sexual oppression

But the issue is never simply whether these events occur. The gambit those on the right seek to make is not just that such things take place, but rather they are endemic, or they are becoming endemic. They are not the exception, they are the rule. But to take the UK once again, the statistical facts paint a very different picture. In an extensive study published by the European Union in 2014 – one which was based on interviews with 42,000 women – it was estimated that 25 per cent of women from the UK had experienced sexual violence or sexual harassment. In Europe more widely that figure indicated that over a fifth of all women had experienced the same.[39] And yet, a study carried out by the Home Office a few years before in 2005 stated[40] that of all cases of sexual violence reported to the police in the UK only 4 per cent are found to be or suspected to be false.

And that 4 per cent – a small percentage in and of itself – is nevertheless inflated by the way some cases which are branded 'false' are also those cases that have been recorded as 'no crime' – for the reason that there is insufficient corroborating evidence rather than the fact that it has been established that the alleged victim had falsified the allegation. Sometimes people contact the police when they have, for whatever reason, no memory of a period of time, and are worried something had been done to them during that period of blackout. When such a claim can't be established, this too can be registered as being 'false' although the victim might not have named any alleged perpetrator.

But perhaps the most telling statistic of all is the one which surrounds rape prosecution itself. In the period from 2019 to early 2020 police 'recorded 55,130 rapes but there were only 2,102 prosecutions and 1,439 convictions in England and Wales'.[41] At the same time, figures from the Office for National Statistics indicate that the true number of raped women and girls would more likely stand at around 95,000.[42] Another estimate indicates that in the twelve months running up to March 2020, 99 per cent of all rapes reported to police in England and Wales resulted in no legal proceedings against the alleged assailants.[43]

Almost three years after the Me Too movement had exploded, the UK's Crown Prosecution Service prosecuted less people for rape than in any other time in the past for which data exists. In the United States we can observe a similar pattern. One year on from when the Me Too movement first occurred, one study showed that less than '1 per cent of rapes lead to felony convictions'[44] while another revealed that only 4 to 5 per cent of cases are ever prosecuted and that, of every 100 rapes committed, only five to twenty are reported to the police in the first place.[45]

If we are, therefore, living in a draconian dystopia where liberal-feminists and 'politically correct' apparatchiks oversee the persecution and incarceration of vast swathes of men whose only 'crime' is to have looked at a woman the wrong way – that surely must come as some surprise to all the legions of women and girls who have been the victims of sexual abuse and experienced no redress whatsoever. Of course, like many conspiracy theorists, the 'it's political correctness gone mad' constituent are happy to overlook the reality on the ground especially if it contradicts the type of narrative which grants them self-importance – which places them at the head of a culture war fighting for traditional, individual freedoms against the impingements of mirthless, modern-day puritans.

And so they set up the 'witch hunt' narrative by arguing that the forces of liberal feminism and 'political correctness gone mad' have created a situation where 'the victim' is to be believed at all costs, that the logic of this is driven to absurdist conclusions whereby her 'word' overrides any need for trial or due process – 'a replay on the level of farce of the old Soviet tactic of denunciation'.[46] Or to say the same, the principle of 'believing the victim' overrides absolutely the principle of innocent until proven guilty.

But again, the truth here is being warped by an insidious right-wing agenda. When one says that rape victims should be 'believed', I would argue this is not intended in a wholly literal sense. One refers to a cultural and political assumption rather than something which is ratified in advance as a legal and iron-tight principle. To clarify, the victim of a burglary or a mugging can make his or her way to the average police station and give an account of what has happened, with the expectation that the police officers who take his or her testimony are going to hear it with an eye to gleaning the information needed to track down the perpetrator. They will, from the outset, treat the person who has come forward to report the crime as someone who is telling the truth.

What they won't do, generally speaking, is interrogate that same person about aspects of their personal life. They won't ask that person if they like to have a drink, or how many drinks they had had on the night of the mugging. They are unlikely to suggest that the way the complainant is dressed is responsible for setting the crime into motion. They won't ask about that person's personal history and draw details from it that infer the complainant has brought the crime upon themselves. They won't suggest that perhaps they are simply making it up because they had an unsatisfactory evening. They will not ask to take the complainant's mobile phone in order that they can trawl it for intimate information from the complainant's past.

But in the same period that rape convictions had reached a historic low in the UK, not only were police demanding rape complainants hand over their mobile phones for inspection, but an investigation revealed that authorities were actually dropping rape cases for those victims who refused to submit to this kind of 'digital strip search'.[47] And the use of a victim's sexual history as a way to discredit her allegation is, to this day, not uncommon – the most high-profile incident in recent times occurred with the case of the footballer Ched Evans who was convicted of rape, but the verdict was overturned after an appeal court ruling allowed the victim's previous sexual behaviour to be taken into account.[48]

When one understands that a culture has been fostered on every level – from the moment a woman reports her sexual assault to the time the case goes before a judge and jury (at which point the victim can be interrogated by the prosecution about her previous sexual history as a way to undermine her credibility) – one understands why, according to the Rape and Incest National Network, less than 25 per cent of sexual assaults are ever reported to police, which is significantly less than the level for that of violent crimes in general.[49]

And it is in this context that the principle of believing the victim is such an important corrective. It is not something which seeks to annul the trying of a case through a legal process; rather it seeks to correct the bias towards female victims which is built into the background of the legal process itself, a bias which often intrudes into the different stages in that same process – from the moment that the victim comes forward to the point at which a jury of her peers arrives at its decision.

Often jurors suffer from the very same prejudices that the 'political correctness gone mad' lobby seeks to inculcate: that is, they (the jurors) believe there is a 'prevalence of false allegations of rape … that they are routinely made'[50] as opposed to the reality that such cases are extremely rare. Jurors also suffer from other traditional biases; that behaviour surrounding alcohol consumption and past sexual history has bearing on the alleged victim's moral status and thus the veracity of her claims; in short, 'there is overwhelming evidence that jurors take into the deliberation room false and prejudicial beliefs about what rape looks like'.[51]

In cases of sexual harassment, we see a similar trend. In France, 93 per cent of complaints of sexual harassment are dropped or never followed up on by law enforcement.[52] Indeed, an extensive study revealed that in 40 per cent of sexual violence in the workplace cases, the person who makes the complaint is reprimanded or fired, while the accused person is typically not investigated or punished.[53]

In 2021, in the UK, a detailed survey revealed 97 per cent of women aged eighteen to twenty-four had experienced some form of sexual harassment while over three-quarters of all women had been harassed in the public space. That same YouGov survey[54] discovered that 96 per cent of all respondents had declined to report their experiences of sexual harassment, exposing 'a damning lack of faith in the UK authorities' desire and ability to deal with sexual harassment' against women. This lack of faith in the authorities has real and worrying foundations which stretch far beyond UK borders, however.

In the United States, for example, the Me Too movement shone a spotlight on how the bastions of political power deal with the sexual harassment complaints of often junior female staff. The Office of Compliance which is responsible for adjudicating these kinds of complaints within the US Congress presents the victim with a labyrinthine network of bureaucratic measures which curtail her rights and whose smothering pressures are enough to make anyone think twice about coming forward:

The Office of Compliance, which is charged with adjudicating complaints against members of Congress, offers victims little more than a maze of rules. It might more accurately be called the 'Office of Silence,' since proscribing women from talking is ingrained in the process itself. A complaint must be filed with the office within 180 days of the incident. In order make an official complaint, the accuser must submit to mandatory counseling, which usually takes thirty days, and then, if they continue with their complaint, they must complete another thirty days of mediation. During mediation, women must follow strict rules of secrecy, including agreeing to nondisclosure agreements that bind them from talking.[55]

Alex Ronickher, a lawyer who specialized in harassment actions, describes such laws as specifically 'written to create a system to disincentivize staffers from coming forward'.[56] And while the Me Too movement has helped overhaul sexual harassment policies leading to a crackdown on several dozen lawmakers who harass their staff in Congress and forcing a number of resignations, it is worth noting that none of these incidents have led to prison time for a single individual thus far. In other words, the 'political correctness gone mad' narrative which seeks to paint Me Too as a rapacious 'witch hunt' that is spiralling out of control, condemning legions of innocent men to languish in prison, has virtually no correspondence with the reality. It is instead a rather spiteful fairy-tale concocted by those who feel a desperate and craven fidelity to the powers-that-be. But, like all the best fairy tales, such a narrative also requires its own fantasy villain. And it is in this capacity where we now encounter the sinister spectre of the 'Feminazi'!

The spectre of the Feminazi

The term originated in the 1990s, devised by the bloated right-wing shock jock and professional hate-monger Rush Limbaugh, to stigmatize feminists seeking to expand abortion rights for women, but it began to gain more traction in the following decades with the rise of online politics, the Twittersphere, and the so-called Men's Rights Movement. If feminist movements were to be described according to the fantastical remit of 'political correctness gone mad', if the movements against gender inequality, sexual harassment and sexual assault were to be reimagined as joyless and prosaic exercises in inhuman oppression from above, then the Feminazi was to become the personification of this process.

In her figure, the anxieties of vast numbers of men and a good few women were materialized. Those who felt instinctively and elementally discomforted by the struggle to shift power relations in terms of a more egalitarian balance, those who felt they were losing a grip on all the stable verities of traditional gender roles and hierarchies – to these people, ruffled by the winds of change and feeling the ground cracking beneath their feet – the struggle for new freedoms could only ever appear as a series of cold and alien oppressions. In the brittle and frigid figure of the Feminazi such fear and anxiety was given existential expression.

A bête noire, a bogeyman, a 'politically correct' gremlin – the Feminazi exacerbates all those traits in women that men of a conservative and traditional bent seem to despise; she is vocal, demanding, strident, domineering and utterly self-righteous. She is inherently argumentative and antagonistic, puritanically politically correct, shrill and dogmatic, superior and aloof. In terms of her social position, she is usually imagined as someone white, middle-class, professional – and in terms of her politics, a card carrying member of the liberal elite.

This is significant – if feminist movements like Me Too can be reframed as totalitarian in nature then their leaders must be conceptualized in similar terms. The Feminazis are figures of power – elite ringmasters who bring the culture of 'political correctness' to its ghastly fruition in and through the mobilization of a mass movement that descends into the relentless and bloody pursuits of a moral crusade; the unbridled persecution of simple, ordinary folk in the face of a moral panic, the stultifying choking atmosphere of paranoia and the need to conform.

But, as one might expect, this fantasy chimera has little in common with the actual women who are labelled Feminazis on the ground. One of the better known UK feminist campaigners to have been dubbed a 'Feminazi' in recent years is Caroline Criado-Perez. And what of the totalitarian and 'politically correct' nature of her crime? She successfully led a campaign to feature an image of the nineteenth-century author Jane Austen on a bank note. Not perhaps the most evil or insidious action ever to have been enforced on a nation by the 'culture police', but one supposes such things are a slippery slope. If a man has to look at Jane Austen staring up at him from his hard-earned bank notes, then how long will it be before he feels the stern gaze of George Elliot reprimanding him from his chequebook? Or Emily Bronte, looking all windswept and disdainful, from the watermark of his credit card?

There were clearly a good number of people disturbed by this affront to the status quo such that they felt entitled to vent their spleen against the 'Feminazi' who had facilitated it. Criado-Perez received not just the standard, run-of-the-mill rape threats on Twitter that prominent women – women in the public eye – so often receive. She was also treated to descriptions of her own dismemberment, mutilation and murder, the type of stuff which would put one in mind of a Jeffery Dahmer or Ted Bundy: 'threats to her had spoken of mutilating her genitalia, stalking her outside her house, beating and gang-raping her'.[57] One Isabella Sorley[58] tweeted Criado-Perez 'I've only just got out of prison and would happily do more time to see you berried!' Despite the unintentional hilarity of the spelling, these kinds of threats are saturated with violence, bile and utter, utter rage. They make one question fundamentally the security of one's own well-being.

Criado-Perez received a deluge of threats like these, but the police only took action against two of her tormentors, Isabella Sorley – and her partner John Nimmo (who had threatened to anally rape Criado-Perez); the first eventually receiving a jail sentence of twelve weeks and the second a sentence of eight weeks. Not the most severe of punishments, perhaps you will agree – but the vast number of people who piled in to terrorize and intimidate Criado-Perez suffered no consequences whatsoever. And all because of the decision to put a female author's face on a banknote. When one looks at this, the fanatics and intolerants in question seem less like the 'Feminazi' endeavouring to affect what was essentially a mild reform and more like the scores of inadequates, buzzing with viciousness, that at once swarmed in to monster her.

Another notorious 'Feminazi' on the UK political scene is Laura Bates. Her crime? In 2012, she founded the 'Everyday Sexism' project inviting women on social media to provide accounts of the type of everyday experiences of sexism they'd had. *The Guardian* journalist Zoe Williams would note the parity between this and the Me Too movement, writing that both were trying to create an 'inflection point for resisting injustice' whereby 'everybody is emboldened to speak out at once'.[59] Bates was, in turn, branded a Feminazi, and like Criado-Perez she experienced 'torrents of abuse, including graphic rape and death threats, directed at her personally'.[60]

Again, one has to question where the extremism here really lies: with the person who is trying to make visible incidents of sexist injustice which pulse just beneath the surface of society and yet often go unremarked upon – or the people who are promising rape, dismemberment and murder for the raising of such issues in the first place. On the 'Feminazi' label, Bates comments with sharp acuity, '[i]t's a term that flags something to other attackers. It's very much part of a group attack, like a trolling thing. I would associate the word Feminazi with a mass attack, somebody signalling to their mates: "I'm having a go, here, come and join in." And then you get bombarded.'[61]

In other words, the 'Feminazi' designation purports to identify someone who is extremist and intolerant, closing down any views which aren't acceptable to her puritanical standards of a 'political correctness gone mad' – but in actual fact the 'Feminazi' label becomes the licence by which large numbers of men and some women are able to target those women who have a public profile and expose sexist oppressions. The concept of the 'Feminazi' was never designed as a kickback against intolerance; it is, rather, a ruthless political strategy which unleashes the foulest stigma and the most violent of threats as a means to silence those voices which challenge the status quo and its hierarchy of everyday sexism and misogyny. As Criado-Perez comments on the 'Feminazi' stereotype:

Because feminism is experiencing this new wave, more people are talking about it, more women are saying, 'Yes, I am a feminist.' And with that comes the attempt to shut women up and delegitimise what they are saying. It's not engaging with any of the facts of inequality; it just dismisses women on the basis that we're authoritarian. It's a very anti freedom-of-speech term to use, and it's so often used by men who claim feminists themselves are anti free speech. No one seems to notice that women are routinely silenced. It's a very dishonest engagement.[62]

Prospects for change

What is a radical social movement? What does it mean? It is the process by which more and more people become aware of the collective nature of their oppression and this sets into motion the possibility for great change. Journalist Elizabeth Schulte describes Me Too in the following terms: 'Ordinary women's experiences of harassment and abuse at work, at school, in their families, and on the street, which many women have come to accept as a fact of life, were now out in public … #MeToo exposed the outrage that simmered just below the surface that had few outlets to be heard.'[63] For the rotten edifice of power and position which props up the status quo is always revealed most clearly in the moments when the cracks begin to fissure across it. And with this comes the possibility of change.

And yet, there are those who greet the possibility of such change with a savage sense of anger. Not only figures who are in danger of losing immanent power and position but also smaller, non-descript people, who don't have much power in the first place, but experience the prospect of social transformation with a feeling of cringing dread. The concept of the 'Feminazi', the need to envisage the Me Too movement as a 'politically-correct' witch hunt or a left-wing form of McCarthyism – these are notions which allow such people to put the genie back in the bottle. By slotting these components together to craft an ideological vision of the world in which those struggling against injustice are the perpetrators of it – the 'political correctness gone mad' thesis helps to uncork the worst and deepest forms of misogyny; forms of discrimination and oppression that have accrued through the ages – and to unleash these against the forces which threaten change.

Given the gains of the sexual revolution, the number of women in work, the fourth-wave feminism of the last decade – the staid, straight-laced conservativism which would once have countered these things by asserting directly that women should know their place in either the bedroom or the kitchen seems absurdly antiquated. But an argument which seeks to fortify traditional gender roles and forms of oppression from the purview of liberation itself, an argument which appears to don the mantle of sober rationality over and against forms of rampant hysteria – is an argument which can mobilize misogyny and hatred in order to close down and silence those women who clamour for their freedoms a little too loudly. It is a much more effective argument.

Of course, it is nothing new. Behind the mask of 'it's political correctness gone mad', behind the struggle against the 'Feminazi', behind the shock jock who is prepared to say really 'risqué' and 'politically incorrect things' and the journalist who is prepared to write them – we encounter the same archaic and fusty figure, that of the Victorian patriarch of yore who finds 'loud' women to be an affront, who understands that sexual harassment and sexual abuse are just a part and parcel of the world, while simultaneously wishing that those who are the victims of such things would show a little more dignity, a little more decorum, by keeping it to themselves and not making such a fuss. Above all, someone who is terrified by the prospect of change.

3

Black Lives Matter stole my statue

George Floyd

It happened an ocean away in a non-descript Minneapolis suburb. And it was ordinary in terms of its everyday horror. But it was captured on camera. After a report of a forged bill, police were called and an officer would, without provocation, draw his gun on one George Floyd – a middle-aged Black man who was then arrested and 'restrained' on the floor. The police officer kneels on Mr Floyd's neck for over nine minutes, while the pinned man fights to breathe, croaking out the fear for his life, before finally – and in abject terror – he begins to beg for his mother. A moment of the most terrible pathos, for George Floyd's mother had died two years before, and yet – instinctively, involuntarily – it was to her benevolence her middle-aged son turned in his most desperate moment.

Eventually he becomes non-responsive. The cop does not remove his knee. The pinned man's pulse is checked. Still the cop does not relent. George Floyd is declared dead at the hospital one hour later. The whole time the cop who is doing this appears almost nonchalant, his eyebrow cocked – at one point he puts his hand into his pocket. He has the swagger of vicious arrogance, the complacency of a stupid, unfeeling bully whose miserable and sadistic life is shielded by petty officialdom and the generic authority of a uniform. Officer

Derek Chauvin looks like someone who has learnt that he can use his fists with impunity; *yes, that most of all* – he looks like someone who knows he can get away with it.

It would be easy to dismiss what happened to George Floyd as an aberration; indeed many papers and news outlets have taken exactly this line. Chauvin was, so the story goes, a 'bad apple', a psychotic, hate-filled and brutal cop who just happened to cross paths with Mr Floyd, while the latter just happened to be in the wrong place at the wrong time. And yet, as comforting as it might be for some to represent this crime as an isolated and arbitrary incident there is clearly much more to it than that. Like Mr Floyd, I too have had the experience of carrying a counterfeit note and trying to use it in a shop. The difference lies in this. When I offered the cashier the money, she raised the note up, looked at it in the light, before tentatively explaining that it was a forgery. She sounded almost sorry.

For my part I apologized profusely. I remember feeling embarrassed, even though I had no idea that the note was a dud. In the end, I just reached into my pocket and paid with another. But what didn't take place is as telling as what did happen. The cashier didn't call the authorities. She didn't give the police a physical description of me, so that they could track me down. No one pulled a gun on me. No one stood on my neck for almost ten minutes. No one deprived me of the ability to breathe. And no one deprived me of my life. Instead, I walked out of the shop and into the sunlight, and never gave the incident a second thought. Until it was brought to mind many years later, by the George Floyd case and the horror of what had happened to him.

But why was I treated any differently? If I told you it was because of my incredible good-looks, you might be tempted to cry 'fake news'! The difference lies in something much more prosaic, much more mundane. The melanin content of one's skin. I am white. George Floyd was a Black man. And as a Black man, living in the United States in the early twenty-first century, Mr Floyd was a candidate for more intense and even deadly forms of physical repression on the part of the police. African Americans account for less than 14 per cent of the US population but make up almost 24 per cent of all fatal shootings by police since 2015. In the same period, African Americans were more than 50 per cent more likely to be arrested on drugs offences even though surveys show whites use drugs in comparable numbers. African American drivers are 20 per cent more likely to be stopped than their white counterparts. The list goes on. The results of such systematic biases are clear; in 2019 African Americans constituted 13 per cent of the overall population and yet at the same time they made up almost a third of the US prison population.[1]

Such systematic discrimination is facilitated by a series of political and cultural expectations; Black people are more likely to be violent, to commit crimes, to be unreasonable and belligerent, to be more ignorant, to be worse parents … in a word … to be less *human*. These are the kind of latent, semi-conscious feelings George Floyd would have experienced on a regular basis; they were at work in the hearts and minds of people he sometimes encountered and yet who knew nothing about him, and they were at work in the society more broadly in the moments before he stepped into the store on that fateful day carrying that counterfeit bill.[2]

Chauvin's slow, methodical and unbearable extinguishing of George Floyd's life was far from an aberration. It was that which had been set into motion by a social system that had been systematically structured in terms of racial prejudice; the everyday occurrences – the petty harassments, snide assumptions and slights – which form a background to a deeper dehumanization; one which would allow an emissary of the state to gradually crush the life out of one of its citizens with callous arrogance and utter disregard. But what had led to such a climate of racism? How did we get to this point?

Historical context

As difficult to imagine as it is today, the ancient world was almost entirely free from racism. There are, perhaps, a handful of paragraphs in the ancient sources which hint at something like racial discrimination, and there is only one recorded account of someone being killed for the colour of their skin. Even here the claim is sketchy. It occurs in a passage recorded in Greek by a Roman citizen named Appian who talks about a group of Roman soldiers preparing for battle in the first century AD. They step out of their garrison where they encounter an Ethiopian at the front gate and 'as they considered this a bad omen they immediately cut him in pieces'.[3]

No doubts they considered the Ethiopian to be someone from a mysterious, uncivilized and remote region and that his 'foreignness', his 'otherness' – his 'primitiveness' perhaps – in some way felt threatening to the prevalent Roman military culture and its set of imperial assumptions. This was expressed through the superstitious violence the mere presence of the man unleashed. But did the soldiers associate his foreignness, his 'otherness' as being something intrinsically bound up with his skin colour? It is certainly not impossible but it is by no means certain either. After all, in the ancient world, ethnicity tended to be demarked in terms of culture or environment; the ancient Greeks derided non-Greeks as barbarians, not because of the colour of the skin, but because they considered non-Greeks of any background to be unlettered and uncultured, and when such people endeavoured to speak Greek, they made a mangled and unsophisticated 'bah-bah' sound that the Greeks satirized with the onomatopoeic word 'barbarian'.

The Roman architect Vitruvius, for his part, explains the 'Ethiopian character' in terms of environmental conditions, arguing that Ethiopians (and other peoples from hot places) have longevity, good health and are dark-skinned, both intelligent and cowardly – because their blood has been dried up by the sun. In contradistinction, Vitruvius understood that Germans had white skin and were courageous but dim-witted because they lived in a wet climate which didn't dry up their blood, and so they had more of it to lose in a battle, and were less vulnerable as a result.[4]

Even when the ancients conceptualized people in terms of 'blood lineages' which demarked one clan or tribe from another, this did not translate into 'ethnic' accounts of 'biological' superiority or inferiority whereby the tone of one's skin could act as a marker. The Ancient Greeks and Romans couldn't conceive of Africans constituting a 'Black race' not least because no ancient Greek or Roman conceived of themselves as being members of a 'white race' by which 'Blackness' could be thrown into relief. Brutalities, oppressions, subjugations and massacres of foreign peoples – all of these events were prolific and sustained throughout Antique history but they were never rationalized or understood in accordance with a conception of 'race'.

I say this because it gives some indication of the massive sea change that had to take place in order to create the political and cultural landscape of a modern world where race and racism play such a significant part. Race, as an ideological concept, really began to take shape in the seventeenth century when it evolved out of the fundamental contradictions that were opening up between the natural resources and indigenous peoples in the Americas, Africa and the Far East, the nascent capitalism which was developing in parts of Europe, and the new forms of global imperialism which helped to provide the material basis for it. The Spanish and the Portuguese (and later the English, Dutch and French) were all ravenous in terms of their competitive struggle to loot and plunder the 'New World', exsanguinating its rich resources – its silver-riven mountains, its tabacco fields, its sugar crops and the repositories of gold that local civilizations such as the Incas and Aztecs possessed in abundance and could be looted without limit.

But the genocidal voraciousness with which the 'conquistadores' prosecuted their murderous endeavours in the continent had the result of not simply draining natural resources but also decimating whole populations, the same populations whom the Europeans required to provide the massive pools of labour in order to produce and secure their colonial booty. The death count inflicted against the indigenous Americans provides another great chasm of darkness that opens up in the historical record; the latest estimates suggest that a population which was probably around 60 million by the time Columbus made his baleful voyage across those gloomy Atlantic waters, had suffered – one century later – a death toll of 56 million; that is, over 90 per cent of the total population of the Americas had been wiped out.[5] Many of these had been killed by the wars of conquest the Europeans unleashed, the majority, however, had their lives ended by wave after wave of foreign imported diseases such as measles, small pox and the bubonic plague.

Increasing numbers of Africans were introduced to the Americas in order to compensate for this dearth of labour. At first they tended to be indentured labourers; that is, people who would labour to pay off the 'price' of their passage across the Atlantic, who were often worked into the ground for years afterwards on colonial lands, subject to iron discipline such as physical beatings, and these same labourers could sometimes be bought and sold in the period for which their labour had been leased. But despite these undoubtedly draconian practises, the labourer in question would eventually be freed and often provided with some small amount of money and resources so that they could go on to stake a claim for themselves on the land or in the newly developing townships.

In this sense, indentured labour proved to be an unreliable means to ensure the massive production targets the great imperial empires sought to achieve, for the labour population was transient and mobile, and could not be systematically concentrated for any significant period of time. The revival of slavery – which had existed, for the main part, on the periphery of various European, Arab and African kingdoms and regions – was a more 'effective' and 'productive' means of resolving the labour question in the Americas. The number of kidnapped and enslaved Africans began to rise, providing the physical impetus for the extraction of the various cash crops and natural resources that could be sold to fill the coffers of the first global empires (Spanish, Portuguese) – and would, from there, filter through to the Northern cities of Europe and an ever more complex banking system which heralded the rise of a modern bourgeoisie.

The 'radically' new orientation in labour proposed a level of destruction which was almost without limit. In the West African kingdoms, rulers were often coerced into delivering their own peoples to enslavement by the threat or fact of European military intervention, or sometimes rulers were made complicit by the promise of goods such as guns, ammunition, tools and other small manufactures – but, in any event, the population losses that resulted from the vast swathes of stolen people helped retard economic development in Africa, reducing the capacity of indigenous work forces and gutting local industry. As a consequence, those regions tended to become more dependent on European goods and for the same reason their political direction was more and more determined by European interests, often resulting in wars between various African states sponsored by European powers as they further consolidated their grip on the brutal and violent process of trafficking human beings.

The Marxist historian Walter Rodney, in his seminal work *How Europe Underdeveloped Africa*, cites an estimate of global population development from 1500 to 1900; Asia, he points out, went from having 257 million to 857 million, Europe climbed from 103 to 423 million, but Africa only went from 100 to 120 million in those same 400 years.[6] These figures can't be conceived of as having pinpoint accuracy, of course, simply because the ability to measure populations in the centuries gone by was less sophisticated. But they certainly suggest the massive hole that was blown into the African landscape by the violence of the slave trade and the irradiating effects which would cripple the birth rate and stifle economic development in various regions for the centuries to come.

But most grievous of all was the tragic destiny of the stolen peoples themselves. The number of victims taken from their homeland to be transported across the Atlantic is usually put at around 10 million, but as Rodney points out such a figure fails 'to cover mortality in transhipment. The Atlantic crossing or "Middle Passage" as it was called by European slavers, was notorious for the number of deaths incurred, averaging in the vicinity of 15–20 per cent.[7] As well, there were also 'numerous deaths in Africa between time of capture and time of embarkation, especially in cases where captives had to travel hundreds of miles to the coast. Most important of all (given that warfare was the principal means of obtaining captives) it is necessary to make some estimate as to the number of people killed and injured so as to extract the millions who were taken alive and sold. The resultant figure would be many times the millions who landed alive outside Africa.'[8]

A new ideology

To implement such a murderous and violent restructuring of the global population necessitated a new form of ideology. In the medieval period of Western Europe consciousness for the vast majority was very much a religious consciousness; specifically that of Christianity in its Roman-Catholic variant. But there were ways in which this type of ideology did not chime with the vast project of social engineering the colonization of the Americas and the transatlantic slave trade required. Christianity, in its Pauline variant, had built into it a strong streak of universalism, the idea that every human being is sculpted in God's image, that we are the children of a common ancestor; that the branches or tribes of the human world are all, ultimately, descendants of Adam.

Catholic critics such as Bartolomé de las Casas in the sixteenth century argued against the slave trade on precisely this basis, and he also affirmed that the indigenous societies the Spanish were in the process of exploiting and destroying 'equalled many nations of this world that are renowned and considered civilized, and they surpassed many others, and to none were they inferior'.[9] A common belief of the period was that the 'Indians' themselves were the descendants of the ten lost tribes of Israel, and that in 'discovering' the Americas, the Spanish and the Portuguese had encountered paradise on earth. All of this helped create the beginnings of a rich dissenter tradition that would punctuate the history of the slave trade and the conquest of the Americas.

At the same time, however, a different type of religious perspective was emerging. The Roman Catholic Church had been wracked by a series of challenges levelled by more heretical and plebeian tendencies such as the French Cathars, the English Lollards and the Bohemian Hussites. To combat these proto-Protestant heresies, among other things, the Roman Catholic Church introduced the Spanish Inquisition in the fifteenth century. But the Inquisition was also introduced at a time of great social-structural change; that is, it was introduced at a time when the feudalisms of old were being transformed by great kings, often in combination with a nascent bourgeoisie, generating the Absolutist monarchies that would take hold for the centuries to come. In addition, these monarchies created the embryonic basis for a state that was to some degree able to overcome the fragmented character of feudal medievalism, drawing together regional populations through a deeper and more universal network of taxation and military service, the earliest iteration of what would eventually become the nation state.

Once such a geo-political unity was beginning to take form and more and more exert its hegemony through the specific religious ideology the monarch and the ruling group propounded – the possibility of defining those who exist as in some way 'other' to the ethos and identity of that unity opened up. In 1492 – the same year Columbus made his famous voyage – Isabella and Ferdinand, the monarchs who had united much of Spain by fusing the kingdoms of Castile and Aragon, expelled all the Jews, and in the decades to follow Muslims too would be given their marching orders.

The Inquisition took shape in this rapidly shifting environment and in line with the priorities of an emerging Absolutism; it was set up in 1478 at the bequest of Isabella and Ferdinand, and consecrated by Roman Catholic law in and through a papal bull. Among other things, the Inquisition hoped to root out those Jews and Muslims who had converted to Catholicism as a means to avoid persecution but were, in fact, clandestinely practising the 'heretical' ways of their former religions. Such people were referred to as *marranos*. But they were not simply stigmatized and tortured for the nature of their religious ideals. They were also classified in a more 'fundamental' sense; the 'genuine' and 'authentic' members of the body politic were described as having 'pureza de la sangre' or 'pure blood' in contradiction to these Jewish and Muslim converts who were considered outside its parameters and lacked this same 'purity' of blood.

Laws were introduced which forbade the marriage of Christians with converts in order to preserve the 'purity' of the bloodline with the result that not only did the state and its backers attain a greater sense of what we might nowadays call 'ethnic' definition which threw into relief the 'other' and the 'outsider' more definitively – but also the persecutions of Muslims and Jewry allowed for confiscations of wealth and property on a vast scale further filling the coffers of state, and providing a rationale for the complete subsumption of the region under Catholic rule with the takeover of Granada – the last bastion of Islamic power on the Iberian peninsula – in 1492. The notion of 'pureza de la sangre' formed the beginnings of a radical break with previous Catholic theology for it emphasized inherent differences between social groupings rather than the universality that had previously united all 'tribes' as the sons of Adam.

Such ideology fell short of a coherent and systematic conception of racial hierarchy, it is true, but it provided the germ which would eventually yield one. In the seventeenth century, a nascent capitalism had successfully broken through feudal barriers in both England and the North Netherlands, and along with it came the semblance of a modern state in which the creation of a 'national population' could more and more be used to throw into relief notions of 'aliens' and 'outsiders'. At the same time, England had already embarked on its own imperial journey, having begun a broader colonization of Ireland with 'plantation', having founded the colony of Jamestown on the American mainland, and having formed the East India Company which would lead to British colonial domination of the Indian subcontinent a century and a half later. In Jamestown, the colonists there began to deploy slave labour a little over ten years after the colony had been founded.

This combination of the development of the first nation states whose unfettered capitalism would allow for the creation of vast and sweeping global empires was also happening alongside a technological revolution which heralded the modern age of science and the beginnings of Enlightenment ideology; the colonial endeavours led to the discovery and classification of vast numbers of animal species from across the world, along with the new materialisms which would map the laws of motion and matter culminating in Newton's great work *Principia*, in 1687.

The systematic classification of the material world that marked the emergence of modern science was gradually fused with the early grain of notions of blood purity that had arisen at the time of the Inquisition as the theological justification for excluding Jews and Muslims from a predominantly Catholic society. In this way, a pseudo-science began to develop; something which projected the hierarchy of matter and animal species in the natural world onto human social relations in the period in which Western European elites were beginning to subjugate peoples across the globe to their own imperial demands and requirements. A new theory of race began to take shape; a pyramid of peoples where the white man stood at the apex, separated out from all others by a moral, intellectual and spiritual superiority which was ingrained biologically. As one moves further down the pyramid, one encounters a series of lesser races which eventually shade back into nature once again becoming identical with the animals, the 'brutes', the 'beasts' – dumb, inarticulate and wholly beholden to their physical impulses.

The political economist William Petty was one of the first to try to set down this new system of racial classification in a written treatise. William Petty was also one of the founding fathers of political economy, developing a theory of 'laissez-faire' governance which reflected the nascent market capitalism that was coming to challenge the rigid feudal tariffs of yore, while in the same moment, he pioneered more efficient methods to survey lands, such as those in Ireland, which were to be forcibly confiscated and doled out to Cromwell's soldiers after their bloody interventions in that region. Truly a barometer of his time Petty wrote:

> *Of man itself there seems to be several species, To say nothing of Gyants &*
> *Pygmies or of that sort of small men who have little speech …'tis very possible*
> *there may be Races and generations of such … there be others [with differences]*
> *more considerable, that is, between the Guiny Negroes & the Middle Europeans;*
> *& of Negroes between those of Guiny and those who live about the Cape of*
> *Good Hope, which last are the Most beast-like of all the Souls (?Sorts) of Men*
> *whith whom our Travellers arre well acquainted. I say that the Europeans*
> *do not only differ from the aforementioned Africans in Collour … but … in*
> *Naturall Manners, & in the internall Qualities of their Minds.*[10]

This new and systematic theory displaced the old Christian theology of the universality of mankind and its joint collective heritage with a pseudo-science that increasingly emphasized the innate differences supposedly carried by bloodline and demarked by skin tone; a fantasy formulation of a world driven by the immaculate and innate perfectibility of European whites in the same period when the tawdry and bloody processes of imperial looting, conquest and murder were being affected on a global scale by European powers in reality. The new racelogy offered the ideological 'justification' for the unadulterated violence which imperial conquest necessitated, by classifying vast sections of humanity as sundered in a purely physical and animal-like existence. The spiritual and technological progress of humankind more broadly was devolved onto its whiter layers; thus the prosecution of genocidal violence against the lower orders could be reimagined as the inevitable and necessary development of human potential understood as white 'civilization's' march through the world.

To reduce other human beings to little more than the status of animals through this type of raceology was effective in justifying the worst atrocity of the period, that of the transatlantic slave trade. The new raceology provided the 'rationalization' by which Black Africans could be reduced to the status of objects, of things, of beasts of burden – but it also headed off another danger from the perspective of the colonists. The economic oppressions of poor whites were grievous in their own right, often leading to uprisings, and in the early period of American history the rebellious energies of Black slaves and poor whites sometimes tended to link up, as was the case with Bacon's Rebellion in 1676 whereby thousands of Virginians – both Blacks and whites, slaves and freedmen, civilians and indentured servants – rose up against the colonial governor William Berkeley, chasing him from Jamestown and setting fire to the settlement. As a result of that uprising, the colonial elites responded by consolidating the awakening awareness of the new racial categories in and through an intensified legal framework.

The Virginia Slave Codes of 1705 made it illegal for whites to work for Blacks (up until this point there were a dwindling minority of people in the landowning class who were of African descent and who could command white labour), new property rights were established for slave owners and poor whites, all Black servants were granted the same legal status as slaves, slaves could be whipped, branded or mutilated merely for associating with whites, Blacks were prohibited from owning arms and so forth. The aftermath of Bacon's rebellion fused developing notions of race and racial superiority into a political and legal infrastructure that not only allowed for the unadulterated deployment and exploitation of Black labour on a slave basis but also helped ensure that Black labour was isolated, increasingly set against its white counterpart in order that the possibly of unified resistance and rebellion be curtailed.

As the slave trade began to pick up pace, as its sheer lucrativeness drew in more speculators, ships captains, merchant seamen, investors, overseers, mercenaries, plantation heads, insurers – the tendency of those orchestrating the trade to see those who were the victims of it as either sub-human animals or merely disposable objects was infinitely enhanced as the ideology of racial codification seeped into plantation culture like a disease. As a consequence, the cruelty towards enslaved Blacks would come to know no limit.

The great Marxist historian C. L. R. James describes the conditions of the slave ships: 'Night and day thousands of human beings were packed into these "dens of putrification" so that no European could stay in them for longer than a quarter of an hour without fainting … The close proximity of so many naked human beings, their bruised and festering flesh, the foetid air, the prevailing dysentery, the accumulation of filth, turned these holds into a hell.'[11] To these bleak, inhuman conditions was added the brutality of the ships masters: 'To the slave-traders they were articles of trade and no more. A captain held up by calms or adverse winds was known to have poisoned his cargo … one captain, to strike terror into the rest, killed a slave and dividing heart, liver and entrails into 300 pieces made each of the slaves eat one, threatening those who refused with the same torture. Such incidents were not rare.'[12]

Perhaps one of the most infamous incidents occurred in 1781 when it was revealed that, after a navigational error which led to more time spent at sea, the Zong slave ship jettisoned more than 130 slaves – men, women and children – into the cold waters of the Atlantic. If those same slaves had died of 'natural causes' – that is, if they had died from dehydration while remaining on the ship, the slaving company wouldn't have been able to receive an insurance settlement; but by murdering a large number in order to exploit a legal loophole, the slavers were eligible for compensation for every slave who was killed.

These kinds of incidents were simply the tip of the iceberg. According to the *Encyclopaedia Virginia*, it is estimated that '[b]etween 1500 and 1866, Europeans transported to the Americas nearly 12.5 million enslaved Africans, about 1.8 million of whom died on the Middle Passage, their bodies thrown into the Atlantic.'[13] The historian David Olusoga describes how, after the bodies were cast overboard 'they were devoured by the sharks that, over the centuries of the Atlantic slave trade, learned to seek out slave ships and follow the bloody paths of slave routes across the ocean.'[14] The conditions on the plantations were equally grim. James describes the situation in San Domingo (present day Haiti) whereby at its height, half a million slaves extracted sugar cane.

The stranger in San Domingo was awakened by the crack of the whip, the stifled cries, and the heavy groans of the Negroes who saw the sun rise only to curse it for its renewal of their labours and their pains. Their work began at daybreak: at eight they stopped for a short breakfast and worked again till midday. They began again at two o'clock and worked until evening, sometimes till ten or eleven … The sugar plantations demanded an exacting and ceaseless labour. The tropical earth is baked hard by sun ... the reaping of one crop was the signal for the immediate digging of ditches and the planting of another ... the extraction of the juice and the manufacture of the raw sugar went on for three weeks a month, sixteen or eighteen hours a day, for seven or eight months in the year.[15]

The 'domestic' conditions of the slaves offered no respite. James describes how they:

[w]orked like animals, the slaves were housed like animals, in huts built around a square planted with provisions and fruits. These huts were about 20 to 25 feet long, twelve feet wide and about fifteen feet in height, divided by partitions into two or three rooms. They were windowless and light entered only by the door. The floor was beaten earth; the bed was of straw, hides or a rude contrivance of cords tied on posts. On these slept indiscriminately mother, father and children. Defenceless against their masters, they struggled with overwork and its usual complement – underfeeding ... their masters gave them half-a-dozen pints of coarse flour, rice, or pease, and half-a-dozen herrings. Worn out by their labours all through the day and far into the night, many neglected to cook and ate the food raw. The ration was so small and given to them so irregularly that often the last half of the week found them with nothing.[16]

On top of all this, there were the methods of discipline required to enforce such a hellish existence:

Irons on the hands and feet, blocks of wood that the slaves had to drag behind them wherever they went, the tin-plate mask designed to prevent the slaves eating the sugar-cane, the iron collar. Whipping was interrupted in order to pass a piece of hot wood on the buttocks of the victim; salt, pepper, citron, cinders, aloes, and hot ashes were poured on the bleeding wounds. Mutilations were common, limbs, ears, and sometimes the private parts, to deprive them of the pleasures which they could indulge in without expense. Their masters poured burning wax on their arms and hands and shoulders, emptied the boiling cane sugar over their heads, burned them alive, roasted them on slow fires, filled them with gunpowder and blew them up with a match; buried them up to the neck and smeared their heads with sugar that the flies might devour them; fastened them near to nests of ants or wasps; made them eat their excrement, drink their urine, and lick the saliva of other slaves. One colonist was known in moments of anger to throw himself on his slaves and stick his teeth into their flesh.[17]

It makes for difficult, harrowing reading, and it is almost impossible to imagine that people might treat other people this way. But it is also important to understand that the slave owners who had more and more been warped into these sadistic, brutal, suspicious, paranoid and grotesque caricatures of humanity – had lost all human sensibility, all such feeling – as a result of imbibing the toxic ideology of race and racism for decades and even centuries; an ideology that had helped drive economic exploitation through the slave model to an absolute nadir in terms of the excruciating and unrelenting objectification of people as things. This is what demarked the transatlantic slave trade from all other forms of slavery which came before. The racial codification that allowed a person to be reduced to a purely physical utility; something to be worked into the ground, drained of every iota of physical energy, bled dry before being discarded like a husk.

The resistance of slaves

But to the sheer numb and deadened inhumanity of the slavers, history offers up the incredible dignity and resistance of the slaves. A deep wellspring of humanity. For the story of the transatlantic slave trade is also a story of resistance and rebellion on the part of the slaves themselves. The first slave rebellions in the modern age took place in what is now South Carolina in 1526. The details are sketchy, the records scant, but it appears that after an early settlement was ravaged by disease and conflict, a group of African slaves set fire to the house of the settler leader, one Lucas Vázquez de Ayllón, before 'the Africans ran into the forest, never to be seen again'.[18]

We do not know the names of those slaves, we know virtually nothing about them, but they are responsible for inaugurating a series of rebellions in which slaves not only broke free from their captivity by incinerating their callous masters, but also escaped into the forests, swamps or mountains – often to build their own settlements there, or to mix with the indigenous peoples in secret, illusive communities which would eventually become the basis of many creole cultures such as the Garifuna people who are descended from Black-Caribs or the Mascogos who were the descendants of the Native American Seminole people and escaped African slaves.

These ex-slave communities or Maroon communities as they became known, were precarious and precious outposts of freedom and resistance, set against the dark expanse of colonialism, racism and imperial power that had facilitated the extraction of such great wealth over and against such human suffering. In Jamaica, large numbers of free Blacks, slaves and indigenous Americans coalesced into various and diverse Maroon communities that repeatedly inflicted ambushes and defeats on the occupying power, the English.

In the eighteenth century, one group of Maroons, led by the now legendary 'Nanny Maroon', waged a successful war over the course of a decade against English occupation, and was able to establish and hold its own region, 'Nanny Town', in the Blue Mountains overlooking Stony River. The Maroons fought a guerrilla war, employing ingenious tactics of surprise and camouflage, melding into the shape and form of the forest such that British soldiers told tales in fearful whispers of the trees themselves coming to life before separating one's head from one's body.[19]

Maroon communities had also formed against French occupation. In San Domingo (present-day Haiti) the Maroons led resistance movements which targeted large-scale plantations, freeing slaves and often killing slavers, sometimes poisoning the drinking water of the plantation owners. Even more significantly, it was a Maroon leader, Dutty Boukman, who declared war on the French plantation owners in the early 1790s, thereby sparking the Haitian Revolution, perhaps the greatest slave revolt known to history.

Here the slave class – largely uneducated and illiterate, living in scant conditions and subject to the most fearful military discipline – were able to defeat first the white oligarchy which oppressed them, then the soldiers sent out by the French monarchy in order to quash the revolt, then a Spanish invasion which looked to capitalize on the unrest, then a British invasion, and finally the defeat of a second French army – some 20,000 soldiers strong – sent out by Napoleon himself. Ultimately the freed rebels were able to declare themselves as the Republic of Haiti in 1804.

This feat of organization and endurance, in the words of its great chronicler C. L. R. James, provides 'one of the great epics in revolutionary struggle and achievement'.[20] Napoleon, widely considered the greatest military mind of the nineteenth century was outflanked and outfought by the superb tactics of Toussaint Louverture, a man who was himself born into slavery. A voracious reader and autodidact familiar with the works of Epictetus and Machiavelli, Louverture would go onto be inspired by the ideals of the Enlightenment and the French Revolution, ideals which would incentivize the radical movement from below, channelling the rebellion into the creation of a revolutionary new society.

Away from the islands of the Caribbean and into mainland America where Lord Sugar had been supplanted by King Cotton on the great landed estates of the South, rebellions were also brewing. In 1831, a great shadow was cast over the land in Virginia, even though the sun was still high in the sky. The solar eclipse was witnessed by a slave and a preacher named Nat Turner. For him, the meteorological event was filled with great and ominous meaning; it was as though a vast dark hand had reached out across the sun taking it as its own.[21] Turner saw the eclipse as a harbinger of the future, a signal to Black empowerment and emancipation, and he gathered together scores of slaves and some free Blacks who then travelled from district to district, house to house, freeing slaves and slaughtering many of the whites unfortunate enough to cross their path (though sparing a few poor whites whose economic condition was little better than that of the slaves themselves).

The rebellion was put down brutally by local state militia but Turner's premonition would be brought to fruition only a few decades later after the country erupted into civil war in 1861. In 1863, Lincoln's 'emancipation proclamation' changed the legal status of slaves in those Confederate states that were in an active state of rebellion from 'enslaved' to 'free'. Lest one thinks that freedom was simply handed down from above to the slaves through legal writ by a more enlightened element in the white bureaucracy of power – one must remember that Lincoln himself had only moved towards the politics of emancipation hesitantly and under the pressures and exigencies of the war itself. By freeing the slaves by way of legal proclamation, the number of Union soldiers was rapidly swelled by Black recruits; indeed Black soldiers came to number over 180,000 or 10 per cent of the total number of the Union troops. They fought heroically and ferociously because, as Fredric Douglass would reflect, they 'had a deeper interest in the defeat and humiliation of the rebels than all others'.[22]

It is highly unlikely the Union forces would have triumphed without the Black soldiers; the emancipation of the South was unthinkable without this mobilization of the subject Black population from below. And here one must consider not only the Black soldiers but also the increasingly revolutionary mood which was developing among those Black people still subject to the slave system in the South; slaves fled from the plantations in droves, risking their lives and those of their families in order to act 'as scouts, guides, and spies for invading Union armies'.[23] At the same time, they often took direct action against the masters by sacking their property or engaging in protests like those of the women of Magnolia who went on strike, refusing to return to the fields. In that particular instance, the slaves stopped working, but not completely; the masters, trying to re-establish discipline, would eventually enter the slave quarters only to be met by the chilling spectacle of a gallows the slaves themselves had fashioned and erected. Perhaps, in that ominous stillness, those slave masters understood. The end was neigh. Slavery's time had come.

As Steven Hahn argues, when seen in this light, the American Civil War becomes more than just a war – indeed it might arguably be seen as the 'largest, most successful slave revolt in history'[24] or at the very least, one of them. As the system of plantation slavery had collapsed and Union armies flooded into the South occupying the territories there, a new period was inaugurated – that of Reconstruction. For the twelve precious years following, the uplifted ex-slaves achieved political representation – sixteen Black ministers served in Congress, several in the US Senate, alongside over 600 in state legislatures and hundreds more in local offices from sheriffs to judges. A process of land redistribution was pressed whereby large swathes of land in South Carolina and Georgia were reserved for Black ownership and use, and the Freedmen's Bureau Act authorized the land which had passed into governmental hands as a result of the dispossession of the old slave oligarchy to be rented or sold to ex-slaves.[25]

A counterrevolution

However, the remnants of the old slave owning oligarchy still had considerable power and – terrified by the mobilization of a newly freed Black population – they responded with the most vicious forms of violence. In the direct aftermath of the Civil War, the terror organization the Klu Klux Klan was formed, headed by ex-Confederate soldiers – battle-hardened militants acclimatized to bloody violence and steeped in the philosophy of white supremacy. Similar organizations and chapters opened up across the whole of the South, targeting Black political leaders and prominent officials for intimidation and assassination and sometimes too the whites who supported them.

But the clandestine terror of the Klan was supplemented by political lobbying on the part of the old Southern elites which synergized with Republican fears at the radical egalitarianism that the defeat of the Confederacy had opened the door to. The mobilizations of free Blacks had provided a powerful impetus to popular struggles more generally – Reconstruction had seen, for instance, the first state-funded public schools along with more equitable tax laws and increases in bargaining power on the part of landed labourers. In addition, Black empowerment provided a key incentive to the burgeoning feminist movement; the women who spoke at what some people consider to be the inauguration of the feminist movement, the conference at Seneca Falls in 1848, had often made their bones by first speaking as abolitionists.

For such reasons, the Northern political elite was inclined to come to some kind of rapprochement with its former adversaries in the South. The president who succeeded Lincoln, Andrew Johnson, ordered the lands which the Federal government had taken possession of – and which were to be redistributed to the freed Blacks ('40 acres and a mule') – to be returned to their former owners. This was highly significant because it left the Black population dependent on the white owners once more, this time in the role as paid labourers or share croppers.

To this, was added another vital legal and political caveat. Although the 13th Amendment which came into law in 1865 had prohibited both slavery and forced labour, it nevertheless made a crucial qualification – 'except as a punishment for crime whereof the party shall have been duly convicted'. As the period of Reconstruction reached its end, not only did the free Blacks face the terror tactics of the Klan, but – as a result of having their right to own land curtailed – they often found themselves charged with petty misdemeanours like vagrancy or loitering. Such charges were then translated into long-term prison sentences that allowed the now unified state to enforce a form of collective labour on large numbers of Black people without compensation once again. The era of the chain gang had been born.

Once more, a new injection of racist ideology was required to justify the shift. Here, the image of the Black person as criminal begins to attain definition. To the racism of old – that which described Black people as sub-humans and particularly animalistic – was now added a sense of ravenous criminality; Black people were depicted as being wanton criminals in thrall to their animal instincts. In particular, Black men were stigmatized as sexual predators lurking in the shadows waiting to pounce on vulnerable white women.[26]

The 1915 film, 'The Birth of a Nation', epitomizes this ideology at its very height; it describes the period of Reconstruction as a period in which slovenly Blacks are able to take over the political process through corruption and sheer numbers, disenfranchising the whites and endeavouring to put an end to a more traditional and noble form of life. Most of the actors are white people dressed up in 'black face'. One scene depicts a leering and brutish Black man who attempts to rape a white woman. The latter throws herself off a cliff rather than submit. The end of the film is a triumphant one; a group of Klu Klux Klan militia intimidate a group of Blacks into not voting. The 'horde', the 'animal-like masses', have been held in check.

The need to disenfranchise Black people politically went alongside the need to criminalize them socially such that their labour could be conscripted into the prison chain gangs. Political disenfranchisement took place through the evolving Jim Crow Laws, a set of legal measures which enforced apartheid by segregating transport, schooling, libraries and so on, leaving those facilities or institutions that were meant for Blacks desperately underfunded and often not fit for purpose.

At the same time, this assault on education for Black people, along with their impoverished economic status, was complimented by a series of literary and means tests which more and more made it impossible for Blacks to vote. Gradually all the great gains of Reconstruction were swamped under a counter-mobilization that managed to discipline Black labour in the most exploitative ways while removing at a stroke the political rights that freed Blacks had achieved; all of this was facilitated by the racist image of the Black person as inherently inclined towards criminality.

From 1955, a new wave of Black resistance began to emerge targeting the apartheid. In that year, a fourteen-year-old African-American child, Emmett Till, was accused of whistling at a white woman working behind the counter in a store. The claim that the child had done this was later found to have been fabricated. The husband of the woman along with another white man abducted the child. They beat him and mutilated him before tossing Emmett's body into a river.

It was one of those incidents which are known to history. An incident of such bleak injustice and callous cruelty that it acts as a flashpoint revealing vividly the broader forms of discrimination and oppression at work in the society at large – and by so doing, becomes the moment at which is shaped the outlines of a greater movement of resistance and rage. The child's mother (Mamie Elizabeth Till-Mobley) insisted on having her boy buried in an open coffin so that people could see the devastation which had been inflicted on Emmett's swollen, unrecognizable face. The press reportage – along with the image of the 10,000 mourners who, dignified but angry, had turned up to pay their respects to the slain boy – provoked a wave of protest and rebellion that passed across the whole nation.

For the following decade the Civil Rights movement encompassed boycotts, such as those sparked by Rosa Parks refusing to give up her seat on a segregated bus, the Freedom Rides whereby Black and white activists risked their lives by travelling through the South on desegregated buses, the occupations of universities, the strategy of non-violent resistance, the sit-ins, the marches of millions upon the capital led by figures such as Martin Luther King. Such protests and demonstrations linked with the anti-War movement, the feminist movements, the burgeoning gay rights movement – to generate the intoxicating atmosphere of freedom and change which was rippling across the panorama of political and cultural life in the mid-to late 1960s. In 1964 and 1965, the Civil Rights movement attained one of its major goals and put an end to the legal system of apartheid by compelling the introduction of the Civil Rights Act that ended segregation in public places and banned discrimination in the work-place, and the Voting Rights Act which followed it, and which prohibited racial discrimination at the ballot box.

This was, however, far from the end of the story. The American authorities had come to see some of the political organizations and leading figures that emerged out of the Civil Rights Movement as existential threats to the establishment order. The FBI introduced the COINTELPRO programme which saw leading figures of organizations such as the Black Panther Party falsely charged with crimes, imprisoned and even assassinated. Individuals and groups were smeared, false stories were planted in the media, leaders of the Civil Rights movement such as Martin Luther King were wire-tapped and the FBI even sponsored a group of paramilitaries constituted from former members of the Minutemen – an anti-communist and fascistic organization devoted to suppressing violently those considered to be un-American. Numbering many thousands of members in the late 1960s, by the early 1980s the Panthers numbered little more than a handful, such had they been decimated by the state campaign of systematic violence and intimidation directed against them.

Perhaps even more significantly, after the defeat of American apartheid, the state would once more re-orientate its tactics in the suppression of the Black population. In this case, it involved combining the stereotype of the Black person as an innate criminal – a stereotype that had been nourished under Jim Crow – with the issue of drug use. Under the Nixon presidency, the state declaimed loudly its intention to fight against the scourge of drugs, declaring that drugs were 'public enemy number one'.[27] This explicit drive to treat drugs not as a health issue but as a criminal one was part of a deeper political strategy that represented a realignment of the Republican Party more broadly. The 'Southern Strategy' saw Nixon concentrate on Deep South whites, in particular those sections that were disaffected by the Civil Rights movement and felt that – with the end of apartheid – the political power and social superiority they maintained over the Black population was increasingly in jeopardy.

Of course, after the great victories of the Civil Rights movement, it was much more difficult for politicians to mobilize this inflamed and toxically racist element with a direct appeal to racist language. So instead, Nixon turned to the language of 'law and order'. In fighting the drugs war, law and order would be restored; or to say the same from the perspective of the racist white layers – the Black population would be repressed through new means because it was the Black population that the war on drugs was truly calibrated to target. One of Nixon's central advisors, John Enrilichman, reflected on the strategy in the following terms:

We knew we couldn't make it illegal to be either against the war or Black, but by getting the public to associate the hippies with marijuana and Blacks with heroin, and then criminalizing both heavily, we could disrupt those communities … We could arrest their leaders, raid their homes, break up their meetings, and vilify them night after night on the evening news. Did we know we were lying about the drugs? Of course we did.[28]

In the Raegan era, the strategy was intensified. In 1982 Raegan announced 'the war on drugs', a campaign that took place against a backdrop of severe economic crisis and helped legitimate a broader neoliberal assault on healthcare and social services that would disproportionately affect the Black population. In this context, the notions of gangs – groups of urban youth, feral and violent – increasingly came to feature as a media staple. These shady figures were more and more presented as exclusively Black or Latino drug dealers whose presence was a ubiquitous and perpetual threat to good, hardworking American citizens, themselves most often depicted in the guise of the 'traditional' white working family.

It was an example of what might be called 'dog whistle' racism. The great Civil Rights movement had achieved not just legal equality but also the recognition amongst larger numbers of the population that notions of racial inferiority were a hallmark of ignorance and an obstacle to the creation of an enlightened and civilized society. For this reason, there was required some secondary concept – like the notion of gangs – which the mainstream media could then use as a placeholder for the derogatory depiction of other races, particularly that of African-Americans.

In actual fact, as already referenced, the level of drug use amongst whites and Blacks in the United States is rather similar in scale but whereas the whites of the suburbs who in the Yuppie era tended to use the more expensive cocaine – the poorer urban Blacks most often used 'crack', a far cheaper derivative. In 1986, as part of its 'war on drugs', the administration introduced the 'Anti-Drug-Abuse Act' which further shifted the focus from rehabilitation to purely punitive measures by putting into place mandatory minimum sentences for drug offences. But one such minimum sentence of five years would be applied to a crack user for the possession of just five grams of crack cocaine, while the user of cocaine in its normal form would not be subject to the same unless they were in possession of 500 grams. This 100:1 disparity was clearly a cynical and contrived attempt to more effectively criminalize a particular section of the population on an implicitly racist basis. And when Raegan took office in 1980 the prison population stood at 329,000 – but when he left office in 1989 that figure had almost doubled to 627,000.[29]

The Democratic administration, which succeeded Raegan, followed the ideological programme he had set out; the same emphasis on punitive measures was consecrated by Bill Clinton with the appalling 'three strikes law' which mandated life sentences for anyone convicted of three crimes no matter how petty. Again, this disproportionately targeted ethnic minorities who tended to live in poorer and more deprived areas. And again, the same codified racial rhetoric was used to justify the onslaught; the racism of the past where Black people were described first in terms of subhuman animals and later in terms of feral criminals – was now condensed into the type of language which was highly suggestive, racially speaking, but without referring to a conception of Blackness outright.

So, for example, while Bill Clinton went about massively expanding the prison population through a programme of 'law and order' by which the state was able to target poor Blacks in particular, Hillary Clinton – his own personal

Lady Macbeth – worked to justify such politics, playing on the worst fears of the populace by describing roaming 'gangs of kids' who were in some way less than human – 'no conscience, no empathy' – before using the now infamous term 'super predators'[30] to classify them. Here, distilled into a single phrase, we get both the idea of Black youth as animalistic and as inherently criminal – relayed in such a way as to mobilize those racial tropes that had been built up over the centuries, but without explicitly using the words 'Black' or 'African-American'.

Bill Clinton, for his part, voted to retain the disparity in punishment for those who use cocaine and those who use crack, a disparity that the Sentencing Commission would go on to describe in the following terms: 'The 100-to-1 crack cocaine to powder cocaine quantity ratio is a primary cause of the growing disparity between sentences for Black and white federal defendants.'[31] At the time of Clinton's first election win in 1992 the prison population stood at 847,000 while when he left office in 2000, that figure had climbed to 1,334,000.[32]

These trends continued in the following administrations, both Republican and Democrat. A 2016 expose discovered how, in the United States, 'approximately 39 per cent of the nationwide prison population (576,000 people) is behind bars with little public safety rationale' – that is, the crimes in question were almost all non-violent, lower level offences and that this section of prisoners 'should not be in prison'.[33] In 2011, the US Supreme Court ordered the state of California to drastically reduce its prison population as a result of an overcrowding that had 'resulted in extreme suffering and even death, a deprivation of the inmates' rights that violates the Constitution'.[34] The state of California appealed this judgement, but what was particularly interesting was the rationale for their appeal. They argued that the prison population shouldn't be reduced because to do so would deplete the pool of cheap prison labour.[35]

Of course, Black people in particular provided and continue to provide a disproportionately large amount of this cheap prison labour. In 2016, it was reported that around '1.75 million Black men were under federal, state and local criminal justice supervision', by far the highest number of any ethnicity. What makes this statistic all the more disturbing is the fact that it represents 'about double the 872,924 Black men who were enslaved in 1850'.[36] And it is not just Black prison labour which is grossly undervalued. Such forced labour is supplemented by broader economic trends in which Black men experienced the largest pay gap in the United States of any ethnic minority relative to their white counterparts: 'On average, Black men earned 87 cents for every dollar a white man earned' – while at the same time '[b]lack women's share of the high-wage workforce – jobs that pay more than $48 per hour, or about $100,000 annually – is less than half their representation in the overall workforce'.[37]

It is easy to imagine that racism is simply a product of fear, of ignorance, of a lack of education, of bitterness and alienation, of suspicion and distrust, and of misery. And racism feeds off these factors, without a doubt. But underlying them is a political strategy that has been unfolded over centuries. From the transatlantic slave trade, to Jim Crow apartheid, to the mass incarceration of the modern epoch and the police brutality that is its inevitable corollary – racism takes shape as the means by which a powerful elite is able to exploit and enforce the labour of the poorest sections of society on a systematic and institutional basis. The means by which a social relation of the most vicious exploitation can be 'justified' by those who have benefited from it, generation after generation, century after century.

At this point we must return to that video in which a state official places his knee over a civilian's neck for more than nine minutes, gradually and excruciatingly draining him of life until none remains. To those who argue that Derek Chauvin – George Floyd's murderer – was an aberration, an anomaly, a bad apple, someone who was thoroughly unrepresentative of the character of society more broadly – one might point out that behind the present incarnation of Derek Chauvin, as he appears in all his cocksure arrogance, pressing the head of George Floyd into the pavement in brutal daylight – lingers the ghostly silhouettes of his predecessors in the past; the Derek Chauvin who was a small-town sheriff, only at night he would don a white-clothed mask in order to join his 'brothers' in the ghastly 'entertainment' of burning crosses on lawns or hanging brutalized, Black bodies from the arching branches of shadowy trees; or an earlier incarnation still, the Derek Chauvin who was an overseer of a great landed estate where he would whip the slaves until their backs bled or brand their bodies with hot iron allowing the wounds to sizzle in the high, unrelenting sun.

For what happened to George Floyd forms a link in a chain of systematic oppression and mass murder, one which ropes back through the centuries. And it was this which the Black Lives Matter campaign was able to bring to light with such pathos and such pain, articulating the experience of Black people in America with a simple and deathly slogan – that 'I can't breathe' – the unbearably poignant words uttered by George Floyd just before his death; but words which had been croaked out by other Black men in the moment of their murder including Eric Garner, including Elijah McClain, including Javier Ambler, including Manuel Ellis and others. That 'I can't breathe' was no longer simply the words of an individual in his death agonies – they were the words of a whole people who had struggled and fought to break the chains of slavery, who had smashed the political and legal forms of apartheid through the most heroic acts of demonstration and revolt, and yet still they found themselves smothered by a miasma of racism and ignorance, still they found their lives to be disposable in the very place they had come to call home.

Those words resonated around the world. From 'the Black Trans Lives Matter' demonstrations which broke out in the heart of Brooklyn to the streets of Amsterdam where protestors chanted in their thousands, 'I can't breathe'. From the socialists in Sri Lanka who gathered in the capital's Liberty Plaza waving placards which sported the words 'Justice for Floyd', to the moving mural of George Floyd which was daubed onto the bullet-scarred wall of separation that segregates poverty-stricken Palestinians from Israel proper. In France too, Palestinian flags flew at a Black Lives Matter protest in the Place de la Republique, Paris. That there are affinities between two states which have both evolved a top-heavy police apparatus adept at brutalizing on a racist basis the peoples they have displaced and impoverished goes without saying. Indeed Israel's police, military and intelligence services have provided training for American law enforcement in terms of use of force and crowd control. But the global explosion of Black Lives Matter revealed something else; it revealed the intimate and powerful connection that exists between peoples – worlds away – the struggles from below which recognize collective forms of oppression and whose solidarity crosses racial and geographical lines. The very essence of internationalism.

The backlash against Black Lives Matter

For this reason, the reaction to the protests on the part of the powerful was always going to involve the endeavour to downplay them. To delegitimize them, to undermine them ideologically in and through a media campaign that mobilized the narrative of 'political correctness gone mad' while at the same time trying to reassert many of the racist tropes that the Black Lives Matter campaign had evolved to counter. In looking at cases of police brutality and even police killings through the stereotype of the Black person as having an innate predilection for criminality – media sources could minimize the value of the life that had been stolen.

The New York Times, for example, published a piece on Michael Brown – the unarmed teenager shot to death by a police officer in Ferguson in 2014. Their journalist, John Eligon, observed that Brown had 'lived in a community that had rough patches, he [Brown] had dabbled in drugs and alcohol … [h]e had taken to rapping'.[38] In actual fact, Michael Brown did not have a criminal record (not that the shooting of an unarmed teenager is made any more viable had it been so) – and yet, that 'community with rough patches', that 'dabbled in drugs and alcohol', are all attempts to criminalize the teenager's character along with that final but absurd flourish – 'taken to rapping' – the clearest racist marker of all. The irony here, of course, is that many of those who are using these codified racial pointers in order to suggest that young Black victims who have been killed by police are culpable for what has happened are also the same set of people who tend to insist that the police who commit these atrocities are not motivated by any racial considerations whatsoever.

Indeed the methodological endeavour to whitewash the racist nature of the killings of Black people by police became the central thrust of those ideologues who wished to counter the Black Lives Matter campaign; such a strategy reached fruition with the 'All Lives Matter' slogan which became ubiquitous after the slaying of George Floyd and the mass protests which followed it. The 'All Lives Matter' slogan is slippery in the extreme; it offers up what appears to be a disinterested statement of fact grounded in Enlightenment ideals of universal equality. In this sense, it can masquerade as a progressive stance rather than a backward and reactionary one.

Following the killing of George Floyd, the then vice president of the United States Mike Pence – part of the overtly racist Trump administration – was asked by a news channel over and again to confirm if he believed that Black lives matter. But rather than answer affirmatively, Pence retreated into the vaguer and more indefinite proclamations of eighteenth-century Enlightenment thought in order to aver that 'all of us are created equal, and endowed by our creator with certain inalienable rights. And so all lives matter in a very real sense'.[39]

And to be sure, it would be hard to disagree with the idea that 'all lives matter'. But such a statement is being proffered as a response to a set of oppressions in the present day that have developed out of a specific context; that is, the racism that is a consequence of a series of historical and social forms which have evolved in accordance with the need of the most powerful to exploit and fetter Black labour and Black populations on a more intensive basis. The violence that results in the much higher frequency of unarmed Black men being killed by cops can't be understood without recourse to this kind of history. How many of the cultural and political assumptions towards Black people in the present day on the part of the emissaries of the state are rooted in such a historical context.

The 'All Lives Matter' slogan works to counter the thrust of Black Lives Matter by stamping the universality of the generic individual onto a situation whose injustice grows out of a key set of historical specificities that affect some individuals over and above others. By saying that 'all lives matter', one places all citizens on an abstractly equal basis thus absolving the real forms of concrete oppression which apply to specific groups.

'The All Lives Matter' rallying cry, then, allows it to appear as though some people – by asserting that 'Black Lives Matter' – are privileging one group and in some way trying to raise the value of their lives above everyone else's. Of course, this is utterly disingenuous. If a community experiences an earthquake or a famine, and solidarity and aid pours in from across the world because people feel that 'Bangladesh', for example, matters – one would have to be a special type of silly to start cluttering up the airwaves with the bleating insistence of 'hey, but don't all countries matter?'

In the same vein, the 'Black Lives Matter' slogan doesn't imply the devaluation of other ethnicities and races. What it implies is the recognition of a particular group – in the United States and elsewhere – as having suffered persecution, slavery, apartheid and as continuing to endure economic oppression and murderous racism on a regular and systematic basis. It implies the understanding and solidarity which develop in accordance with this. The 'All Lives Matter' slogan is not, therefore, about being even-handed or fair-minded or promoting some form of equal standard and universal humanism. Rather it involves the sly and surreptitious endeavour to occlude and paper over the inhuman horrors of racism and poverty. The attempt to divert people's gaze.

The argument that the Black Lives Matter movement was valuing Black lives to the detriment of other groups (whites) became syphoned into arguments about 'political correctness' more broadly. Notions of 'political correctness gone mad' allowed for a group of people – who had been the victims of racial categorization and oppression for centuries – to be reimagined as the oppressors; to step forward as those capable of imposing their 'will', their 'politics' and their 'culture' on society in an increasingly totalitarian fashion in and through the Black Lives Matter movement.

When the protests were at their most intense, following the killing of George Floyd, a slew of articles appeared in newspapers and websites around the world that took this particular angle. According to the narrative, not only had the protests become 'more violent, more destructive, and more divisive'[40] but now it was more and more impossible to voice any dissension against the movement because of an atmosphere of heightened 'political correctness': 'If you aren't posting #BLM, you're racist. If you ARE posting #BLM but you say it in the wrong way, you're racist. If you're white and you're silent, that's violence. If you're white and you're speaking up, you're talking over Black voices and only they should be heard. If you're white, you're privileged and racist; your "fragility" means you're also racist if you deny it.'[41]

The writer of these lines, Sarah Downey, goes further still. The stifling of free speech along with the increasingly divisive and violent nature of the protests had led to a 'politically-correct witch-hunt' that is comparable to McCarthyism in the 1950s, except people are being rooted out for being 'racists instead of communists'. In a similar vein, the Black Lives Matter movement is akin to what happened in Nazi Germany where 'normal citizens … turned on each other over the supposed moral high ground'. With a dramatic flourish, Downey concludes, 'Stalin's socialist Russia killed 20 million people. Do we really need to run that experiment here?'[42]

The ironies abound: the clumsy conflation of McCarthyism with Nazism and Stalinism as if these things are abstractly identical and represent the same set of social interests when in fact they were differentiated and discrete phenomena with very different political directions and ends. McCarthyism, for instance, was predicated on the fear that America was in imminent danger of turning 'communist', that the reds-under-the-bed type subversion would secure power through its infiltration of American politics and culture, and that the American way of life – replete with liberty and free speech – would be fatally undermined. The ironic thing is how this McCarthyite ideology parallels Downey's own arguments to a tee – she herself is evoking apocalyptic images of the 'red menace' in order to justify a 'fight back' – 'Why people think this can't happen in the US, I don't know. But it's happening, and I see it. Socialism kills people ... Stalin's socialist Russia killed 20 million people.'

Downey is by no means alone in describing Black Lives Matter in these kinds of terms. Phillip Hammond of *Spiked* argues that the movement has 'increasingly come to resemble ... the McCarthyism of the 1950s'[43] while *The Independent's* proprietor, Evgeny Lebedev, writes how the Black Lives Matter movement 'risks abolishing freedom of thought' in a similar vein to the USSR '[u]nder Stalin'.[44] Others, such as the Canadian politico and one-time Liberal Party board member Justin Neufeld, have drawn explicit parallels between the Nazis and BLM with Neufeld tweeting: 'A BLM fist in the air is no different than a Nazi salute.'[45]

Such parallels are commonplace. But the regimes which Downey and others reference in order to better illuminate the totalitarian nature of Black Lives Matter – were also regimes that were hugely powerful and capable of imprisoning, and (in the case of Nazism and Stalinism) murdering millions of their political opponents. So, if one is going to argue parity between, say, Black Lives Matter and McCarthyism or Black Lives Matter and Stalinist totalitarianism – one must first contend with the basic question: How many people has the Black Lives Matter movement actually imprisoned? How many people has it had killed? It feels slightly ridiculous to even pose these questions, because the answer, quite predictably, is zero.[46] And when you consider that figure in all its stark simplicity you begin to understand that all the rumblings about BLM, all the ominous allusions to its totalitarian nature – are little more than props in a performance that evokes the type of sweeping persecution that has a great dramatic and theatrical resonance, but absolutely no basis in fact whatsoever.

In reality, it has not been Black Lives Matter protestors who have been able to harness the state in order to put their political opponents in prison; rather, it is the state which has been mobilized against Black Lives Matter protestors in brutal and systematic fashion. George Floyd was murdered in late March of 2020 – by early June that year over 10,000 BLM protestors had been arrested around the United States in a massive repression which saw 'police forces regularly use pepper spray, rubber bullets, teargas and batons on protesters, media and bystanders'.[47] Later that same year, it was reported that hundreds of these protesters were languishing in prison facing 'tacked charges and threats of life sentences. Others have been charged with "assaulting" police officers where there's no evidence of violence and no reports of injuries. Some arrested protesters have been transferred to immigration authorities.'[48]

One can see once again how the 'the political correctness gone mad' narrative operates; in creating the chimera of a 'politically correct witch hunt' unleashed by the Black Lives Matter campaign – one is able to simply reverse the poles; that is, those who are oppressed and disempowered are, by a strange sorcery, converted into those who wield violence and oppression; in the same moment, the people who fight to maintain the status quo and the ideological forms that reinforce it are reframed as a marginalized and maligned group who are being crushed underfoot by an arbitrary and dictatorial power.

So, for example, right-wing media pundit Tucker Carlson described how the Black Lives Matter movement is in the process of eliminating the police and replacing them 'with an armed "woke militia" to take over cities and increase the power of the Democratic Party'.[49] This kind of thing is ridiculous such that it seems almost laugh-out-loud comical. It feels like satire. But there is more to come. Those who describe the Black Lives Matter campaign as a 'politically correct witch hunt', not only allege physical persecution, but also try to frame things in terms of a culture war in which the movement is able to eradicate all ideological dissent and impose absolutely its own cultural and political standards. But how is it able to achieve this? For commentators like Downey this is done by the way the Black Lives Matter movement links with notions of 'intersectionality' and 'white guilt' such that all white people are branded as inherently and inescapably racist – 'If you're white, you're privileged and racist; your "fragility" means you're also racist if you deny it.'[50] On this basis, 'white voices' are increasingly drowned out.

On the notion of 'white guilt' and the methodology of intersectionality which underpins it, I have some sympathy with what Downey and others are arguing. There is a tendency on the part of some radicals and activists to retreat into the type of fragmented identity politics that might see whites inexorably set against Blacks because the former – whatever their stated political convictions – are regarded as unconsciously and instinctively racist and the automatic beneficiaries of systematic and institutional racism through the nature of their own 'white privilege'.[51] But such notions and methodologies form a part of a much broader spectrum; there are also more class-based approaches to the issue of racial injustice which see its overcoming as predicated on the unity of Blacks and whites locked together, arm in arm, struggling to bring about change from below.

Indeed we know that the Black Lives Matter protests of 2020 were more 'ethnically and racially diverse' than anything which had come before in US history, and that, of the protests which broke out in the major US cities, a majority of protestors (54 per cent) were actually white.[52] In addition, a PEW survey discovered that two thirds of all US adults supported the Black Lives Matter protests.[53] In such a context, it is especially important for the powerful to be able to quell such resistance from below by 'demonstrating' that the movement in question is less about racial justice but more about one group or ethnicity seeking to stamp its own standards on 'polite society' in an increasingly totalitarian fashion. To show that the movement is inherently parcelized, divisive and sectional – less concerned with equality and more concerned with the imposition of its own self-righteous power on others. Notions of 'white privilege' and 'intersectionality' can be usefully co-opted in the endeavour to suggest that the BLM movement wants to stigmatize and repress white people more generally as being irredeemably and inherently racist.

Other times, however, the critique of BLM is achieved in a more oblique fashion. It poses the prospect of an 'indigenous culture' (read white) being overwhelmed by the dictates of a 'politically correct' bureaucracy which is facilitating the whims of the 'other' (read Black) such that the former is in danger of being extinguished by the latter. In the UK, for example – and in the aftermath of the killing of George Floyd and the massive protests which accompanied it – many journalists in the mainstream media sought to portray Black Lives Matter in these kinds of terms; it was argued that the campaign was increasingly imposing a sterile conformity on 'traditional culture' in and through a mirthless and tyrannical sense of 'political correctness gone mad'. Perhaps the most notorious example of this was the debacle which followed the 'Fawlty Towers' incident. 'Fawlty Towers' is a 1970s comedy programme beloved by many and seen as a staple of mainstream culture, particularly because its humour – awkward and irreverent – is often felt to be quintessentially British.

Following the explosion of Black Lives Matter protests in 2020 in the UK, a small British cable channel decided to pull a single episode of 'Fawlty Towers' from its roster, an episode which, they argued, contained racial slurs. The exact motivation behind this decision seems unclear to this day; it's possible UKTV were trying to show genuine support for a movement that was sweeping through society, in order to strike out against racism – it is possible too that they were acting for purely commercial reasons; showing solidarity with Black Lives Matter would help gain kudos with younger audiences that tended to be sympathetic towards the movement.

But whatever UKTV's rationale for withdrawing that episode from their schedule, what we do know is that they weren't forced into it. Nobody from the Black Lives Matter movement contacted them, nobody from the movement put any kind of pressure enjoining the cable channel to drop the episode. In all the anger and shock that had come about from seeing a middle-aged Black man slowly murdered without reason or provocation, nobody considered the antidote to this sort of racist atrocity to be found in strong-arming a small cable-TV station into removing an episode of a 1970s sitcom from its playlist. And, if anyone had desperately wanted to see that particular episode of 'Fawlty Towers', it could still be viewed easily and freely in a hundred and one other places.

Of course, these latter facts were drowned out in the media furore that followed. The 'Fawlty Towers' debacle was, in a sense, too good to be resisted – on a superficial level, at least, it confirmed the narrative of 'political correctness gone mad'; it allowed the media to conjure up the spectre of a totalitarian movement, populated by 'wokes', 'lefties' and 'radicals', that was now successfully imposing its will, striking out at a cultural artefact beloved by ordinary people. The same false dichotomy was created: the same opposition between a totalitarian left-wing political movement, aided and abetted by a metropolitan political elite, over and against the ordinary people as imagined as a belaboured and rapidly vanishing 'British' majority who were seeing their cultural and political identities obliterated by the phenomenon of 'political correctness gone mad'.

All the usual suspects added their voices to a cacophony of outrage; puce-faced, middle-aged white males – wealthy and established journalists and TV presenters with platforms that allowed them to reach millions – trumpeting their outrage about 'cancel culture' and the way in which 'political correctness' was systematically closing down the possibilities of free speech. TV presenter Piers Morgan described the cancellation of 'Fawlty Towers' as 'insane political correctness',[54] Tom Slater writing in *The Spectator,* opined ruefully that it was the result of those 'who whipped up the mob',[55] while Brendan O'Neill warned how 'the crazed witch hunt' had finally come for 'the sitcom that is often voted Britain's best ever'.[56] For someone who is obsessed with the danger of witch hunts, Mr O'Neill is rather adept at the shrieking denunciation and does not shirk from using it. But is there any truth to any of this?

As with most stereotypes, one can always find a grain of truth. I envision cultural and political standards to be like a vessel, bobbing up and down on a particularly choppy sea, buffeted one way and then the next by great waves. The great waves represent large social groups whose movements and interests pull the vessel one way and then the next. So, there is a sense in which a building social movement reflecting the interests of large numbers of oppressed people does assert its power and momentum in order to 'bend' culture, to reshape it in accordance with that movement's goals and aspirations. As the disgust against racism and the systematic murder of Black people and other civilians by the state machine boils over – culture more broadly is 'warped' by the gravity of such a shift. That cable station was 'compelled' to drop the episode of 'Fawlty Towers' – rightly or wrongly – as a response to the building momentum of the Black Lives Matter movement.

Other programmes such as 'Little Britain' were removed from streaming services like BBC Iplayer and Netflix. 'Little Britain' is a 'comedy' programme in which various sketches were performed, including the hilarious portrayal of a Thai mail-order bride called 'Ting-Tong' (it's funny 'cause she's called "Ting Tong" – you see "they" (the Asians) sound funny when they speak and "Ting-Tong" wittily reflects that). 'Little Britain' also adopted the hilarious practise of "black face" whereby its public-school-educated and upper-class white male "comedians" smeared themselves with black pigment in order to better ridicule the obese Black character ("Desiree") they had decided to parody. But again the critical distinction lies in this: the decision to remove such programmes from the online section of the BBC roster was not brought about through some totalitarian enforcement from above whereby Black Lives Matter used secretive and powerful functionaries in the state to control the media and remove any and every programme that the movement had deemed to be ideologically unacceptable. No, the programmes were removed because the corporation in question had detected a change in the weather; as Dr Katie Donington, a senior lecture in history states – [t]he representation of Black people as caricatures was part of a process of undermining their full humanity',[57] and more and more sections of the British public had come to recognize this.

In other words, the loss of these programmes' popularity, which was reflected in the public mood in a post-Black Lives Matter epoch, was simply part and parcel of what culture is; that is – a process of change by which the values of yesteryear are destabilized as new standards emerge. Of course, movements like Black Lives Matter *do* impact such a process, they provide sea-change moments by which larger groups of people are no longer prepared to buy into the cultural assumptions of the past as the movement pulls more people into its moral remit through its collective scope and power. But this is primarily a question of cultural transformation, not physical force. It does not involve totalitarian means.

'What about the statues?' the critics invariably ask. One of the main pieces of 'evidence' in the endeavour to brand the BLM movement 'totalitarian' has been the issue of the destruction of statues of people who were involved in the slave trade or those who had fought for the politics of white supremacy. In the UK, the BLM movement burst into the consciousness of a generation when the statue of Edward Colston was, quite literally, pulled down from its pedestal and cast into the cold waters of Bristol harbour. Colston had been a seventeenth-century slaver responsible for helping to traffic 84,000 enslaved Africans, of whom 'around 19,000 died in the stagnant bellies of the company's slave ships during the infamous Middle Passage'.[58]

It seems almost impossible to imagine that anybody could oppose the removal of such a ghastly artefact designed to honour such an inhuman entity, and yet, oppose it they did. Screeds of words were put to work in countless papers and websites in order to raise the same ideological vision: attacking Colston's statue first and foremost exhibited the anti-democratic and totalitarian nature of BLM and was as well part and parcel of a culture in which an unnamed 'other' begins to more and more erase the history of ordinary 'British' people in and through the action of 'political correctness gone mad'.

Again, such charges, when scrutinized, reveal themselves to have about as much substantiality as mist. On the count of the move to destroy the statue being undemocratic and totalitarian – it was swiftly revealed how, in fact, for 'years, members of Bristol's Black community, historians and campaigners had been lobbying for the statue to be removed',[59] all to no avail, with the rather slippery conservative elements in the city council – through dissembling tactics and delay – even managing to veto a plaque that was to have been placed on the plinth of the statue and would have made some acknowledgement of the enslaved and murdered who had passed through Colston's bloodied commercial hands. In other words, it was not that the BLM campaign had acted against the democratic process; if anything they had realized it in and through a mass mobilization – over and against the ossified and conservative bureaucracy that had hitherto undermined and stifled it.

The idea that destroying such a statue represented an attack on 'British' culture, on 'British' history, was equally insidious. The statue was a monument to a certain type of culture, a certain type of history – that much should be acknowledged. A historical moment in which a small and wealthy elite were able to enshrine and glorify its own ability to truck in human flesh in and through the most despicable acts of violence and mass murder. But the destruction of the statue at the hands of protestors represents a historical moment in its own right. The right of generations of the oppressed as they endeavour to carve out a very different type of world with a very different set of standards and expectations.

Those who feel themselves being discomforted and even outraged by the removal of such statues are not exercised by the sense that something called 'British history' is being negated, but more the fact that a certain type of history is being challenged; that is, the history of the powerful, the history of elites being in a position to impose their will on the vast majority and structure society in accordance with their own aims and interests. People who feel an instinctive affinity with the status quo and the sense of stability it offers, and for the same reason are offset and deeply unnerved when the historical record is being shaped – not by established authority – but by masses and masses of ordinary people in the process of changing the world.

But beyond all the ridiculous fantasies of totalitarian 'political correctness gone mad' that are generated by this kind of fearful mindset, the simpler and starker question will always linger. What kind of history should one support? That which is written out from below by great social movements fighting racist, sexist and classist oppression? Or that which is written out from above and seeks to stabilize society often on those same unequal principles? Or to say the same, what is genuinely more problematic, what really fills you with the greater ire or the greater regret? The spectacle of 19,000 voiceless human beings consigned to cold, watery graves? Or a statue of the man that murdered them, its old eroding metal gradually sinking into the Bristol harbour?

4

Trans people are a menace to god-fearing toilets

Trans people and the 'political correctness gone mad' narrative

In late 2016, much of the UK mainstream press carried the same story, one which involved trans people and 'political correctness'. Oxford University had, according to the reportage, decided to 'ban' the words 'he' and 'she'. The Orwellian flavour of such an edict garnered the attention of the world's press. Amrit Dhillon, writing for *The Times of India,* reported how the prestigious university had decided to get rid of the pronouns 'he' and 'she' in favour of 'ze' because 'use of the incorrect pronoun might offend transgender students'.[1] The same writer concluded that this was yet another example of 'political correctness' going 'too far'.[2] According to Dhillon, the 'political correctness' movement had 'already infiltrated gender, race, religion and gays, leaving only transgender people – transgender sensitivities have come to dominate public discourse. These days, everything is about this LGBT demand or that LGBT demand.'[3]

The first thing to note about Dhillon's article is that it simply wasn't true. Oxford University issued a statement shortly afterward refuting the claim it had demanded students use the pronoun 'ze'.[4] But that mattered very little in the scheme of things. The sober correction received far less media attention than the slew of articles which had carried the sensational error. As the old saying goes, a lie runs around the world before the truth even has the chance to get its shoes on. But the lie employed here was of a specific type. And that helps explain why it was picked up so swiftly, and repeated in newspaper columns which appeared across the globe.

For it was a lie which factored into a very particular world view; a world view in which a specific group of people – in this case trans people – are able to appeal to a 'liberal elite' in order to impose their own political standards on society more broadly in a totalitarian fashion. In such a vision, trans people appear as a distinctive lobbying group of some considerable power able to stamp politics and culture with their own rigid set of values. Those who might draw attention to the sinister absurdity of these 'politically correct' demands are themselves censored, repressed and beleaguered; browbeaten into conformity by this modern-day brand of politically correct puritanism – 'the Stalinist thought police are at it again, tyrannising us with their edicts'.[5]

The realities of transphobia

As with any narrative of 'political correctness gone mad', this specific narrative provides us with a surreal and topsy-turvy inversion. It relocates a marginalized group – in this case trans people – in a position of great power and influence, and thereby helps disguise the vulnerability of that same group and the social oppression and discrimination it is subject to. In the United States, for instance, trans women are over four times more likely to be murdered than cisgender women. Black trans women are seven times more likely to be murdered than the average member of the general population.[6]

In the UK, from 2018 to 2019, there was a surge in hate crime against trans people of some 37 per cent, with 2,333 incidents recorded.[7] In Brazil, in the period from October 2019 to September 2020, 152 trans people were murdered, while in that same time frame the murders of trans people experienced a 6 per cent spike on a global level (in comparison with the previous year) with at least 350 losing their lives to transphobic violence.[8] In the United States, statistics reveal that trans people experience significantly higher levels of unemployment, lower incomes, lower rates of college education, deeper levels of poverty and worse levels of health compared with the average.[9]

In the UK, a YouGov report discovered that two out of every five trans people had had to deal with a hate crime in the year 2017. One in four had experienced homelessness and more than a quarter, domestic abuse. One in eight reported having been physically assaulted either by colleagues or customers in a work context.[10] And in the higher echelons of power, trans people have scant representation. According to a study published by Atlantic Council, '[a]mong more than 519,000 elected officials in the United States, there are … only forty-nine trans and gender non-conforming elected officials (or 0.009 per cent), and thirty-three of them are trans women.'[11] In the UK, of the 650 members of parliament, at the time of writing, there is not one openly trans person, and nor has there been in times gone by.

The lack of political representation. The obstacles to opportunity in terms of both employment and education. And finally, the homelessness, the poverty and the murders. None of these statistics are conducive to a group which has a 'totalitarian' ability to impose its dictates on others; but that, if you will, is the miracle the 'political correctness gone mad' narrative accomplishes. It makes those who are impoverished, wealthy; while those who lack power, come to brim with it; those who experience prejudice and intolerance are reformulated as the ones who refuse to countenance any other standard or opinion but their own. Such a narrative, however, is comprehensively contradicted by reality itself; by the status of trans people as a beleaguered and persecuted group, and the consistent and relentless oppression they face. Perhaps for this, they are demonized all the more – in inverse proportion to their real-world vulnerability. This has been achieved by targeting trans women in particular – that is, people who are born biologically male but at the core of their being experience their identity as a woman, and are sometimes able to transition as a consequence.

Trans women have been attacked on several different levels, but perhaps one of the most effective ways has been the way they have been abstracted, separated out from society proper – in and through the irrational and ugly demonization of them as sexual predators. Such a portrayal has focused on the issue of the use of toilets in particular. The 'argument' provides the 'rationale' to deny trans women access to women's toilets, and, more generally, to other female spaces such as changing rooms and so on. Allowing trans women to access female bathrooms, endangers the safety of 'genuine' women, so the argument runs. Perhaps the most high-profile advocate of this line of thinking is the author of the *Harry Potter* series, J. K. Rowling. Rowling writes: 'When you throw open the doors of bathrooms and changing rooms to any man who believes or feels he's a woman … then you open the door to any and all men who wish to come inside.'[12] This, in turn, ends up 'offering cover for predators'.[13]

J. K. Rowling's comments are the standard fare – the bland commonsensical type of thinking which tends to categorize her thought on the issue and that of her fellow travellers. But when considered in any detail, the lack of nuance at once becomes problematic. If a sexual predator wishes to access a 'female only' toilet in order to attack a woman, does he really need to gain legal permission to enter? One could dress up as a woman, whether or not the bathroom in question is trans inclusive. In fact, those established but infrequent cases where men have dressed up as women in order to assault women in toilets have, historically speaking, nearly always involved bathrooms that wouldn't have been legal for a trans woman to use in the first place.

A study conducted by PolitiFact in the United States, for instance, found that in the period from 2000 to 2016 only three incidents were recorded of biological males having dressed up in women's clothes in order to commit a crime in a woman's bathroom. Whether any of the biological males in question were transgender is unknown, but, significantly, all these crimes took place in cities which had not chosen to implement laws allowing transgender people to access their bathroom of choice. Indeed that same study concluded: 'We haven't found any instances of criminals convicted of using transgender protections as cover in the United States.'[14] Perhaps unsurprisingly, a landmark 2019 study (also conducted in the United States) revealed there 'is no evidence that letting transgender people use public facilities that align with their gender identity increases safety risks'.[15]

Of course, the bigger issue here is that the narrative is subtly blurring the focus. It purports to shine an objective and dispassionate light on the issue of trans women, but the true focus isn't trans women at all. The real issue is CIS men – heterosexual predators who align with the gender they were assigned at birth (male), but who are dressing up as women. But here the two categories become blurred. Partly because those who are in control of the narrative insist on denying the status of genuine womanhood to trans women.

Sometimes they might do this in a vulgar gutter press way as when journalist and 'militant feminist' Julie Birchill entered the debate in order to describe trans women in *The Observer* newspaper as nothing more than 'a bunch of dicks in chic's clothing'.[16] Sometimes it's done a little more subtly. Rowling, for example, professes some level of sympathy for trans people, and yet, throughout her articles she assumes category of women which trans women by their very nature stand in opposition to. She writes how, in the current and oppressive climate of 'trans activism … Women must accept and admit that there is no material difference between trans women and themselves'.[17]

The separation here is subtle but immutable; on the one hand, there are 'trans women' and on the other, there are the women 'themselves'. The conclusions which flow from this are inevitable. If trans women are not genuinely women, by identifying themselves as such they are simply labouring under a delusion. What is at stake ceases to be that which is most fundamental to their being but merely an idea that they have about themselves. However, argues Rowling, '"woman" is not a costume. "Woman" is not an idea in a man's head'.[18] Like many other transphobes, Rowling speaks of something called 'trans activism', a word she imbues with great dread, but one which also harmonizes with the sense that trans identity is simply a (false) idea that someone has chosen to adopt. Thus 'trans activism' becomes the process by which that same false idea is disseminated to others. In such a context, the 'idea' can be fought against by 'genuine women' who might intellectually or morally refute it, thus preserving their own authentic and fundamental sense of self from a concept that threatens to transgress it.

And if the nature of a trans woman's identity is based on a simple misconception – 'an idea in a man's head' – then no matter how firmly the person in question believes in that idea, it cannot change the objective fact that they have no place using those facilities which are designated for 'genuine women'. If a man, labouring under the delusion that he is a woman, enters that space, he does so – whether he is aware of it or not – on an illegitimate basis.

And if one is able to establish – either through the much more inflammatory and vulgar prejudice of the 'dicks in chic's clothing' or the more subtle but constant opposition between women and trans women which Rowling proffers – that trans women are illegitimate, that their very nature constitutes an anachronism, a mistake – then their presence in female only spaces automatically becomes problematized. It becomes questionable, worrying even. And thus a subtle elision is achieved; if trans women using 'women only' toilets is in some way questionable; the question inevitably becomes – do they have some other more shady motivation? In this way, the link is gradually and subtly shaped, the unstated fear, the instinctive suspicion … the connection between trans women and sexual predation.

The historical context

The truly tragic thing, of course, is that we have been here before. There is a dark history here. In England, homosexuality had been considered a crime in one form or another from the time of Henry VIII up until 1967 when it was partially decriminalized. In the modern era, gay men would often use public toilets as places to meet and have sex, places where they could remain anonymous and escape persecution and stigmatization. Increasingly the police targeted these locations and men 'were frequently arrested, prosecuted and often jailed'.[19] Perhaps, in order to facilitate such persecution, the men who were the victims of it were more and more portrayed as oversexed and predatory; shadowy deviants lurking in public toilets in the dead of night, waiting to pounce on unsuspecting men and even children. Indeed the myth of the gay man as paedophile was a popular currency in such times, for the appeal to the safety of children was one which could be mobilized in order to justify the ongoing repression of gay men by police, and the state-sanctioned violence and incarceration which went along with it.

On the other side of the pond, at around the same time, a young Black man named Samuel Younge Junior pulled over at a gas station desperate to use the toilet. According to the segregation laws of the period (though officially repealed by that point), the white proprietor denied him access to the main toilets which were reserved for whites. At which point, words were exchanged and the proprietor shot Younge Junior dead. The segregation laws were often particularly strict when it came to the issue of toilets, for they had been historically 'justified' by the sinister evocation of the Black man as rapist, looking to target vulnerable white women, and isolated bathrooms were often portrayed as prime locations for this. As Gillian Frank, a lecturer at Princeton University in Gender and Sexuality, puts it, '[t]here was this idea that black men were … oversexed predators … White men felt that [white women were particularly prone to this] in bathrooms – and they felt it was their role to police that space.'[20]

Prejudice is, by its very nature, irrational and emotive; deep-seated and instinctive feelings which have been woven into the human psyche at the most elemental level. Of all these feelings, fear is paramount. When we use the bathroom, when we go to the toilet – especially if we are in a public space – we often feel at our most vulnerable. And it is at that point we are subject to fear. Racism, homophobia, transphobia; these things can never be justified according to a rational and humanistic narrative; rather they are better purveyed by endeavouring to prick those deeper elemental and unconscious currents of fear which flow beneath the surface of the psyche, and which we inherit from the forms and structures of social oppression bequeathed to us by history.

The image of trans women as deviants or sexual predators who must be cordoned off and separated from 'real women' in this context is simply part of a series of prejudicial narratives. Narratives that have been shaped over the decades and centuries and use the public bathroom as a locus of fear through which the demand to single out and ostracize oppressed groups can be made. But when we draw upon a rational and sober assessment of the facts – when we ask the question who is it that is actually most abused, most attacked in public bathrooms – such facts at once fatally contradict the sinister and emotive demonization of trans women. A report from UCLA's Williams Institute recorded that almost 70 per cent of transgender respondents relayed they had experienced verbal harassment when using gender-segregated facilities, while 9 per cent of all respondents recounted being physically assaulted on at least one occasion in those same facilities.[21] Often such assaults are brutal, for their brutality is underwritten by that instinctive fear and disgust which prejudice so effectively channels. Bryann Tannhill, as a forty-one-year-old trans woman, recalls her first experience of being attacked by men when she was just nineteen:

> *Three men, drunk, very large. They kicked me so many times in the ribs. I tried to cover my face to protect my face. As I'm laying there, pretty much lifeless, a guy whips out his penis about to urinate on me. That's disgusting … People did come to my aid. The police came. The EMTs came. They put a tube in my throat. The police officer says, as I'm sitting in the gurney, 'This never would have happened to you if you weren't wearing a dress and trying to fool men'.*[22]

When one considers the visceral nature of such prejudice, such demonization, and the way in which the violence is systematically rationalized by the mechanisms of state – 'This never would have happened to you if you weren't wearing a dress and trying to fool men' – one has a sense of the danger trans people experience if they are forced to use gender-segregated public restrooms and how the documented abuse and harassment reflects this fact. But while the statistics are clear in showing that attacks or harassment of trans women in public toilets are commonplace occurrences – there has, to my knowledge, never been a confirmed case of a trans woman attacking a biological female in a public restroom. Not ever.

The fear-mongering mythology which is built up around the public restroom in order to incite loathing against an oppressed minority isn't the only bigoted relic from the past that has been revivified in order to be used against trans people in the present. If trans gender is not so much a state of being, but merely a mistaken 'idea in a man's head' then there always exists the possibility that such an idea might be 'corrected'. In fact, a 2018 survey from the UK government's Equalities Office, which interviewed 108,000 people, recorded that almost one in ten trans men said they had been offered 'conversion therapy', while one in twenty-five said they had undergone it.[23]

Of course, conversion therapy has a deeply sinister history; just as trans people are now told that their identities are somehow false, illegitimate, superficial and cosmetic – so too have gay people been told the same, that the experience of their sexuality is an aberrant 'choice' which they have talked themselves into making but which might be 'corrected' with the appropriate forms of 'therapy' or 'treatment'. In such a fashion, prejudice and oppression take on a 'scientific' guise, the veneer of medical respectability is used to gloss over what is a harrowing and life-destroying process for those subject to it. One transgender woman reported on her own experience of conversion therapy and how it 'resulted in 23 years of depression, alcoholism and suicidal thoughts, until I transitioned in 2011'.[24] Her experience is once again commonplace.

The sense that transgenderism (and homosexuality for that matter) is simply an idea or ideology that deluded people cling to rather than being a significant aspect of one's own humanity is reflected in the subtle shift in language that is employed on the part of transphobes. Instead of describing their agenda in terms of one which is levelled against trans people and their fundamental human rights, they shift the tone in order to speak about 'trans ideology' or 'trans activism' – thereby suggesting the issue at stake isn't the essential being of the people they are targeting for discrimination, but an abstract and insidious 'idea' – part and parcel of a corrupting political agenda.

And once you decide that the essence of a trans person is not a matter of their fundamental personhood but rather some type of ideological contagion they have contracted, you can then start stoking the fear that such an insidious idea can be spread to others. In particular, children can pick it up – it can be taught as part of a 'politically correct' agenda in schools, and thus confuse and corrupt young and vulnerable minds, preventing them from simply being allowed to be children, helping turn them into deviants. Recently the truly obnoxious so-called 'left wing firebrand' and once-upon-a-time MP George Galloway waded into the 'trans debate' in order to decry those 'woke' schools which, he argued, were deluding children into believing there are '99 genders' and indoctrinating them on 'anal sex' and 'how to masturbate'.[25]

What the truly gruesome Galloway was railing against with all his fusty bombasts seems to have been the concept of sex education in the twenty-first century, a concept which should include even those minorities who fall outside Galloway's ideal of the god-fearing family constituted in and through the sacred and unbroken union between a biologically born man and woman. But once again, we have been here before. The need to turn back the clock, to keep children cloaked in a fug of Victorian ignorance on the flimsy pretence of protecting them has a long historical precedence and once more we see how the prejudice of the present links up with the bigotry of the past.

In 1988, in the UK, a Conservative government introduced the hated Section 28; a law which aimed to 'prohibit the promotion of homosexuality'[26] in British schools so that, in the words of then Prime Minister Margaret Thatcher, children 'who need to be taught to respect traditional moral values'[27] would not have those same wholesome moral values undermined. The language of keeping children safe has always provided an effective cloak for prejudice and repression. In the 1970s, the anti-gay campaigner Anita Bryant led a homophobic campaign called 'Save our Children'. The danger to children from homosexuals was, for Bryant, apparent for, as she went on to argue, '[s]ince homosexuals cannot reproduce, they must recruit, must freshen their ranks'.[28]

Lucy Meadows

Such hate preaching not only adversely affects children. It affects too those who would interact with them, those who would care for them and teach them. Take the case of Lucy Meadows. Lucy Meadows was a teacher. She had also been born a biological man. She was, from all accounts, someone both ordinary and kind. Traditional even. After all, she was a Christian who cherished her faith and was active in the local church. At this point in her life Lucy was called Nathan. Nathan was married, and according to his partner 'was very traditional in his approach to marriage and relationships: protective of myself and our family and very much engaged as provider'.[29] At the same time, there was a part of Nathan which was never quite at home in the world. The feeling of being limited, constricted, unable to express something so fundamental that, at points, it was like struggling to breathe. Nathan would play video games, and in these games his avatar would always be female. Because it just … felt right. Felt truer somehow. One year, the family did fancy-dress for Halloween, and Nathan dressed up as 'Morticia Adams'. Although the occasion was light-hearted and fun, something about that felt right too. Like being able to breathe: 'I could see in her face that she was relaxed in a way she never was as Nathan: as though a great weight had been lifted off her shoulders.'[30]

Nathan became Lucy, transitioning in Christmas 2012. She was nervous about the change, but also expectant, for the time was right and 'I couldn't put it off any longer.'[31] She was nervous too about returning to school – as she would later write '[t]eaching is a stressful job'. But it was as well one she loved doing – 'I work alongside a great staff in a happy school.'[32] Lucy also believed that the experience of becoming her true self would not diminish others but rather help to 'educate the people around me and children at school – I am a teacher after all!'[33] Despite its travails, Lucy's life was a rich one, and despite what would eventually happen, I think it was a profoundly optimistic one too.

The same cannot be said for Richard Littlejohn. Richard Littlejohn is a journalist for *The Daily Mail* newspaper. You have almost certainly never met him. You might not have read his writing or even have heard of him. But you do know him. For Richard Littlejohn is that kid at school – no, not the big bully, but the little sidekick; red-faced and sweaty, with a furtive gleam in his eye – smarmy and spiteful. The one with a keen mental radar for those kids who are different, for the outsider – those who don't quite fit in. He hones in on such people, he targets them, he seeks to expose and humiliate them – all in order to raise a grin from the bigger boys. He's that person who comes sidling up to you with cruel eyes and a sly smile in order to tell you that the Bible 'talks about Adam and Eve … not Adam and Steve' before smirking illicitly, thoroughly delighted by his own poisonous cruelty.

Richard Littlejohn knows – has always known – that there is white and there is black, there are those who fit in and those who don't, those who are part of the culture and the insidious outsiders, those who are British-bred and those who are foreigners, those who are normal and those who are deviant. After all, he has spent much of his professional career exposing and ridiculing the people who are different. Whether it's about demonizing immigrants, ridiculing lesbians or lashing out against the poor and vulnerable, Richard Littlejohn has never stopped trying to raise a grin from the bigger boys.

When Lucy transitioned, she sent a letter to the governors and the teachers of her school to let them know what was happening. An overwhelming majority were supportive. However, the letter was leaked. And like hyenas, the gutter press targeted Lucy in a pack. They contacted friends, family and colleagues all in the hunt to discover the type of salacious information that might establish how someone like Lucy had no place working in a school. Reporters lifted pictures of Lucy's family from Facebook without any right or permission. They camped outside her doorstep in the mornings. Lucy would have to leave her house through the back door. There were many, many supportive and kind comments which Lucy had received from the children she taught and from their parents. Only one parent had objected to her, saying that his son was 'confused' by Lucy's transition. And yet, as Lucy's ex-partner relates, the press weren't interested in 'the many, many positive comments that parents gave out in her support. No: they cared only about the man with the confused child and his petition.'[34]

The flagbearer, the commander-in-chief of this toxic rabble was the puce-faced and perpetually enraged Littlejohn himself. He took to his column in the *Mail*, a column with a readership of millions, in order to decry Lucy Meadows – a woman he didn't know and had never met – asking whether anyone had considered the 'devastating effect' that Lucy's transition would have on the children before trumpeting furiously: 'He's not only in the wrong body … he's in the wrong job'.[35] Lucy had chosen to fully become herself, humanely and freely, and in so doing the 'Adam and Steve' contingent of the gutter press would crucify her with their lack of imagination and empathy, their banal brand of dumb self-righteousness. In March 2013, she took her own life. At the inquest, her coroner, Michael Singleton, singled out the role of the newspaper which had provided hate preacher Littlejohn with his pulpit. *The Daily Mail* had, according to Singleton, conducted a campaign of 'character assassination' and 'ridicule and humiliation' against Lucy Meadows. Finally the coroner turned to the reporters who had gathered there, saying simply but poignantly '[a]nd to you the press, I say shame, shame on all of you.'[36]

The freedom to become yourself

What happened to Lucy was both a tragedy and a crime. But it is also an issue that goes beyond that of trans lives, becoming a question of human freedom in the most profound and universal sense. Our bodies are born into certain biological templates which constitute male and female – though even here things aren't clear-cut (intersex conditions, for example, where one has some features which might stereotypically be associated with the opposite sex or is born with sexual anatomy which doesn't clearly fit the boxes of exclusively male or female). But whatever our biological beginnings, the achievement of manhood or womanhood is most profoundly a process of becoming, a social process. From the moment we enter into social relations, into culture, we begin to draw in the material by which a sense of self is formed in much the same way a foetus in the womb draws sustenance from amniotic fluid. We inherit, unconsciously and organically – from our family life, from the society more broadly – a series of cultural and social sensibilities on which our developing personhood is nourished. So, for example, one might experience oneself as being a little girl by virtue of the fact that the society in which you live deems it fit that you wear pink dresses and play with dolls. Womanhood is the dialogue between the developing personhood of an individual and the set of social relations in which they are located. As the existentialist and feminist philosopher Simone de Beauvoir put it so succinctly: 'One is not born, but rather becomes, a woman.'

Likewise, one is a little boy by weaving certain unstated and unconscious feelings and sensibilities about masculinity into the person you are becoming. You might come to understand, in the society in which you live, that being a little boy involves playing battle-games and climbing trees as opposed to skipping rope or playing netball, for instance. You will also inherit some of the emotional and spiritual sensibilities that can help inform such practical activities. As a boy you will probably learn it is your lot to be more decisive, more aggressive, whereas as a girl you might come to sense that you are expected to be more yielding, more nurturing and so on. And yet, such values are assimilated in the context of one's own personhood, and for that reason, they are often subverted, reshaped and changed as one adapts them to oneself. For instance, this particular little boy might feel calm and relaxed when he is combing the long, sinuous hair of an elegant and pretty doll. While this particular girl might find that boring and stultifying; she might cast her eye to the window and the outside where she longs to be climbing trees or rolling around in the mud.

We used to call such a girl a 'tomboy'. And there is something wonderful about that. There is something wonderful about a child exploring the world in accordance with those sensibilities and feelings which truly chime with who she feels herself to be. To go exploring, to climb trees, if she so wishes, just as there is something wonderful about that boy who is happier enacting fairy tales of beautiful princesses with dolls under the soft-light of the magical kingdom of his own imagination. But what would one make of an adult – a particularly blustering red-faced middle-aged journalist for example – who went up to that little boy and berated him for being 'unnatural'? Who screamed at that little girl for being a deviant and existential threat to society as a whole? My feeling is that we would probably regard the journalist as the odd one in that kind of situation. I think we would probably want to keep *him* away from children.

The sense that gender is an elastic social category, capable of being transformed in and through the life processes of human beings themselves rather than an immutable and static biological 'fact' is something which has a long historical pedigree. In her wonderful book, *Intercourse*, Andrea Dworkin reserves a large part of a chapter to honour the courage of Joan of Arc while providing a luminous window into the psychology of the youthful rebel and skilful military strategist. Joan was the lowest of the low in terms of social standing. Born in the fifteenth century, in a region of present-day France, she was born female in a social world which devalued women, saw them as chattel to be sold into marriage as a way of cementing property relations, and demanded their absolute submission to men in terms of every aspect of their lives. She was also born into a peasant family in a small village so she was at the bottom rung of the class ladder too.

And yet, in some way, somehow, Joan was absolutely intransigent. She refused to bend before patriarchal expectation – she defied first her father, who had demanded she be married, and then the man who tried to sue her for 'breach of promise' for refusing his offer. At the age of seventeen she escaped both her house and her village, in order to struggle against an even more powerful adversary, the English invaders who had ransacked so much of the territory as the bloody grapple of the Hundred Years' War unfolded and Joan was sucked into its maelstrom. But she remained passionate and intransigent – her determination and self-expression guided by a devout religiosity and an open dialogue with some of the religious female martyrs of the past, while at the same time she refashioned herself in the guise of a more masculine identity: 'She had arrived in Vaucouleurs wearing a red peasant dress made out of a coarse material; she left dressed like a man, never to dress of her own free will like a woman again.'[37]

The rest, as they say, is history. Joan was able to propel herself to the head of a great army which scored a series of victories driving the English into retreat, freeing up occupied villages and towns as she stormed ahead eventually liberating the city of Orleans. Joan was able to achieve these quite heroic feats of courage and strategy partly because she had bound herself to the identity and mores of a certain type of masculinity:

> *Living among men, sleeping 'all in the straw together,' seen bare-breasted, Joan accomplished an escape from the female condition more miraculous than any military victory: she had complete physical freedom, especially freedom of movement – on the earth, outside a domicile, among men. She had that freedom because men felt no desire for her, or believed that 'it was not possible to try it.' She made an empirically successful escape from a metaphysical definition of female that is socially real, socially absolute, and intrinsically coercive. She did not have to run the gauntlet of male desire; and so she was free, a rare and remarkable quality and kind of freedom – commonplace for men, virtually unattainable for women.*[38]

Some theorists have been tempted to see in Joan one of the earliest recorded examples of a transgender man. I think that this is possibly problematic. It is very difficult to say for sure how much of Joan's 'transgenderism' was a self-conscious and practical strategy to evade the confines and oppressions of patriarchal power and how much of her identification with maleness stemmed from the unslakeable and elemental awareness – the emotive and intuitive certainty – that she was in some way fundamentally a man at the core of her being. After her capture, and under the pressure of the Inquisition which had been brought in to interrogate her from her prison cell, she was recorded as saying 'that she preferred man's dress to woman's.'[39] By this point at least, we can say that such identification had no 'practical' value; indeed the defiance it implied would eventually cost Joan her life.

But whatever the case, Joan's example – her gender rebellion if you like – demonstrates how the mutability of gender standards and identity in the context of social life is often tied up with the freedom of the individual and their need to realize the set of potentialities which accord with their authentic personhood. Joan's heroic and courageous demand to be truly herself, to realize that set of ambitions and actions which flowed from the core of her being were met with derision, disgust and horror on the part of a patriarchal establishment that demanded fixed and rigid gender roles and an imbalance of power between the sexes as a way to preserve its own privileges and position. As Dworkin writes: 'The Inquisitors wanted her stripped, violated, submissive; out of her male clothes … Chained and female, the men were no longer afraid of her; and it was a rape, or an attempted rape, or a gang-rape, that caused her to resume male clothing and go to her death'.[40] In 1431, Joan was burnt at the stake. She was just nineteen years old. One can't help but imagine there would have been a good few 'Littlejohns' in the crowd that day, the malicious joy of their furtive and rat-like features illuminated by the glow of the rising flames.

Modern realities

As history progresses, more sophisticated forms of social organization evolve. In the modern world a complex division of labour concentrated in the great cities implies the free flow of labour from one job to the next, a vast selection of possible workplaces even within the context of a single industry. Industries themselves rise and fall; new ones are called into being as the material powers which drive social development are refined and reformulated and new technologies come to the fore. Along with the expansion of production, there is a corresponding increase in the possibilities of consumption, at least if you have the material means to take advantage of them. Supermarkets are laden with goods from around the world – Tahitian vanilla, Ecuadorian cocoa, Baltic sturgeon roe, Arabian hummus, Spanish cava and Scottish black pudding all sit, cheek by jowl, on the same set of shelves. The broader panorama of the world is pulled together in and through the ghostly mesh of a vast global market which means that people are often driven to migrate from nation to nation, from countryside to town, from one setting to the next – in search of new employment, new relationships, new opportunities – on a scale unimaginable only a handful of decades before.

The creation of new possibilities, new horizons – in and through the fluidity and frenetic pace of modern existence simultaneously facilitates the development of an individual personality that is riven by a richer set of potentialities; which is brought into alignment with a more complex and diverse set of social relationships, and which experiences in itself the ability to transcend the more traditional and static social, sexual and gender roles inherited from the past. We start to see the first glimmerings of a world in which radically new arrangements in family life are made possible, lesbians can be surrogate parents, gay men can get married, people from different ethnic and racial backgrounds can have children without fear of racist stigmatization. And those who experience their true state of being as different from the biological sex they are born into are able to transform their bodies and their lives in accordance with these deep-seated impulses, weaving and shaping their identities into the fullest and most authentic forms of self-expression.

The creation of a richer and more multi-sided personality on an increasingly social scale, seeking to break out of the confines of more traditional and patriarchal templates is something which is greeted by the Littlejohns of this world with a mix of derision and dread. For it is the unfolding of human freedom as a complex of new needs that see the human personality transcend the limits of the purely 'natural' or 'biological', the limits which are defined by the 'Adam and Steve' constituent in such ossified and fearful terms. And yet, the force and weight of the past still rests heavy on the present.

For example, we continue to live in a society where the lives of women are heavily regulated by men, where individual men have often reaped an array of benefits which come from such arrangements without always being consciously aware of it. In Australia, a 2020 survey revealed that on average each week, more than a quarter of all women spend over ten hours doing unpaid housework. Only 8 per cent of all men, however, do the same. At the same time, almost 45 per cent of women with children spend over five hours a week caring for them, while only 32 per cent of men do the same.[41]

In the United States, women do an average of four hours unpaid work per day compared with the men who only do two and a half hours. In India, women expend six hours per day of unpaid labour managing the household whereas the men expend only 52 minutes.[42] In the UK, in a 2016 survey from the Office for National Statistics, it was estimated that, on average, women do twenty-six hours a week of unpaid work compared with men who do only sixteen hours.[43] As well, it is estimated that the unpaid work of all women in the UK from the ages of 18–100 is worth 700 billion to the UK economy as a whole.[44] On a global scale it is estimated women's unpaid labour is worth $10,900,000,000,000.[45]

In other words, it is not only that the average individual man benefits from the extra labour provided by women on the domestic front – from the extra attention his mother might lavish on him as a child to the greater amount of work his wife puts in around the house, preparing meals, organizing the kids. These things – which can be assimilated, unconsciously, as normal and inevitable aspects of one's everyday existence – on a more fundamental level work to sustain a broader system that is saturated with the vast amounts of uncompensated labour that women provide. Such incredible discrepancies are most effectively maintained when they are rationalized and justified according to certain instinctive and ideological sensibilities.

The sense, for instance, that women tend to be more nurturing, tend to be more adept when it comes to taking care of children, perhaps more suitable to domestic work rather than work outside the household. If one feels, furthermore, that such differences between men and women are in some way natural and innate – then the image of the traditional family in which gender roles are very carefully mapped to these notions of what femininity and masculinity are, can become a comforting and stabilizing idyll in a social world which often seems disrupted and torn asunder by the forces of change. The traditional nuclear family becomes a repository of harmony and an idyllic past in which gender roles were innate and unchanging, where what it is to be a man or to be a woman is a simple, natural fact which accords with a biological essence that need not be problematized by off-the-wall notions of '99 genders' and men who 'pretend' to be women and vice-versa.

The veneration of the nuclear family provides a tonic to those who are dismayed by any sense of social instability and the forces of change. But beyond this, it also provides a template where the subordination of the woman to the man can be rationalized culturally. Can be used to better structure a larger system of exploitation where the patriarchal standards of the past are applied and adapted to the present with the result that a great amount of unpaid, uncompensated labour is pumped into the economy month after month, year after year – from the vast number of women who find themselves in some way limited and reined in by such cultural identities and expectations.

New modes of being that take flight in the world threaten to subvert the traditional family unit – through alternative arrangements leading to the creation of families with an openly gay parent or parents, for example. Or the extension and expansion of the condition of masculinity or femininity itself, the notion that such states of being are about more than the biology you are born into, but part of a richer set of possibilities by which one's authentic self might be realized. In manifesting these potentialities and freedoms, one is brought into collision with the ossified and fixed structures of a more general form of social exploitation of which the traditional family unit becomes the chief emblem.

In undermining and transforming this relation by their very existence, trans people, gays, single-mothers and so on, don't simply unnerve a few fusty and old-fashioned individuals of a conservative bent. Rather they present an existential challenge to the way in which a broader mode of social exploitation is organized and facilitated. The hatred and the rancour that are so often directed at them are not only spiteful and nasty and small-minded and ignorant. More fundamentally, it represents the old world shivering with fear and repulsion having just taken a glimpse of the new. As the writer and activist Jules Joanne Gleeson points out, 'transphobia and transmisogyny … [are] … pervasive and structuring aspects of society'. In seeking to suppress transphobic lives, they also seek to solidify the 'interconnections … [within] … the political order more generally … From this view, trans liberation is not so much a struggle to win particular rights, but one part of a broader movement overturning inter-locking oppressive systems.'[46]

One of the most effective claims allowing transphobes to smuggle in their prejudice is the claim that they are acting in order to protect 'women themselves', that the argument they are marshalling is in some sense a feminist one. Indeed many older generation feminists and those who describe themselves as 'radical feminists' have helped buttress the anti-trans case; figures such as the well-respected and influential academic Germaine Greer have taken to the podium to explain that transgender women are 'not women'. In Greer's case the prejudice is almost palpable in terms of its emotive impressionism – she argues that trans women are clearly not women because they do not 'look like, sound like or behave like women'.[47] What's interesting about Greer's comments is how clearly they collate with earlier forms of prejudice; lesbians in the 1960s who chose to cut and crop their hair, or wear more 'gender neutral' clothing or were physically bigger, were typically described as 'butch' – and for many of the conservative commentators in that period, these women were not really women either, precisely because they did not 'look like, sound like or behave like women'. Of course, what they really meant was that the queer women in question did not 'look like, sound like or behave' according to the conception of womanhood those commentators held dear; that is, a conception of what was 'innate' and 'normal' to womanhood; a concept which emphasized a specific type of female beauty designed to be pleasing to heterosexual males, tied to a delicate sense of passivity, both yielding and nurturing, tender and submissive.

In the broader historical panorama, such a concept of womanhood arose out of the exile of women into the domestic sphere, there to be the child bearers and rearers, largely subordinate to the economic and legal power of the male. In the 1960s, in the context of the sexual revolution and second-wave feminism, the possibilities of what it meant to be a woman were being infinitely expanded and the more conservative elements of society sensed that at the core of their being. The demand for 'women to be women' – or as Greer puts it in its more modern incarnation, to 'look like, sound like or behave like women' – is the demand for the return to a more patriarchal standard; it is as much about disempowering women as is the domestic abuse – the beatings, the rapes, the murders – which husbands inflict on wives, or the incarceration of women and their forced-feeding which once the state inflicted on suffragettes. The prejudice against trans women and the overwhelming violence they are subject to flows from the same place; such things are designed to help fortify and secure a static and traditional template of womanhood that is easily slotted into the structures of exploitation women are subject to in the modern world.

Or to say the same, the opposition between biologically born women and trans women that the transphobes pose – is an entirely false and artificial one. The idea that the critique of the trans woman as woman, the denial of her as woman, is a feminist one and helps protect women – is a notion which works against the *raison d'être* of feminism more generally, that is, the empowerment of women, their ability to realize the fullest series of potentials on the spectrum of what it means to be 'woman' over and against the type of toxic and oppressive masculinity that would straightjacket womanhood in terms of a narrow and fixed definition.

Women who choose to pursue careers rather than have children, women who have lots of sex with lots of different people, women who marry other women, women who like to dress in men's clothing, women who are born biologically male; these are all iterations of the same phenomenon; the social and historical processes by which the unfolding condition of womanhood is able to reach a fuller and more multi-faceted expression, whereby women themselves are able to win through to their fullest freedoms by expanding their possibilities in the richest and most diverse of ways. Those who attack trans women in the present – though they are not always aware of it – are the equivalents of those fusty patriarchs of the past, for as the writer Jessie Muldoon comments, the attack on both trans women and trans men 'only serves to reinforce gender stereotypes, not to undermine them in any way and … this will impact cis women also'.[48]

The fetishization of the natural

For this reason, the logic of such attacks works along the same depressingly familiar lines. Yesteryear's stereotypes functioned by averring that women are 'naturally' more passive, more nurturing, better suited to looking after children; that is, such stereotypes worked to enshrine certain social and patriarchal arrangements as eternal and immutable and grounded in the biological nature of the men and women who are encompassed by them. Those people who resisted such arrangements, who endeavoured to define their lives in contradiction to such biological templates were often seen as in some way 'deviant' or 'unnatural'. Homophobia, for example, stigmatized sexual relationships conducted outside the traditional male-female paradigm as unnatural – for they could not yield the pregnancy the sexual act has evolved to achieve.

There is, of course, a glaring inconsistency to these types of arguments. The 'natural' model doesn't just rule out homosexuality. It rules out the use of birth control (although one feels that might hearten some of its advocates). But it also rules out foreplay – animals don't devote any time to that because it has no bearing on procreation. What about kissing? That serves no biological imperative either, so it's off the table. Speaking of tables, the romantic dinner beforehand? Animals don't place much emphasis on culinary ritual so that too is ruled out in advance. The cigarette after? You should be so lucky. Even conversation is out of the question. In other words, if you choose to reduce human sexuality to only that which is natural – that is, the single flashpoint of conception – then you simultaneously annihilate all that is human in it. And that, dear reader, seems, well, rather ... *unnatural*.

Transphobic prejudice operates along the same lines. That is, it endeavours to reduce what it means to be a man or a woman to the purely physical condition of being male or female; it reduces the social to the biological and thereby relieves us of what most truly makes us human; that is, the fact that we come to ourselves in the midst of society, we individuate ourselves through our social contact with others, for our identities as human beings are not written out across the mysterious code of our DNA but are instead shaped in the crucible of the history, culture and language we enter into. Our sense of self can only ever reach fruition in such a context. That is not to say that our physical bodies are insignificant, that the natural aspects of our existence are purely negligible; one is objectively born male or female (or some gradation in between) – these are physical facts, but the social essence which underpins what it means to be a man or a woman is so much richer, and that is precisely the reason why it can contradict the bald aspect of a purely biological and natural existence. Indeed human potentiality and human freedom consist in the transcendence of such limits. Or to put it more simply – *it is in our nature to be unnatural.*

For this reason, those ideologies which endeavour to fetishize the 'natural' are often implicated in the attack on what it means to be human, and the possibilities of human freedom and potential that are unfolded therein. Homophobes denounce homosexuality because it is 'unnatural' – the true state of nature embodied in Biblical terms is 'Adam and Eve' not 'Adam and Steve'. Sexist patriarchs demand women devote themselves to children and homemaking precisely because it is in *their biological nature* to be more demure and nurturing. Slavery in the modern age was justified by imposing natural categories on human beings in order to create a hierarchy of races in which some groups were deemed less human precisely because of their 'biological inferiority'. The Holocaust was the ghastly culmination of this process, the process by which the socialized essence of what human beings are is fully and horrifically subordinated to the fetishized characteristics of 'pure biology' in and through the vulgar pseudo-science of race craft.

The claim, therefore, that trans women are not really women is part of this same process. Part of the endeavour to submit what is most human in our personalities to a (crude) biological template, and thus to negate an ongoing process of self-expression, of social change – the striving to call into being new forms of freedom. And now we can return to the ideology of 'political correctness gone mad'. Those who propound this notion are able to raise up a specific societal vision; they depict the antics of a 'politically correct' elite who, influenced by 'trans activists', are doing everything they can to shape and bend politics and culture in the most absurd of ways, all for the benefits of trans people. As we have already seen, this can take on a sinister hue; the suggestion that 'trans ideology' is seeping into schools and corrupting children, the imputation that trans women are likely to pose a danger to 'real women' in toilets, and so on. But to the sinister is added the absurd – these trans activists and their allies are, it is suggested, effete and sensitive to the point of being hysterical; unable to deal with the mildest criticism or rebuke, they are always on the verge of being triggered – 'whiny, wimpy, effete people today who demand protection against the slightest whiff of offence … If transgender students happen to be addressed by the wrong pronoun, let them deal with this little mosquito bite of an irritant, the way we all deal with difficulties.'[49]

Not only does this help to minimize the prejudice trans people encounter – 'let them deal with this little mosquito bite of an irritant …' – but it also allows the people who purvey the prejudice to take on the mantle of common sense against a liberal elite that is so ridiculously 'intellectual', post-modern and 'out of touch' that it cannot see what is the most simple and obvious of 'truths'. A man is a man. A woman is a woman. Human beings are simply the sum total of their biology, for they are born into an inescapable natural essence. Thus the ideology of prejudice is grounded in good old common sense and so – rather than the emotive and unthinking hatred of discrimination – such prejudice appears to be merely an assessment of 'objective fact'. Men are born with penises, women with vaginas – and this is something (so the argument goes) which the majority of 'ordinary people' are able to grasp at once, precisely because they are living in the 'real world' and are able to bring to bear simple common-sense thinking to reality as it actually is. In contrast to this, exists a liberal elite who are so bamboozled by absurd notions of 'political correctness' they are quite capable (according to the narrative) of buying into the most ridiculous, post-modern ideals; for them, someone can self-identify as a cat if they wish.

But the endeavour to reduce the struggle of trans people for acceptance and dignity as merely some ridiculous and fashionable anachronism facilitated on the part of a 'politically correct' elite – is taking place at a time when trans people are being stigmatized, discriminated against, denied access to proper medical treatment, harassed, assaulted and sometimes even murdered in significant numbers and places across the world. The presentation of trans people as a danger rather than a minority group which is endangered; the sense that they are both sinister – that is, a threat to 'real women' and children – and at the same time ultra-sensitive and ridiculous – that is, perpetually ready to take offence at the slightest whiff of 'criticism'; this is the ideological vision that has been called into being by the 'Littlejohns' of this world in their desperate attempt to stifle new forms of freedom and self-expression, to reduce them all to the absurdities of 'political correctness gone mad'. But what does such a deeply ingrained hostility mean for a trans person simply trying to go about their day to day life? The author, educator and queer trans woman Sara C answers that question in clear but poignant terms:

I'm called a snowflake when I ask people to use my correct name and pronoun. I'm called a predator when I want to educate children about people like me. I'm called a threat to public safety when I ask for a safe place to pee, and I'm called weak for not being able to protect myself from violence. I'm called lazy for not being able to find a traditional job, but in traditional workplaces, I'm called a liability or a nuisance. I'm called a deviant when I dare to publicly share my relationships or talk about my sexuality.[50]

5

Cancel culture and the cancellation of the space-time continuum by the woke left

The prophets of cancel culture

If he is a prophet, he is a prophet of a strange stripe. He is stood on the platform, dressed in a dark-blue business suit which is sleek and pristine, and yet it can't disguise the mottled shape of the obese, sagging body underneath. He paces up and down. He has the aggressive posture of an animal staking out its territory – a great ape, a silver-backed gorilla perhaps, only his bleached-blonde hair is thinning; windswept and wispy, it seems to float on his cranium like a breeze. His skin is a burnished tan which, in a certain light, shines a sheen of orange.

He leans forward, lifting his shoulders, emphasizing his bulk; he jabs a finger at some point in the distance as he continues to speak, as the gravity and importance of what he has to say reaches its crescendo. His combative movements are enwrapped by the flabby softness of that ample and aged body, part *foie gras*, part McDonalds. His eyes are small and porcine – they are at the same time intense but strangely vacant, angry but vague. Both present and absent, somehow. As I say, if he is a prophet, he is a most strange one. But he has come with a warning. And he speaks the language of the apocalypse well.

There is a new danger, he tells the crowd. A danger so pervasive and insidious that it is 'driving people from their jobs, shaming dissenters and demanding total submission from anyone who disagrees'. It is an alien contagion, one which has been smuggled into the national heartlands from the forlorn and lonely places which live beyond the borders, 'it is completely alien to our culture and our values' and its ultimate goal is to leave people living 'in fear of being fired, expelled, shamed, humiliated and driven from society as we know it'. A form of 'totalitarianism' that aims to secure your meekness, your obeisance; to make you renounce your belief system, your independence of thought, 'to coerce you into saying what you know to be false, and scare you out of saying what you know to be true'. If you resist, you will be 'cancelled'. And the ultimate architect of such totalitarianism? The 'evil people' on the 'far left'.[1] They are the ones who are bringing this cancel culture to its fruition.

You might imagine that the person making such a speech would be doing it from some illicit location in a land where the mechanisms of the state and a sinister secret police force already hold sway, that the individual in question is a clandestine radical heading some subterranean movement against this shadow of 'totalitarianism'. Ceausescu's Romania. Stalin's Russia perhaps. But the land in question is none of these places but rather the United States of 2020. And the person who is delivering the words is not some ragged, underground freedom fighter or persecuted dissident. The man who is delivering these words is none other than the single most powerful individual on the globe, the then president of the United States. Donald Trump.

✳✳✳

He is sat in a squat wooden cabin. Trails of tabacco smoke hang across the gloom. He is dressed in a tatty jumper with a hood at the back, like a man who knows that at any time he might have to pull that hood over his face, turn his head down, and slip away into the darkness of night. For he is speaking out from a dystopia. And he knows they are coming. This man knows about the past too. Those darkest moments. The times when people have been unvoiced and worse merely for the tone of their skin. He knows that 'people of colour have been silenced throughout history'. He speaks into the microphone so that it can pick up his ragged words in a static, whispery crackle, and transmit them to whoever is out there, whoever might still be listening. Perhaps there is still some sliver of light within the pall of darkness which is overshadowing his world. Perhaps it is already too late. First they came for the Jews. Then the Blacks. Now it is his turn.

He still has his microphone, however. His sense of self, his core beliefs, they remain intact and untouchable. He has witnessed this creeping totalitarianism infiltrate everything he loves: 'It keeps going. It keeps going further and further and further down the line'.[2] Eventually he knows it will get to the point where he and those like him, a persecuted minority, 'will not be allowed to talk', will not even be allowed 'to go outside'. After all, the historical record is a bleak one of repression and incarceration – 'so many people were imprisoned'[3] – and now the same interminable pattern is playing out today. This new totalitarianism is reaching its zenith. From the isolation of his bunker, from the smoke and from the shadows, he will continue to speak out. It is what he must do. It is all he can do.

Who is this man? Who is this lone voice in the darkness? And what of the nature of the evil he is fighting against? In Nazi Germany, illicit radio stations sprang up, braving the Gestapo and the concentration camps in order to broadcast freedoms which had once been taken for granted, like the playing of Jazz music for example. Is he one of their ilk? In South Africa, in the darkest days of the apartheid, Radio Freedom sent out its message of equality and hope in the context of a police state where you could receive up to eight years in prison just for tuning into the broadcast. Is he one of its followers?

The short answer is no. In fact, the man delivering these ominous warnings is one Joe Rogan. The persecuted layers of whom he speaks are 'straight white men'. And the subjugation they encounter is deployed against them by members of the LGBT community in particular, those classical and most lethal of all history's oppressors – 'The most vicious shit is coming from like transgender people or gay people'. And the means by which this totalitarian assault has been carried out? '[T]he cancel culture coming from the left'.[4]

There remain a couple of discordant notes, however. On the day Joe Rogan took to the airwaves to decry the ways and means by which straight white men were being progressively silenced, he also happened to be broadcasting to an audience of some 190 million people. And, despite the level of repression he has undergone being a straight white male in such tumultuous and dangerous times – he has nevertheless managed to amass a fortune of 100 million dollars through his broadcasting, podcasts and public appearances.[5] Cancel culture has yet to cancel him apparently.

***

She is older now, but her course is unchanged. She is a writer. That, by the way, is not just an occupation for her. It is not simply something she does. It is something she is. Something she was always destined to be. Throughout the highs and lows in her life, she has been able to take solace in the imaginary shapes and structures of her mind; a place populated by wizards and witches, centaurs and orcs, great castles and dark forests, the magical and the terrifying, the sacred and the profane. Her mind is a world-building machine; whether she is writing in a lonely cafe at the crack of dawn or a salubrious hotel as the evening melts into night. Whether she is writing as an angst-ridden teenager or a harassed and hassled single-mother, whether she is writing in big scrawly crayon as a child herself or whether she is writing tales of quirky monsters in order to delight her own children – words are her power, and she has always been able to put them to page.

She has known success in her career. It is fair to say she is financially stable. But despite her achievements, she looks back to that time when she had very little, when she would do her writing at the back of some greasy spoon cafe, nursing a cup of tea and the warmth from the radiator, putting off the moment when she has to return to a cold bedsit and the electricity bill that still hadn't been paid. But as hard as those times were, they were simpler too – freer somehow. The political culture of today has changed. It has darkened – a sinister shadow cast across the panorama, as subversive and ominous as any Dark Lord. The principle on which all civilized society is based – that of free speech – has been eroded. The Enlightenment atmosphere of toleration, critical debate and uncertainty has been evaporated, leaving a harder, harsher realm of dogmas that cannot be challenged. Lines of 'political correctness' have become the new orthodoxy – hard and unyielding – and anybody who seeks to question them in a spirit of free-inquiry is likely to have their reputations destroyed, their platform removed, their right to free speech nullified.

And so, she finds herself caught in a world more ominous than any she might invent – 'an intolerance of opposing views, a vogue for public shaming and ostracism, and the tendency to dissolve complex policy issues in a blinding moral certainty'[6] – she finds herself morally denounced in the conflict between the puritans and the heretics; she is shamed, de-platformed, unvoiced, curtailed. She has been … *cancelled*. But she will not be silent. For she knows better than anyone about the travails of a world in which peoples' freedom of thought is cast onto the pyre. A world of sacrilege where witches are held up to be burnt.

Does she act in the spirit of some Enlightenment radical, a Galileo for modern times? Brought to her knees by the power of the Inquisition, and yet – broken and downtrodden – some part of her refuses to recant, still she declaims – *Eppur si muove.* Is she a modern-day heretic whose humanism and rationality have rendered her an outcast and *persona non grata* in a society dominated by regressive and repressive orthodoxy?

Actually no, for if you haven't already guessed, the figure in question is none other than J. K. Rowling, the single most successful author of all time. In 2020, when she was warning about the perils and oppressions of cancel culture she earned 60 million making her 28 on *Forbes*' list of the world's most wealthy celebrities.[7] In that same year, taking to the internet in order to promote a letter in *Harper's Magazine* denouncing the way 'cancel culture' silences dissenting voices, she was able to utilize a *Twitter* platform of over 14 million followers. Her thoughts, views and opinions continue to appear regularly in virtually every big paper or news outlet in the English-speaking world and beyond.

The realities of cancel culture

To put it simply, cancel culture is the idea that those on the radical left hold such power in society, that they are capable of 'cancelling' the views of any public or private figure who doesn't accord with the prevailing 'politically correct' line. In this ideological vision, an increasingly totalitarian left is able to drive an individual from his or her social media platform or his or her job, and into obscurity, censoring and smothering their viewpoint in the process. That is what it means to be 'cancelled'. I've begun this chapter with a consideration of perhaps the three most visible 'martyrs' of cancel culture: Donald Trump, Joe Rogan and J. K. Rowling. I've begun with these individuals because they all effectively purvey the right-wing fantasy of a world that is controlled and regulated by the far left and yet the reality of their careers speaks of global visibility, untapped levels of wealth, and the capacity to have their views disseminated to, quite literally, billions.

But is there any sense whatsoever in which any of these three has been effectively 'cancelled'? Donald Trump was eventually banned from Twitter, this much is true. But this was not the result of him saying 'politically incorrect' things (he had been doing that for years on that platform). Rather it was the fact that his words – specifically the falsehoods he used in describing an election he lost legitimately as one 'stolen' from him – helped incite a riot on Capitol Hill that sought to overturn the democratic result and would lead to the loss of several lives. Twitter suspended Trump's account 'due to the risk of further incitement of violence'[8] – or to say the same, Twitter was banning one of its users from its forum, not from the perspective of a left-wing sense of 'political correctness', but from the purview of a billion dollar company which was worried about verifiably false claims negatively impacting state security. Furthermore, even though his Twitter platform has been withdrawn on this basis, Trump has access to a vast publicity machine through TV, podcasting, newspapers, his PR people and the incredible wealth that has helped him set up his own communications platform[9] with the express aim of rivalling Twitter and its ilk.

In the case of J. K. Rowling, the situation is a little different. J. K. Rowling has experienced a backlash from large numbers of people on the left for her transphobic opinions. While Rowling's transphobia is undeniably offensive and dangerous, many of the people who took part in the critique of it responded in a deeply disturbing fashion. She received online Twitter abuse from people who purported to be progressives but went ahead and showered her with hate, with the most appalling language, with threats of physical violence, threats of rape and death. It was a travesty of bullying, intimidation and the most extreme misogyny, and should be universally condemned no matter what Rowling's views were on other issues. And yet, could what happened to Rowling be regarded as an example of cancel culture?

I tend to think not. Firstly, because despite the energy and viciousness of their bile, the people attacking Rowling were in no position to remove her from either the Twitter platform or any of the other social media and media outlets which allow her to reach audiences of billions. They were in no position to ensure that her publishers fired her, or that her books ceased to be manufactured and distributed. In other words, they had no ability to 'cancel' her whatsoever.

In addition, while the online abuse was undoubtedly coming from those on the left in Rowling's case, the 'trolling' phenomenon clearly isn't confined to one side of the political spectrum – one only needs to look at the abuse the few prominent left wingers face on Twitter and other forums; politicians like Alexander Ocasio-Cortez, for instance, and the deluge of death threats she receives online from men and women on the right. Undoubtedly vicious and foul – this certainly aims at silencing people whether it be Rowling or Ocasio-Cortez – but such behaviour, ubiquitous on social media, doesn't really fit the cancel culture narrative. One, it is not the sole providence of the left, and furthermore it is largely incapable of manifesting the organized, systematic and 'totalitarian' pressure from above that can shut down the avenues of free speech and compel the loss of jobs.

And yet, despite this, despite the fact that those who are screaming 'cancel culture' most loudly are also those who have their voices amplified and projected into every corner of society by way of the most public of platforms – nevertheless the sense that the force and power of 'cancel culture' is levelling an existential threat against freedom of speech is something that is gaining traction. In 2020, the open letter signed by Rowling was published in *Harper's Magazine*, a letter which levelled a grave warning against cancel culture (though it did not use that specific term). It was signed by a series of writers, academics and luminaries who coalesced mainly around the political centre but there were also a handful of left-wing figures such as the redoubtable and principled Noam Chomsky or the wonderful radical public intellectual Cornel West, alongside several figures on the right like the journalist and Bush-era political advocate David Frum.

Fundamentally, however, the letter struck a liberal tone – very much a handwringing lament in the Voltaire-esque 'I disapprove of what you say, but I will defend to the death your right to say it ...' type vein. The letter averred that the censorship and repression that was once the provenance of 'the radical right' was now 'spreading more widely in our culture' with the result that 'the boundaries of what can be said without the threat of reprisal'[10] have greatly narrowed. The letter didn't use the phrase 'cancel culture' but it was clear that this was the target, and the notion of 'censoriousness ... spreading more widely' was clearly a salvo directed at the left.

While the emotional tone of the letter was ominous and darkly atmospheric, the actual facts were rather thin on the ground. The means by which the letter suggests the increasingly totalitarian power of 'cancel culture' are less about concrete examples and more about baroque and obscure allusions. In the whole piece, only three lines are devoted to figures in public life who have actually been 'cancelled' and even here there is a pervading and mysterious anonymity which characterizes the 'evidence' being proffered: 'Editors are fired for running controversial pieces; books are withdrawn for alleged inauthenticity; journalists are barred from writing on certain topics; professors are investigated for quoting works of literature in class; a researcher is fired for circulating a peer-reviewed academic study; and the heads of organizations are ousted for what are sometimes just clumsy mistakes.'[11]

Naturally this has invited some speculation. The '[e]ditors ... fired for running controversial pieces' is widely believed to be a reference to two specific editors, James Bennet of *The New York Times* and Ian Buruma of *The New York Review of Books*. However, as the *Guardian* journalist Jessica Valenti points out, once one looks into these examples in any detail, a different type of story emerges. In the first case, 'Bennet lost his job for, among other things, running an op-ed section that published a senator advocating the use of military force against peaceful American protesters ... a column that employees pointed out literally put Black lives in danger.'[12] Bennet both defended the publication of the article, while at the same time rather clumsily averring he hadn't actually read it before it was published. Which makes him as an editor seem either rabid or incompetent, liable to lose his job on each count, especially because the issue was one of disregard for public safety. In other words, what happened was not a matter of 'cancel culture' but rather the more prosaic fact of someone being fired because they had proved disastrous at their job. It in no way indicates some form of 'politically correct' and cancelling totalitarianism. It indicates the decision to remove someone from their post as a result of either their incompetence or a more authoritarian desire for bloodshed.

In a similar vein, Ian Buruma (one of the co-signatories on the *Harper's Letter*) had lost his job at *The New York Review of Books* after having published a piece by the disgraced broadcaster and writer Jian Ghomeshi who had been accused by more than twenty women of sexual assault, of having 'slapped, punched, bitten, choked or smothered'[13] them during sexual encounters. Jian Ghomeshi's story (he was eventually acquitted of some of the charges and paid other alleged victims off in settlements) – is not a story about the totalitarian ability of the Me Too movement to repress men; it is another depressing tale of how, even in the time of Me Too, powerful men are still able to enjoy the sympathy of the courts and the media whereas their victims often remain unvoiced, their testimonies disregarded.

As one journalist tweeted: 'Oh look, it's another man whose been accused of sexually assaulting multiple women finding refuge from his so-called "exile" in the pages of (a) well-respected national publication'.[14] Ghomeshi's article in *The New York Review of Books* provided him once more with a global platform and it allowed him to reframe an account of savage sexual assault in terms of one where Ghomeshi himself is the victim, having faced 'enough humiliation for a lifetime', a victim of 'mass shaming'.[15] The choking, the biting, the punching and the slapping, the terror and the humiliation which is part and parcel of the alleged victims' accounts seems to fade away before the more wistful narrative of a life-lesson imparted to a rueful and changed man – someone who had made some minor and incidental 'mistakes' – only to have been brutally ostracized and persecuted, before finally emerging stronger than ever, serene in his redemption. It was, quite frankly, vomit-inducing.

Ian Buruma's dismissal from *The New York Review of Books,* then, occurred because he had chosen to give an alleged sexual predator who was facing the testimonies of scores of women – an incredibly potent platform before the advent of his trial in order to spin the narrative in his own favour. Victims lobbying groups were understandably appalled by this because it reflected the discrepancy in power between alleged perpetrators and alleged victims but Buruma himself remained unmoved even to the point of indifference, eventually reflecting that '[t]he exact nature of … [Ghomeshi's] … behavior – how much consent was involved – I have no idea nor is it really my concern.'[16] One can justifiably argue that Buruma's callousness, his indifference to 'consent' and the victims of sexual assault more generally, warranted a dismissal – on the grounds of his not being able to discharge the ethical obligations of a considerably important and influential editorship.

But even after his dismissal, Buruma continued to enjoy the perks of a lucrative career. He retained a professorship at Bard College. He continued to have his voice heard; that is, he continued to publish in some of the biggest outfits on the globe (Penguin Books in 2018, Atlantic Books in 2020). His journalism is regularly featured in some of the most prestigious and widely read newspapers in the UK and the United States, papers like *The Times*, *The Telegraph* and *The Financial Times*, while he still gives interviews to *Bloomberg* and still receives glowing reviews for his books in outlets like *The Wall Street Journal*. One of his favourite themes in these later writings? The victims of cancel culture.

The *Harper's* letter also makes reference to 'professors … investigated for quoting works of literature in class', thus building the image of a society in the grip of a repressive puritanism that is seeking to suppress books. But again, when one goes to the example this alludes to, the situation is markedly different. In this case a UCLA professor named W. Ajax Peris read exerts from a letter which contained the N-word and also showed graphic images of lynching to the class without prior warning. Some students complained. Naturally the use of the N-word and images of racist murder are going to be particularly disturbing to Black students, while at the same time, one can hardly refuse to acknowledge these things because they are such an important part of the historical record any teacher seeks to impart.

Should Peris have shown a better and more delicate sense of etiquette? Were the students being over-sensitive? Whatever the case, the important thing is that the complaints the teacher received were investigated and this 'investigation was resolved with a critical letter from his department head. He was not subject to widespread calls for termination and will be teaching classes in the fall.'[17] In other words, Peris was not cancelled. As *The Huffington Post* journalist Michael Hobbes comments, '"Peris" case was utterly routine. Students complain about their teachers for justifiable reasons and silly ones thousands of times per week in America. These complaints don't just come from left-wing students: After the 2016 election, a professor at the College of Charleston was targeted by conservatives for dedicating a class to discussing Donald Trump's victory.'[18]

The *Harper's* letter also avers that 'books are withdrawn for alleged inauthenticity'. Once more, when scrutinized, the claim proves to be something of a red herring. It is almost certainly a reference to a novel called *American Dirt*. This was a novel about a Mexican immigrant. It was initially celebrated by figures like Oprah Winfrey in her book club, but soon it began to be pilloried by more discerning critics – not least by Mexican authors (and immigrants) themselves – for its harmful and stereotypical presentation of Mexican lives. The controversy gathered steam and this eventually resulted in a book tour being cancelled with the publisher citing issues of safety and threats of violence issued against the author. Undoubtedly, this is disgraceful, and those who made such threats should be held to account, but when it comes to the broader issue of cancel culture, the book wasn't 'withdrawn for alleged inauthenticity' as per the claim in the *Harper's* letter. Rather it continued to sell in millions and remained in the top ten best sellers list for the best part of a year after the controversy had erupted.

The *Harper's* letter itself is written in the tone of the belaboured liberal dissident – high-minded, shot through with a forlorn sense of gravitas, a last stand before the approaching storm; think John Proctor calling out with anguish, refusing to relinquish his name even as he is marched towards the gallows, or the prisoner Solzhenitsyn, giving voice to this thoughts in the bleakest of times, scribbling notes under the looming shadow of the Gulag Archipelago. The letter exudes self-regard; the writers and signatories are fully moved by the nature of their own sublime sacrifice, the lonely and noble stand they are making before the dark forces which are gathering on the horizon. But for the most part these people are not political dissidents. They are instead a clutter of the most privileged, the most wealthy, the most visible and the most famous – none of them has ever been 'cancelled' and none of them are in danger of being 'cancelled'.

The letter represents a fantasy of persecution which emanates from a liberal and right-wing mindset that consistently confuses having its positions challenged by the emergence of progressive movements and new social standards with a form of totalitarian repression from above. In the context of Black Lives Matter, in the context of Me Too, it is natural and inevitable that the question of the way race is taught in the classroom is subject to critical scrutiny, or that a book receives massive public criticism for its lazy racial stereotypes or that an editor is held to account for a marked indifference to issues of 'consent' around sexual politics. As Valenti argues most cogently, '"Cancelled" is a label we all understand to mean a powerful person who's been held to account. It's a term meant to re-centre sympathy on those who already have privilege and influence – a convenient tool to maintain the status quo.'[19]

And it is also worth noting how some of the luminaries who put their names to the letter are less than consistent. Bari Weiss – another signatory of the *Harper's* letter – has railed against cancel culture as the 'new McCarthyism', but the fact that she is desperately concerned about the crushing of liberal freedoms from above, didn't prevent her from becoming so enraged when a Black editor politely refused to have coffee with her that she reported him to the head office of *The New York Times*.[20] While Brett Stephens, another *Times* journalist who has railed against 'cancel culture', was revealed as trying to get his colleagues in trouble if they criticize him on Twitter.[21] In other words, they are all for freedom of speech, with the caveat that it should really only apply to their own.

The character of the mainstream media

Those who trumpet the need for free speech most loudly – that is, those who use the free-speech argument to level a liberal critique against 'cancel culture' – are often adept at overlooking the conditions in which that speech arises. In the case of journalism, for example – in Britain – amongst the big media outlets and newspapers, a 2019 survey discovered that 44 per cent of their news columnists had been to 'public schools' (fee-paying schools) and yet only 7 per cent of the population as a whole actually attend these schools. Such schools are famously the schools of the elite that help their students develop a network of contacts from an early age, and this very much works to fortify their connections and prestige once they enter into the adult world of work. In addition, another 44 per cent of all news columnists went to one of the two elite universities, Oxford and Cambridge.[22] On top of that, many young people who gain access to journalistic positions often work as interns beforehand – that is, they provide a period of free labour for a top magazine or newspaper with the expectation that they might receive paid work afterward.

Again, only those people who are from the upper echelons tend to have the economic support in order to be able to do this. As well, many of the biggest newspapers are controlled by a small elite of multi-millionaire or billionaire press barons whose interests and ideology are shaped largely in accordance with their elite wealth. At the current time of writing, for instance, 'three-quarters of circulation is controlled by four families. Viscount Rothermere, owner of the *Mail* and *Metro*, is leader of the pack with 35.5 per cent of print circulation, supplemented by website traffic in the UK of 38 million visits per month, according to Comscore. Rupert Murdoch is second with 25 per cent of print, plus 54 million website visitors a month to *The Sun* and *The Times*. Evgeny Lebedev is third, with 8 per cent of print (*The London Evening Standard*) and website visitors of 25 million per month. In fourth position is Frederick Barclay of *The Telegraph* with 5 per cent of print.'[23] *Quelle surprise* – these newspapers are all uniformly pro-big business.

None of this tallies with the image of society the decriers of 'cancel culture' are trying to create. None of this suggests that we are dealing with a media in which the concerns of a 'politically correct' left wing are able to enforce their views in and through a totalitarian form of censorship and repression. In fact, the views which are concentrated and amplified tend to be those of the liberal centre and the right wing – that is, the mainstay of establishment views. The 'free speech' that the elite-educated and upper-class liberals are so concerned with tends to be a free speech that operates within very specific and curtailed parameters; that is, people like themselves with considerable access to the mechanisms of the mainstream media in and through a hierarchy of privilege; and this often produces a rather stale and uniform political consensus. An alternative narrative that better reflects the social interests of the vast majority is that much harder to smuggle in, especially when those from a lower economic bracket are so seriously underrepresented.

In 2017, an event took place which acted as a flaming torch, revealing the great fissure which had opened up in British society between the haves and the have-nots. In July of that year a fire broke out in the twenty-four storey Grenfell tower block, in one of the most deprived areas of London. The fire started because of an electric fault in a malfunctioning fridge, but what was surprising was the rapidity of its spread. It billowed up the surface of the building before gutting the floors on which the residents lived with its heat and flames. It burnt on for more than sixty hours, leaving the building a black slab of charred metal and concrete, set into the surrounding landscape like a smouldering tombstone. And indeed it would mark the loss of seventy-two lives, along with the many others who were severely injured.

It was later established that the fire was the result of cladding which burns easily and had failed fire tests consistently for twelve years before the conflagration.[24] There was only one escape route in the building and no building-wide fire alarm or sprinklers. Residents had expressed concerns over and over, but these were repeatedly brushed aside by the Chelsea Tenant Management Organization.[25]

The Grenfell fire was a tragedy. But it also spoke to a dystopic and divided landscape – for though Grenfell Tower was situated in one of the poorest and most deprived neighbourhoods in London, it was within a stone's throw of the richest. Still smouldering, the blackened, brutalist and threadbare building looked out across the borough of Kensington and Chelsea where the streets were wide and pristine – tended with neat trees, decorated with green squares – and where also the salubrious white Georgian houses had sold on average for £4.3 million each[26] in the year before Grenfell Tower was destroyed.

Even though these neighbourhoods were linked by their geography there was a metaphysical divide which opened up between the lives of the people in one and those in the other, and on that July night in 2017 such a divide was illuminated most vividly by the light cast from a burning building and the lives that were consumed in the inferno. Landlords had accumulated their wealth at the most grievous of costs, their own lives cocooned in safety and luxury, abstracted from the inhuman conditions their business practices and investment packages had set into motion, as the divide between absolute poverty and billionaire wealth fissured across the landscape of twenty-first-century Britain. And it was a divide which had been reproduced in the form and structure of the mainstream media itself.

The journalist and TV presenter John Snow would report on the Grenfell case and his experience of it left him harrowed and haunted, but it also left him with significant questions about the role of journalists and broadcasters in the mainstream media more generally. Snow himself had been confronted by angry Grenfell residents who had written a blog highlighting the dangers of their impoverished conditions but not one mainstream media source had chosen to pick up their story. In a keynote speech at the Edinburgh television festival Snow asked: 'Why didn't any of us see the Grenfell action blog? Why didn't we know? Why didn't we have contact? Why didn't we enable the residents of Grenfell Tower – and indeed the other hundreds of towers like it around Britain – to find pathways to talk to us and for us to expose their story?'[27] The veteran journalist was forced to conclude that the reason was not merely a result of haphazard accident or unfortuitous timing but rather a more structural and systematic issue that went to the root of social organization and class in contemporary Britain: the media, Snow averred, was 'comfortably with the elite, with little awareness, contact or connection with those not of the elite' and that such a disconnection, such a divide, was indeed 'dangerous'.[28]

It is not, therefore, that the majority of the mainstream media work in tandem to 'cancel' or 'suppress' everyday issues of class poverty and structural injustice; for the most part, it is that the emissaries of the media operate in a realm abstracted from the majority of ordinary lives, and their own social and political interests tend to reflect that separation more often than not. When certain new stories (usually those with a more radical bent) come in, the editors simply don't choose to pick up on them because they seem 'irrelevant' or in some way contradict the political narrative of the paper's editorial line. But this does not in any way impact the liberal idea of 'freedom'. After all, anyone, from any class background, is free to submit articles or stories – even if those stories don't get taken up. Likewise anyone, from any economic background, is free to apply for a job as a journalist – even if the majority will never have the financial means or social connections to secure such a position.

In the same vein, though the vast proportion of the mainstream media is in the hands of billionaire barons, it is still referred to as a 'free press'. And why not? I have as much legal right to purchase a major national newspaper as Rupert Murdoch, though the £3067 currently sitting in my bank account means this is unlikely to work out for me. And last but by no means least, the hallowed issue of free speech itself. Despite the fact that it is often difficult to air the sort of grievances which pertain to the fundamental inequality which structures society, as with the concerns the residents of Grenfell had long before the fire – it is not as if their free speech was repressed. It simply wasn't heard. It was never amplified through the mainstream media and into the public fora. Until it was too late.

The liberal notion of free speech, therefore, is pivoted on a social system structured in terms of considerable economic inequality and this affects the parameters of who can speak and what issues are heard; what appears as free speech is severely curtailed and restricted to a minority whom, in most cases, have the economic means and social background to be jettisoned into the more prestigious positions and roles in the media in the first instance. Yes, anybody has the abstract right to speak out but the deeper and more profound inequalities help determine the limits of exactly what is said.

But what if those limits were stressed? Tested? And ultimately breached? What if a set of more radical views was able to penetrate the 'public' discourse on a comprehensive and society-wide basis, views which better reflect the political and social interests of people like those who had lived in Grenfell Tower and the neighbourhood there? In 2015, something happened which did indeed allow the consensus of the political establishment to be breached, if only for a short time.

The event of Jeremy Corybn

Up until 2015, the two main parties of British politics, whilst vying with each other for votes in parliament, nevertheless carried the same essential economic policy. After the financial crisis of 2007–8 a Conservative-led coalition cemented the politics of 'austerity' in 2010. Put simply, austerity was the endeavour to transfer the single biggest sum of money from the people at the bottom of society to the people at the top in British history. The bankers, financiers, investors and moneymen who had facilitated the crisis with their reckless brand of casino capitalism were not to be punished for their financial flagrancy but rather rewarded to the tune of £500 billion[29] in the form of a bailout package which was issued in 2008. It allowed the financiers and bankers not only to keep their exorbitant salaries but in the years that followed they were able to claim bloated bonuses and hiked salaries on a scale that was inconceivable to the person in the street.

The austerity politics, the decision to bail out those at the top by crippling those at the bottom with the debt, was something which both major parties committed to. The Tories brought in the austerity measures in 2010. And in 2013, the Labour Shadow Chancellor Ed Balls signed his party up to the austerity package that the Tories had introduced.[30] In 2019, a report by the Institute for Public Policy Research concluded that austerity was to blame for 130,000 'preventable' deaths in the UK amongst the layers of the most vulnerable and impoverished. Had the government and the leading opposition party focussed on taxing the super corporations that little more heavily, those lives could have been saved and it is doubtful one banker or billionaire would have gone hurtling to his or her doom.

The horrific audacity of the bailout was as a bloody scar across the visage of a nation wracked with crisis, and as such, it demanded some form of ideological band aid. Along with the economics of austerity, a political culture arose in which the central problems of society were not conceived of in terms of the unbridled speculation that had unleashed the financial crisis but rather with the poor majority themselves, be they immigrants, people on benefits, the working-class or struggling single mothers. Programmes proliferated across mainstream TV; dubbed as 'poverty porn', they purported to show the reality of a bleary and belligerent underclass which was milking the benefits system dry, feral and prone to violence, spilling out into the streets in a profusion of boozy, vomit-stained ignorance and rage.

Alongside this, the right-wing press – day after day, week after week – carried stories of immigrants claiming benefits at the expense of 'authentic' (read white) English people and the sense of racism and a bunker mentality of 'protect our borders' was increasingly ramped up to its zenith, coalescing perfectly with the Brexit vote in 2016. The Tory Party, as one might expect, had a vested interest in promoting this atmosphere of paranoia and suspicion for it neatly deflected one's gaze from the sleek and feted heads of finance who had gorged themselves sick on the national economy; in 2013, the Conservatives launched vans which cruised through the capital, sporting slogans on the side that read 'Go Home or Face Arrest' as a way of highlighting the 'sinister' spectre of 'illegal immigration' and promoting the government's draconian response. The then Home Secretary Theresa May went on the record with her rather bloodthirsty desire to 'create, here in Britain, a really hostile environment for illegal immigrants'.[31]

The campaign would have devastating consequences whereby people who had lived in the country for the majority of their lives were wrongfully upended and deported in the most brutal fashions to places they no longer had roots in. Many of these people were born British subjects, and this was highlighted in the Windrush scandal where scores of Black people were unceremoniously deported. Many others were denied access to medical care and benefits. Some had their passports confiscated. Some died far from their families, alone under distant skies.

One might have thought that any opposition party worth its salt could have taken the chance to point out how, in fact, immigration had consistently proved to be a boon for the UK economy. How much richer culture and society is made from an influx of people from every possible place. Instead, the so-called 'liberal elite' of the Labour Party leadership chose to issue a cup which read 'Controls on Immigration … I'm voting Labour'.[32] Just as the party of 'opposition' had colluded with the endeavour to penalize the poor for the economic irresponsibility of the rich, so too did it collude in the ideology which sought to disguise this. On the plus side, every crank, ultra-nationalist and xenophobe now had something from which to sup.

In 2015, however, something happened to shatter this consensus. Jeremy Corbyn was elected as the leader of the Labour Party. Corbyn was on the marginalized far-left of the party and had remained in the shadows on the backbenches for decades, taking part in community initiatives and supporting grassroots movements as a local MP, all at a remove from the baleful glare of the press and the political mainstream. In 2015, he found himself elevated into a position of leadership for the main opposition party, and at once began to articulate his own set of more radical and egalitarian politics. As part and parcel of this, he challenged the austerity narrative. He pointed out that immigration was to be celebrated for the 'enormous contribution to our society'[33] immigrants make. The issue of scant resources in the health service was not a consequence of uncontrolled immigration but instead the result of austerity politics imposed from above. It wasn't immigrants who drive down wages but rather 'exploitative employers'.[34] Corbyn aimed to put the blame for the crisis squarely on the shoulders of those who had helped facilitate it – the wealthy and the bankers rather than the poor majority. At the economic level, he proposed a break with austerity politics and an end to the biggest redistribution of wealth from the bottom to the top in British history.

The political establishment reacted with unlimited venom. Not least the members in the higher echelons of the Labour Party itself who worked to sabotage the leadership eventually mounting a coup in 2016 that sought to remove the democratically elected leader. It failed but a fresh leadership election was called, and the rebel MPs tried to stymie the results by introducing new and undemocratic voting restrictions. Hundreds of thousands of poorer, younger people had flocked to the Labour Party, heeding Corbyn's anti-austerity, anti-corporate, anti-war message, and the elite politicians in the party who had fulminated the coup understood they couldn't win a new leadership contest through democratic means.

So they introduced a voting fee of £25 – clearly on the grounds that the people who were swelling Corbyn's ranks were likely to be poorer and less able to cover the cost. It didn't work. 180,000 new supporters joined the party within forty-eight hours of the leadership election being declared.[35] In the event Corbyn won a resounding landslide. But so magnanimous was he in victory, that he invited all the elite politicians who had plotted against him back into the party, even giving some key positions in the Shadow Cabinet. The mode of conciliation – even of those who had threatened to undermine the democratic process through an illegal action – was to remain a hallmark of Corbyn's political strategy right up to the point where it cost him the leadership.

But what is important for the purposes of the current chapter is how the mainstream media responded to Corbyn. How they responded to a figure that had been catapulted into the very centre of the public debate and yet was amplifying an anti-austerity and left-wing narrative that broke fundamentally with the economic and political consensus which had developed amongst both the main political parties in the decade before.

The first issue to take up is that of the coup itself. In the lead-up to the coup, in the first half of 2016, the mainstream media played the role of facilitators. A series of resignations by right-wing anti-Corbyn MPs at the very top of the Labour Party were enacted, very much in the vein of a group of people who had been forced into a grave but spontaneous decision imposed by the dictates of conscience. Corbyn was intolerable as leader and anyone of moral principle should now make their voices heard in opposition. But the presentation belied the reality. In actual fact, the coup was not based on a spontaneous and overwhelming sense of ethical outrage that had developed in the moment, but rather the action was part of a coordinated and premeditated political strategy cultivated over many months and from behind the scenes by the anti-Corbyn MPs.

It eventually transpired that these right-wing MPs had links to the PR company Portland Communications and a Labour source would reveal that within a month of Corbyn's election the previous year, the plan had already been hatched 'to get rid of him'.[36] But as one MP after the next announced his or her resignation, the media and the TV stations gave them virtually unlimited time to register their anti-Corbyn sentiments, fully bolstering the impression that the Leader of the Labour Party was deeply unpopular and clinging to power by anti-democratic means – but failing to reference the vast upswing of hundreds of thousands of grassroots members who had flooded the Labour Party to support the anti-austerity movement.

The same line was trotted out by the rebel MPs and the media; Corbyn was unelectable – despite how, in the very moment this was being asserted, the Labour Party was on its way to becoming the biggest mass party in Europe precisely because of Corbyn's policies. One wouldn't receive this information even from the main state broadcaster and the supposedly impartial BBC which was said to be above partisan political interests. In reality, the BBC behaved in a remarkably partisan and corrupt way when it was revealed that, in order to support the MPs who were briefing against Corbyn – it's chief political editor Laura Kuenssberg had engineered a plan to have the anti-Corbyn Labour MP Stephen Doughty on one of the BBCs flagship political programmes and that – half way through – this MP would become suddenly distressed, leading into a spontaneous 'on air' resignation.

The resignation had been coordinated in advance, a calculated and cynical manoeuvre on the part of the public broadcaster[37] to do the Corbyn leadership as much damage as possible under the auspices of covering the political news. Even the language these journalists used was freighted; for instance, it was pointed out by a leading Channel 4 journalist that broadcasters were consistently referring to the members of the right wing of Labour as the 'moderates'[38] as a means to distinguish them from the Corbyn tendency with the inevitable implication that the latter were the extremists.

Thus were the state broadcaster and right-wing of the Labour Party found to have been acting in collusion in order to pave the way to remove the only leading political figure that was fighting against the austerity narrative. If their counteraction was base and contrived, the reportage which was provided by virtually all the mainstream newspapers strayed into the territory of inflammatory propaganda and out-and-out character assassination. From the very beginning Jeremy Corbyn was smeared consistently and across the board. Papers like *The Daily Mail* painted him as a terrorist sympathizer, 'the bomb-maker's friend',[39] a supporter of the IRA – largely on the back of the fact that Corbyn had protested atrocities carried out by the British army in Northern Ireland like Bloody Sunday where twenty-six unarmed civilians were shot (many of them fleeing), along with photos that showed Corbyn appearing with the then Sinn Féin leader Gerry Adams. The problem with such guilt-by-association tactics was that Tony Blair and Bill Clinton had also appeared with Gerry Adams, and for the same reason as Corbyn – to help negotiate a peace settlement in Northern Ireland.

In addition to his IRA 'sympathies', Corbyn was adduced as having shown support for Black September, a pro-Palestinian terrorist organization which had, among other things, murdered nine members of the Israeli Olympic team in the infamous Munich massacre. How was Corbyn's connection to such horror established? On a 2014 visit to Tunis, Corbyn had been pictured holding a wreath under a canopy of branches which also ran 'alongside the graves of Salah Khalaf, Hayel Abdel-Hamid, Fakhri al-Omari and Atef Bseiso, three of whom have been linked to Black September'.[40] The fact that Corbyn was in proximity to these other graves was enough to glean his secret sympathy for the terrorist cause of mass murder, despite the fact that the wreath Corbyn actually laid was on the graves of Palestinians who had been killed in an airstrike, a completely separate incident that had no connection with the activities of Black September. The story was spun by *The Daily Mail, The Sun, The Times, The Daily Telegraph, The Daily Express* and *The Metro* newspapers; or to say the same it received repeated coverage week after week in much of the national media despite the sheer tenuousness of the 'evidence' for the allegations on display.

The lengths that the mainstream press were prepared to go to in order to cultivate the image of Corbyn as a threat to national security reached their preposterous heights when the same collection of newspapers provided yet another cacophony of noise, again decrying the monstrous Labour leader for his appearance at one more ceremony in order to pay tribute to the dead. On this occasion, it was a gathering at the Cenotaph on Remembrance Sunday to honour those lives lost to war. Here, the sheer toxic menace of Corbyn's anti-patriotic views was established by the fact that the Labour leader hadn't 'bowed his head low enough to honour the war dead' with live footage showing the dastardly 'Mr Corbyn slightly tilting his head downwards for a few seconds before turning and walking away'.[41] Last but not least, the maverick Labour leader's utter hatred for his own country was revealed by *The Daily Mail* which noted how, while everyone else 'cheered on England against the All Blacks' in 2019, the sinister and subversive Labour leader himself was 'caught taking a nap on a train', utterly indifferent to the patriotic fervour which was sweeping the nation.[42]

Over the years he was leader, Corbyn was depicted in the press as an anti-black racist (*New Statesman*),[43] an arch misogynist (*Daily Mail*),[44] 'undereducated', 'humourless' and 'third-rate' (*Sunday Times*),[45] a rabid anti-Semite (virtually all the papers and TV channels) and last but not least (and most surreally of all) *The Sun* even alleged[46] that Corbyn had worked as a Russian informant and asset during the Cold War. In the event, it was the allegations of anti-Semitism which did the most damage. For the reason that the other allegations were simply spurious smears and easy to disregard once they had been looked into in any detail, but the charge of anti-Semitism was more difficult to refute.

And that was because there has always been a section of the radical left who have bought into a critique of capitalism that is based on a Jewish banking conspiracy; in addition, the just and humanitarian critique that should be levelled against Israel's illegal and ongoing occupation of Palestinian lands and the IDF's brutality in Gaza is sometimes marred and distorted by a virulent and toxic anti-Semitism that frames the issue less in terms of a military colonial state and more as a world conspiracy in which the Jews have unlimited power and hold unlimited malevolence. As hundreds of thousands of new members flocked to join the Labour Party and support Corbyn's anti-austerity, anti-war and pro-Palestinian message – it was perhaps inevitable that some would carry the toxic spore of anti-Semitism into the party. That there were some genuine incidents of anti-Semitic behaviour in the Corbyn period is simply beyond debate. As Bebel once ruefully ruminated, 'anti-Semitism is the socialism of fools'.

But the media went further. Collectively, they began to paint an image of the Labour Party as riddled with anti-Semitism, sometimes to the point where it presented an existential threat to the lives of its Jewish members.[47] The British political commentator Helen Lewis took to the pages of *The Atlantic* in order to explain 'why British Jews Are Worried by Jeremy Corbyn'.[48] *The Daily Mail* carried a headline quote warning 'Jeremy Corbyn is the biggest global threat to Jews'.[49] Even left of centre papers like *The Guardian* sought to establish a 'necessary' connection between systematic anti-Semitism in the Labour Party and the Corbyn leadership by suggesting it was no coincidence that 'anti-Semites think Labour is the party for them'.[50]

The media amplified the voices of those Jewish figures and political groups which were anti-Jeremy Corbyn, describing them as 'mainstream' while either ignoring or downplaying those Jews and Jewish groups which were pro-Corbyn; groups like the Jewish Voice for Labour, for example, or Jewdas (the latter being described as a 'fringe group').[51] By portraying all British Jews as having one single opinion and speaking with one uniform voice (i.e. that all

true Jews were instinctively and automatically opposed to Corbyn's Labour) –
the mainstream media came dangerously close to reproducing the type of anti-
Semitic logic they supposedly abhorred.

What didn't come through was Corbyn's history of campaigning against
anti-Semitism. As a local councillor in 1977, Corbyn had organized a defence
of the Jewish population from neo-Nazis who were on the march. In the
same period, he had orchestrated a campaign to save a Jewish graveyard from
property developers (the graveyard was saved). And as the public intellectual
Leo Panitch pointed out, Corbyn's parliamentary resume on the issue of
combating anti-Semitism pretty much speaks for itself: 'A recent compilation
of the number of motions he advanced in Parliament to defend Jewish people,
alongside other public stances he took to tackle anti-Semitism – to denounce
Holocaust deniers, to commemorate Jewish resistance to fascism, to pressure
the police to do more to protect synagogues against vandalism – came to
well over 50.'[52] Of course, very few people in the mainstream media thought
it necessary to draw attention to these kinds of facts, no doubt because they
contradicted the political narrative that was being woven as part of a collective
media campaign against the Corbyn leadership.

Another aspect which received scant media attention was a parliamentary
report on anti-Semitism in the Labour Party which found 'no reliable,
empirical evidence to support the notion that there is a higher prevalence of
anti-Semitic attitudes within the Labour Party than any other political party'.[53]
In addition, the number of complaints in the Labour Party from the years
2017 to 2020, and which related to anti-Semitism, represented 'about 0.05
per cent of the membership at the time'.[54] And yet, when the British public
was polled on the issue, when they were asked in a random sample just how
many members of the Labour Party had been the subject of anti-Semitic
complaints – the average figure was returned of some 34 per cent; or to say
the same, the public perception of the level of anti-Semitic complaints which
had taken place in the Labour Party during the Corbyn tenure was hundreds
of times more than the actual number of registered complaints. *Ergo*, the
mainstream media's onslaught against the Corbyn leadership had proved
remarkably effective.

The sustained media assault along with the orchestrated and illegal coup from the higher echelons of the Labour Party itself would set the stage for a General Election in 2017 which Corbyn lost by a whisker. In the event he was 2,227 votes away[55] from the chance of being Prime Minister. But there was one other event which stymied his chances. In the aftermath of the election it was revealed in a major investigation that the Labour Party elite had resorted to deliberate sabotage; that is, party funds were syphoned into the anti-Corbyn faction within the party as a means to 'undermine the party's objectives'. Other anti-Corbyn Labour officials refused to share information with the Leader's office, while still more were revealed as having come into the office 'to do nothing for a few months' in the run up to the critical election. The report concluded that 'an abnormal intensity of factional opposition to the party leader' had 'inhibited the proper functioning of the Labour Party bureaucracy' and contributed to 'a litany of mistakes'.[56]

The man that Corbyn lost to, however, was a very different social type. Alexander Boris de Pfeffel Johnson is a scion of the British ruling elite; his well-practised affectation of bumbling affability belying a résumé which screams of his ability to lie, cheat and manoeuvre in the pursuit of the type of power that – to people such as himself – seems nothing less than a birthright. Jeremy Corbyn, a plant-loving pacifist who liked to tend his own allotment and make his own jam, would appear on the podium often a little scruffy, dressed in the kind of donkey jacket which was once the provenance of the raffish radical of the 1960s anti-war movement. He lacked not only Johnson's affectations but also the latter's fundamental sense of dishonesty.[57] As a speaker Corbyn's delivery came from the heart; but such sincerity often occurred alongside a stumbling awkwardness. He didn't always get the lines right. In every way, Corbyn was the diametric opposite of his simpering and slick patrician rival. And, although the press had accused Corbyn of holding virtually every type of prejudice known to humankind, in actual fact you will never find a quote from one of Corbyn's interviews or an article he has written which evidences racism or sexism of any kind.

Not so, with Johnson however. Johnson is on the record as having described Black people as 'picaninnies' with 'watermelon smiles', gay people as 'bumboys', comparing Muslim women who wear burqas to bank robbers and saying they look like 'letter boxes', justifying anti-Islamic prejudice on the grounds of it being 'natural', and suggesting that Malaysian women only go to university in order 'to find men to marry'.[58] In addition, he described working-class men as 'drunk, criminal, aimless, feckless and hopeless'[59] while saying that the children of 'poor working mothers' are more likely to 'mug you on the street corner'.[60] As the editor of the flagship Conservative magazine *The Spectator*, Johnson ran a 2004 article which blamed working-class football fans who had been unlawfully killed because of overcrowding during the Hillsborough tragedy for their own deaths, citing them as 'mindlessly' violent and 'drunken'.[61] Such visceral prejudice, virulent sexism and an aloof disregard for the lives of ordinary people is far from remarkable and perhaps speaks to the fact that Johnson (like many MPs) passed through the upper-class 'public school' system and was weaned on its decadent ethos of empire, imperialism and elite individualism (something part and parcel of building so many of the patrician rulers of the political class in the UK today).

And yet, while there was no actual evidence of an iota of racism or sexism on Corbyn's part, and while Johnson's political career often seemed to form a single sustained projectile vomit of those things – nevertheless the attitude of the mainstream media to both remained entirely different. Corbyn tended to be lacerated for all the racist, sexist, anti-Semitic things he had never said, while 'Boris' as the press cheerfully dubbed him, was seen as more of a harmless buffoon, as someone whose quaint out-of-touch, 'non-politically correct' views made of him a bit of a character, an archetype of a fading brand of the 'Englishness' of yesteryear, much like cheery red telephone boxes or crumpets dolloped with hot melting butter. When 'Boris' made negative comments about Muslims, for example, which led to a 375 per cent[62] spike of incidents of abuse against that minority – many in the press were inclined to describe such incidents as 'gaffes' rather than a form of hate-speech, again feeding into an almost comical narrative where an accident-prone Prime Minister was good-naturedly stumbling across the political landscape before tripping in a slapstick fashion every once in a while.

And while Jeremy Corbyn was being excoriated relentlessly by the mainstream press for his supposed anti-Semitic sympathies, the fact that the Tory government, which Johnson stood at the helm of, had been cozying up to the far-right government of Viktor Orbán in Hungary – a government which had been concentrating its own power base through an inflammatory and demagogic anti-Semitic narrative – went little remarked upon. Perhaps even more surprisingly, while much of the press passed a fine-toothed comb through every paper Jeremy Corbyn's writing had appeared in – with the hope of finding an article written by someone else in an anti-Semitic tone to establish guilt by association – they rather remarkably overlooked a 2004 novel written by Boris Johnson replete with every type of racial slur but most incredibly of all, the novel was actually structured on the premise of a conspiracy whereby the Jews control the media and are able to 'fiddle'[63] elections at will.

In 2019 when Boris Johnson was being quizzed on the BBC's flagship political programme 'Question Time' in the run-up to the election that year, the presenter asked him if honesty was important to him. As Johnson began to sputter the inevitable lines about just how important the truth was, the audience at once burst into spontaneous laughter. But in the evening broadcast of the same programme, the BBC – a supposed bastion of political impartiality – edited out the laughter[64] in much the same way a prostituted state might censor any criticism of its tin-pot dictator.

When one considers the collective campaign of slander carried out by the press against Corbyn along with the illegal coup mounted by the right-wing of the party bureaucracy and the electoral sabotage it was able to enact in the run-up to the 2017 election – one is dealing with perhaps the single biggest subversion of democracy in British political history. Without these factors, it is virtually certain Corbyn would have been Prime Minister. And this is vitally important to any consideration of 'cancel culture'. According to the 'cancel culture' narrative – the political class and the organs of the media have been so thoroughly permeated by an intolerant and dictatorial set of 'radical left' sensibilities, that they work to destroy the reputations and careers of those they consider to be acting outside this ideological remit; that is, those who have right-leaning or even liberal views.

But the Corbyn phenomenon shows the reality of what happens when someone to the left of the political spectrum occupies a significant position in the political mainstream. If the 'cancel culture' narrative held water, then

Corbyn should have been fortified and elevated by the elite establishment and the forces of 'political correctness gone mad'. Boris Johnson, on the other hand, with his litany of 'anti-politically correct gaffes' (read racist, homophobic, sexist hate speech) should never even have made it into the Houses of Parliament, let alone to the highest office in the land. Yet despite the so-called pervasiveness of cancel culture – just like his counterpart in the US Donald Trump – Boris Johnson was raised to be the leader of the nation. Indeed the ugliness of his prejudice was even transformed by an often supine media into the mark of authenticity – someone who wasn't a member of the 'politically correct liberal elite' and was prepared to 'speak his mind'.

Far from cancelling Johnson, the real life centre-ground liberals in the Labour Party and the media demonstrated time and time again that they preferred him to the genuinely left-wing candidate Jeremy Corbyn. And behind all the hue and cry, this was for the simplest reason of all. Boris Johnson favoured the austerity politics which better preserved the economic interests of the upper classes, the section of society which the majority of those politicians had been drawn from. Jeremy Corbyn, on the other hand, challenged those same austerity politics. And that is why the person who was truly 'cancelled' – if one can use that phrase – was Jeremy Corbyn himself. Along with many of those associated with the left-wing political programme he was pursuing.

In fact, the only people on the right who were 'cancelled' were those rare individuals who opposed Jeremy Corbyn politically but nevertheless recognized that the campaign against him was making a travesty of democracy. Individuals like the conservative journalist Peter Oborne, someone who was for many years Chief Political Commentator in the right-wing rag *The Daily Telegraph*. Oborne wrote that while he didn't 'hold a candle for Corbyn' and that the Labour leader's politics were diametrically opposed to his own, he – Oborne – also recognized that Corbyn 'possessed personal decency and authenticity, which has scarcely been acknowledged amidst the thousands of hatchet jobs conducted against him in the press and wider media'. In conclusion, Oborne declared that 'Corbyn was never the monstrous figure presented to the British people ... Nor was he an anti-Semite, and there is no serious evidence which suggests that he was'.[65]

Indeed, Oborne went on to argue, not only were the British press complicit in the illegitimate monstering of the democratic opposition to the party in power, but he also wrote an exposé showing how the mainstream media were more and more acting as shills for the Johnson administration: 'It's chilling. From the Mail, The Times to the BBC and ITN, everyone is peddling Downing Street's lies and smears. They're turning their readers into dupes.'[66]

Oborne's claims were buttressed by the statistical analysis which showed conclusively that the mainstream press had been systematically biased against Jeremy Corbyn. One such study from the London School of Economics on journalistic representations of Corbyn revealed how 'Corbyn was thoroughly delegitimized as a political actor … 1) through lack of or distortion of voice; 2) through ridicule, scorn and personal attacks; and 3) through association, mainly with terrorism.'[67]

When Oborne himself tried to challenge this bias in the flagship papers he had hitherto written for, perhaps unsurprisingly he found they no longer had an appetite for his work. Such articles were consigned to the pages of alternative left-wing media, like the much smaller and more conscientious *Open Democracy* whose pages have, on occasion, hosted the words of the current writer too. But perhaps even dubiously, those mainstream papers that purport to provide a left-leaning narrative like *The Guardian* not only followed the narrative of monstering Corbyn in their editorial line, but likewise resisted the endeavour to tell the other side of the story. Indeed, one of the few up-and-coming working-class female journalists who had written for *The Guardian* for several years, Dawn Foster, was 'sacked'[68] after she penned a column drawing attention to the campaign of the centrists within the Labour Party to sabotage the Corbyn leadership. In the article Foster encouraged the then deputy Leader of the Labour Party Tom Watson to spend less time trying to undermine Corbyn and more time trying to support him. At which point, the 'gatekeepers' of the paper intervened in order to have the young working-class journalist removed and, in so doing, revealed *The Guardian's* 'institutional classism.'[69]

The logic of the cancel culture narrative

And this was always the crux of the issue. What the campaign against Corbyn reveals – is that true 'cancellation' is not a product of a phantasmagoria, a left-wing conspiracy where a mysterious cabal of 'politically-correct' mandarins are, with witch-hunting zeal, suddenly able to submit society to their far-left demands. Rather, the political character of the dominant mainstream media narrative tends to be shaped within the context and limits of certain structural interests; the billionaire press barons who are able to buy up so many of the papers, the editors and journalists who are predominantly from the upper classes and have come though the private school system or attended the most prestigious grammar schools, the politicians who are the ones to dominate the mechanics of law-making and have also emerged, in the main, from a higher social-economic stratum.

Now within these limits there surely exists a diversity of views, from the liberal who has some anti-racist sympathies and is tacitly supportive of the anti-racist programme of the Black Lives Matter movement (as long as it presses its claims moderately and through legal channels without inciting the 'mob') to the parochialism of the right-wing conservative who wishes to fortify the national borders against immigrant outsiders. But within such diversity, such differentiation – an unconscious and often unstated unity emerges; one which seeks to fortify the privileges, the connections and the world view of a section of the population whose wealth and power in some sense place them at odds with the interests of the great majority. And when there are political or journalistic voices[70] which genuinely threaten the equilibrium of that status quo, the right and the liberal centre are often brought into proximity with one another and act in consort to neutralize the threat; not as the result of some pre-ordained conspiracy, but because the realm of both politics and the media is dominated by the middle and upper classes of society and they feel instinctively the nature of their own best interests.

And this is precisely what happened with the Corbyn movement. The liberal section of the press and the liberal forces within the political establishment were regularly hostile towards Johnson and his right-wing Toryism, but once they were faced by an anti-austerity movement from below which challenged their economic power and control of the parliamentary machine – they came together with the right in an orchestrated and seamless campaign that sought to decapitate the Corbyn leadership. Their differences were put aside because the establishment as a whole intuited that the anti-austerity movement which

Corbyn had come to head – represented a set of social-economic interests rooted in the poor majority that vividly clashed with their own.

But the 'cancel culture' narrative – like all variants on the 'it's political correctness gone mad' thesis – once again reverses the poles; it abstracts from politics rooted in social interests and instead presents us with a chimera – the mysterious spectre of 'politically-correct' power which engulfs the political establishment in a tidal wave, cancelling out all opposition in and through the depredations and tyrannies of a witch hunt that flows from a form of left-wing totalitarianism. But it is a chimera precisely because there is no social basis for such totalitarian power in reality. Precisely because Black Lives Matter activists, Marxist revolutionaries, trans people, left-wing feminists, those at the bottom, the oppressed more generally – are clearly not the ones who populate the corridors of political power and nor are they the ones who tend to gain positions in the most prestigious media outlets.[71]

The idea of 'cancel culture' is a conspiracy theory that takes the form of a persecution complex, one which evinces the paranoia of a ruling elite, but it also provides an eminently political function; it casts the representatives of that elite as forlorn and persecuted freedom-fighters while the political sensibilities that reflect the interests of those at the bottom are depicted as inherently authoritarian and repressive. But most of all, 'cancel culture' provides a smokescreen; its fantasy evocation of a sinister left-wing totalitarianism helps mask the everyday ways in which the political power of an elite reproduces itself and the way it is able to prosaically and routinely marginalize and exclude those voices that are capable of genuine dissent.

6

The immigrants are eating the white working class!

Xenophobia and the professional politician

In 2010, the then Labour Party leader Gordon Brown and Prime Minister of the UK was on the campaign trail hoping to win a new term as leader of the nation. He had travelled to the Northern town of Rochdale with the hopes of winning voters over, but here he was accosted by an elderly woman named Gillian Duffy who heckled him during an interview he was giving to the press. In the first instance Brown ignored her, but on the advice of aides, he later tried to engage with her as he no doubt didn't wish to appear aloof. In the exchange they went on to have, Duffy described herself as a disillusioned Labour supporter who was concerned about immigration in particular. As Duffy became more and more animated, her indignation reached its crescendo:

> 'You can't say anything about the immigrants because you're saying that you're … but all these eastern Europeans what are coming in, where are they flocking from?'[1]

Brown was eventually able to extricate himself from the angry woman, but he made the rather unfortunate mistake of leaving the microphone, which was pinned to one lapel, still active. The brief conversation in the aftermath, once he felt he was alone with his aides, provided a valuable peek into what goes on behind the PR facade of amiability and engagement the professional politician tries to present.

'That was a disaster. Well I just … should never have put me in with that woman. Whose idea was that? … she was just a sort of bigoted woman. She said she used to be Labour. I mean it's just ridiculous.'[2]

The comments which Brown made in the aftermath, perhaps not unsurprisingly, filled the newspapers and were relayed over and over across the twenty-four-hour news cycle. The incident was dubbed 'Bigotgate'. Brown's PR department went into frantic overdrive, and the dour and rather impersonable Scotsman was then forced to go on a 'charm offensive'; with a painful rictus grin slapped over a halting and uncomfortable apology – Brown appeared on various interviews to try and undo some of the damage, and even met Duffy again in person for a cup of tea and slice of humble pie. All to no avail. Whether this incident caused Gordon Brown to lose the election would be difficult to say, but lose he ultimately did, and what had happened with Duffy had done him few favours on the eve of the election.

For the press and many of the voters, I think, saw it in a very particular ideological light. Brown's personal act of hypocrisy had revealed something about the political class in general: here we had an ostensibly 'liberal' member of the political elite patronizing an ordinary and hardworking member of the public, nodding away her concerns with a plastic grin, before making an exit as quick as possible.

But while there was some truth to this narrative, while Brown certainly was an elite-level career politician and Duffy was an 'ordinary' member of the public – the details of what Duffy had said were obscured in the media furore. Nobody acknowledged the dull thick-headedness of what had been said to Brown by Duffy in the first place: 'all these eastern Europeans what are coming in, where are they flocking from?' – well from Eastern Europe according to the premise of your mind-numbingly stupid question. More fundamentally, no one really acknowledged the racist tone in which the question had been couched: the description of foreigners as 'flocking' very much chimes with a racist rhetoric in which the individuality of the people in question is negated before the image of them as an animal-like 'flock', 'herd' or 'swarm'.

The fact is that Gillian Duffy was indeed a rather foolish and bigoted woman, but the media conflagration focused exclusively on Gordon Brown's reaction and failed to provide any critical account of Duffy's words. In the words of the writer Jason Okundaye, reflecting on the incident some ten years later, 'when Gordon Brown called Gillian Duffy a "bigoted woman" a cultural tipping point was reached where it became more offensive to accuse someone of bigotry or racism, than to actually be bigoted or racist'.[3] Okundaye picks up on something most significant here; the point at which the conversation with Duffy took place, marked something of a sea change in the British political panorama more generally.

Brown was prime minister at the tail end of a period of time whereby New Labour had dominated British politics – 1997–2010 – and in this period net annual immigration had gone up four-fold which saw 'the UK population … boosted by more than 2.2 million immigrants'.[4] In 2004, ten countries from poorer European regions joined the EU such as Poland, Estonia and Hungary and many people from these areas came to the UK to work. In 2007–8 the global economy was wracked by the financial crisis that emanated out from the United States and which caused several major British banks to go under. Brown was having his rather dejected conversation with Duffy on the eve of a new, leaner and more ruthless period in British politics; the ascension of a coalition government dominated by the Tories would inaugurate an austerity political programme designed to bail out the banks with hundreds of billions of pounds plundered from the social safety-net and those at the very bottom of the economic ladder.

Immigration had always been a political football, had always served as a useful tool for the ruling elite. But as the political class pulled off perhaps the most audacious confidence trick in British history under the rubric of austerity – transferring hundreds of billions from the poorest in order to bail out the bankers after the financial crash – the figure of the immigrant became a particularly useful alibi for the crime. The spectre of the unnamed and illusive foreigner could serve as a nifty scapegoat to absorb the type of suffering those at the bottom had been put through so as to bolster the wealth of those at the top. The intangible, interminable shrinking sense of the economy contracting, and your life possibilities being reduced day by day, could be neatly displaced onto the image of a shapeless foreigner, a furtive phantom, who was illicitly stealing away your national birth rights from behind-the-scenes.

The white working class

In such a vision, however, it was not sufficient to simply demonize the immigrant. Another chimera had to be called into being, and this came in the form of something described as 'the white working class'. 'The white working class' was a concept that had arisen in the context of deindustrialization, the defeat of the unions on a nationwide scale, and the ascendency of the neoliberal model in politics. It to some degree encompassed the notion of working-class defeat and destitution but framed it within that all important qualifier 'white'.

'White' was important here because it allowed a key critical shift to be carried out in ideology. The historical defeat of the English working class by a Thatcherite administration that was able to crush its strongest and most militant component (the miners) and implement a series of successive neoliberal reforms to stratify and tame labour along with a series of administrations which followed in Thatcher's wake and consolidated this process – all this could be reframed according to a different narrative; that is, the component of class struggle was one which could be replaced with that of race ('white').

It was no longer the case, therefore, that the working class was suppressed in and through economic exploitation by a ruling elite from above – rather, so the narrative went, the 'indigenous', 'white' working class had reached a point of destitution because it had been 'neglected', 'left behind', 'marginalized' in favour of immigrant labour in particular. The 'multiculturalism' of a liberal elite determined to facilitate the interests of immigrant labour could be counterposed to a 'traditional' 'white' working class whose economic rights and prerogatives were being usurped by a never-ending wave of foreign interlopers.

Class struggle, class conflict, between a financial elite that had increased its vast wealth at the expense of the immiseration of the working class faded into the background before a vision in which a 'white working class' is existentially threatened by the spectre of the foreigner – not only in economic terms but in cultural ones too. The 'white working class' – detached from class struggle in this fashion – ceased to be something with any radical or revolutionary potential, it ceased to be something from which socialist and internationalist struggle might take life; rather it became a purely parochial entity; a bastion of vanishing 'whiteness' in a sea of multi-culturalism.

For this reason, it was more and more described as insular, reactionary, racist, provincial, unthinkingly patriotic, volatile and often rabid. It liked its football, adored the monarchy, decorated its heartlands with Union Jacks, loved its booze and Brexit; it was territorial and combustible, distrustful, uneducated and inherently suspicious of outsiders. It was less 'the working class' and more 'the underclass'.

Such an evocation was supremely useful in the time following the global economic crisis of 2007–8. The economic onslaught which the rich went on to conduct against the poor required more than ever the type of deflection xenophobia might provide while at the same time the role of a right-wing elite could be reconfigured; from the ones who inflicted the most extreme deprivations at the economic level as part and parcel of a more rapacious capitalism to the ones who were determined to defend 'the white working class' as an entity whose life's blood and culture were being menaced by multiculturalism.

In the same instant, the transformation of the working class into an underclass denuded it of its revolutionary possibilities; it became something which could be conceived as being more deferential to notions of Britishness, to patriotism, to Queen and country – and simultaneously it became something reactionary, parasitic and racist. Throughout the period of austerity politics, TV was flooded with what was loosely dubbed 'poverty porn'; images of mainly white people on benefits – often with some substance abuse issues or alcoholism, sometimes belligerent, regularly anti-immigration and 'non-PC' – being wheeled out in front of the cameras to the gawking incredulity of their middle-class betters, the slick interviewers and media savvy producers who had built professional resumes on crafting such spiteful, nasty and sensationalist programmes.

In other words, there was a dual aspect to such an ideological vision. The more powerful in society could present themselves as allies of 'the white working class' in the same moment as they drew attention to the nature of its fecklessness and its unproductivity, its inability to regulate its family numbers, the single-mothers, the feral children, the dependency on benefits. Right-wing Tories and the party of Brexit, UKIP, could promote themselves as being aligned with the interests of the authentic British people – that is, 'the white working class' – over and against the foreigners; while in the same moment providing the image of an underclass that needed to be subjected to the type of labour discipline the austerity project required.

I do not say that any of this was adopted as a conscious political strategy, but rather it happened at a more unconscious and protean level which chimed with the broader political shift of austerity itself. The 'white working class' became a kind of repository for both discrimination and pity; the upper echelons of the society often genuinely regarded those below as an uneducated mob, broiling with resentment, race-hate, and bleeding the benefit system dry – while at the same time seeing them as a bastion of authentic Englishness that was being inexorably eroded by a left-leaning multiculturalism and liberal elite.

The moment at which Gordon Brown had his rather disastrous encounter with Gillian Duffy was also the point at which the concept of the 'white working class' was to become entrenched in the British cultural and political landscape; the media coverage was able to overlook and forgive the racist content of what Duffy had actually said because racism itself had been reconciled to the position of the 'white working class' as an inevitable response to its neglect and social exclusion.

Duffy became an emblem of 'the white working class', just as Brown became the embodiment of a liberal elite which held aloof contempt for the 'white working class' and was incapable of addressing its concerns over immigration because that same elite was fundamentally abstracted from the lives of ordinary British people. To double down on what Brown had said when he had accused Duffy of being a bigot, to point out the truth that she was in fact a racist – nobody in mainstream media seemed to have the gumption to do. For fear, clearly, of being associated with an out-of-touch elite, to be accused of that most heinous of crimes, of being 'politically correct'.

In the years following Brown's exchange with Duffy – up until the advent of Jeremy Corbyn's election as Labour Party leader in 2015 – the Labour Party would pander to racist and anti-immigrant sentiment precisely because (as a genuine liberal elite) they were convinced that the poor majority *did* tend to be racist and parochial, and to not show sympathy with these type of values was to turn your back on an authentic and salt-of-the-earth Britishness (and to haemorrhage votes in the process).

The working class, Brexit and the media

But how much of this has any substance? How true is it to say that members of the working class, white or otherwise, provide a key source from which racist and anti-immigrant feeling is mined? In 2019, *The Guardian* newspaper reported that nearly four out of every ten people in Britain believe that immigration provides a threat to Britain's future, and yet, the majority who expressed such views tended to be those with 'middle-incomes' – that is, have a household income of between £25,000 and £50,000 – rather than 'those who earn least'.[5] In other words, racist attitudes tended to be concentrated more amongst the lower-middle classes than the working classes, generally speaking.

Another study, carried out by the London School of Economics, reported that a depressingly high number of whites living in Britain do have a distrust and suspicion of immigrants, and yet, that number is highest in those areas where there is almost no actual immigration. In such wards 'that are almost entirely white, 90 per cent of White British people want immigration to be reduced'.[6] In those areas where minorities 'make up half or more of the population', however, that number at once reduces by more than 20 per cent.[7]

Or to say the same, 'local diversity does lead to more tolerant white attitudes' and this effect is most pronounced where immigrant labour is most concentrated: specifically in large industries where white British and immigrant labourers often work in close proximity. It is much more difficult to maintain that most inhumane of things – a racist attitude – when you are working side by side with people from other places, when you share your lunch breaks with them, when your children play with their children in the local schools – because the nature of their humanity and its equivalence to your own is constantly impressed upon you by the simple fact of experience.

This was revealed in another way too. While it would be fair to say that the Brexit referendum of 2016 wasn't driven entirely by concerns of immigration, nevertheless such concerns were a key part of the whole 'taking back our borders' rhetoric which surrounded the issue. And a good deal of this was charged with racism and xenophobia; indeed, racist nationalism was emboldened by the eventual decision to leave the EU, for there was an almost five-fold increase in the number of Islamophobic incidents in the week following the referendum.[8]

Here again, the same narrative of the 'white working class' was used to explain the decision to secede from the European Union: in this case it was the 'white working class' in the North that had been particularly neglected whereupon their ignorance, resentment, lack of education and parochialism led to a racist backlash which powered the Brexit vote. The class prejudice on the part of the liberal wing of the establishment was palpable; indeed one particular line of thought[9] went as far as to suggest that there was an 'association' between Brexit voters and 'obesity' – an argument which clearly fed into the svelte and clean living middle-class individual's notion of a parasitic underclass filled with track-suit wearing grotesques, living on council estates, allowing their bloated bodies to expand across the expanse of a fetid food-littered sofa, all the while watching trashy daytime TV and waiting for the gyro check to cash.

But again, the reality revealed by the statistics spoke of a very different social complexion. In actual fact, rather than the working poor of the North, the majority of people who voted 'leave' actually lived in the South of England. Perhaps more significantly, those in the poorest classes provided only less than a quarter of votes for the 'leave' position – instead most of those in favour of the decision to leave (59 per cent) were of the middle classes and lower-middle classes.[10] As the sociologist Lorenza Antonucci argues, the narrative that Brexit was driven by a populist backlash on the part of the poor and the working classes who had in some way been 'left behind' by a liberal establishment was by and large a misnomer: in actual fact 'rather than representing the "left out", Brexit was the voice of this intermediate class who are in a declining financial position. This category of voters represent a group of high sociological relevance also labelled as "the squeezed middle".[11]

That is not to say that a good few working-class people didn't vote to leave. It is not to say either that the working classes are immune from racist and anti-immigration sentiments. But as Steve Fenton argues, the type of 'resentful nationalism' which infuses racism against immigrants tends to inflict workers who are experiencing 'declining' class situations, workers and their families who have lived through deindustrialization and in their later careers or retirement 'can only look back in disenchantment at the fall in prestige of the industry, profession or business to which they gave most of their working lives. Those who are the direct victims of a downward class trajectory – the redundant coal miner, the unemployed steelworker, the shipbuilding craftsman, subsequently forced to work in an unskilled service job.'[12]

Against all the evidence, however, the concept of the 'white working class' as a repository for racism and retrograde and reactionary sentiment became a bastion of the mainstream media narrative, particularly from 2010 onward, and this was only intensified in the aftermath of the Brexit result. Newspapers continually lamented the situation of the 'white working class' – a particularly predominant theme was that of their children, and again the same dualism, the same double standard was applied. On the one hand, working-class teenagers could be demonized as sexually promiscuous, as 'breeding' with abandon, as volatile and violent, in a slew of stories which were reeled off on prime time television and in the biggest newspapers, like the story of 'tearaway teenage mother'[13] Jamelia Humphreys whom, at the age of sixteen, appeared in a Chanel Four documentary called 'Skint' and would also feature in the pages of *The Daily Mail*. At the same time, that same mainstream media would profess a desperate concern for those 'white working class' teenagers living in deprived areas. Papers like *The Express* could in one moment carry a story with a lead that read 'Teenage mum to bring up triplets on the state',[14] and in the next reel out a headline of mournful melancholy – 'What about the white working class?';[15] a headline which overlaid an article lamenting how 'white working class' children and teenagers were being edged out of education through lack of funding and neglect. And why were they not receiving their due? Because (according to the same piece) an '£800 million pot of cash' which should have gone 'to help working class white children in deprived areas' was instead handed to universities in order to facilitate '"wider inclusion" for ethnic minorities'.[16]

The schizophrenic attitude of the media to the mirage it itself had called into being was reproduced in the political class. After Brown's encounter with Duffy in 2010 and Labour's subsequent loss in the general election, the new leader, Ed Miliband at once began to pander to the anti-immigrant line. Whereas Brown had challenged it by calling out bigotry for what it was in the Duffy exchange, Miliband would soften and downplay it, desperately trying to assure those who 'worry about the real impact immigration has, this Labour Party will always respond to those concerns, not dismiss them'.[17] As *The Times* political editor Roland Watson observed at the time, Miliband was drawing up 'policies designed to appeal to the white working class'.[18]

Miliband himself was the son of Jewish immigrants who had fled Nazi persecution; possessed of a rather innocuous personality, he seemed gentle, awkward and bumbling. One felt that he was vaguely unsettled by the tenor of his own anti-immigrant rhetoric, that his heart wasn't really in it. But he was being pulled along in the wake of a political logic driven by the chimeric creation of 'the white working class', as the Labour Party became more and more desperate to assure this phantom entity of its own anti-immigrant credentials even releasing a mug which sported the slogan 'Controls on Immigrants. I'm Voting Labour' – the type of vulgar piece of tat that only a deranged crank would shell out for. Last but not least, Miliband had the promise to be tough on immigration carved into a tombstone-like monument (the 'Ed stone') which laid out the party's pledges. In the event, the tombstone-style design proved to be prophetic, as it heralded the death of his tenure as Labour leader.

Austerity and the rhetoric of the white working class

But while Labour policy was geared towards the fabled 'white working class', it did not shy away from promoting ideologies and policies that were destructive to the poorest in society, to the actual working classes. Under Miliband, the Labour Party also fed into narratives of a feckless underclass that would 'linger on benefits', and promised to be 'tougher than Tories on benefits'.[19] As a consequence, in 2013, the Miliband opposition signed up to the austerity economic measures the coalition government had introduced and which favoured the wealthy; those at the top who had facilitated the economic crash were, it seemed, entitled to unlimited benefits from the state without ever being stigmatized as 'spongers' or 'parasites'.

The Tories – the party which introduced austerity and is in power at the time of writing – continue to exhibit the same vision of political dualism. In 2020, the then Equalities Minister Liz Truss raved about how 'the white working class' had been 'written off',[20] abandoned to its poverty and disadvantage, and yet this speech came at the end of a year in which her administration had voted down plans to provide the most economically disadvantaged working-class children free school meals during a summer of global pandemic and a massive decrease in living standards. The Conservatives would eventually reverse their decision on free school meals, it is true, but only because the working-class footballer Marcus Rashford mounted a campaign which garnered such public sympathy and attention the Tories were shamed into making a U-turn.

We see once again, on the part of both parties, how a fantasy conjuring of a 'white working class' – an underclass – allows for a heightened exploitation of the actual working classes in reality. Again, by racializing a sector of the working class as 'white', one can then draw attention to the minorities that threaten that sector's livelihood and culture, thus diverting one's gaze from those at the top. So Liz Truss goes on to describe how 'diversity agendas' are part and parcel of the process by which 'the white working class' is 'written off'.[21] And why are such 'diversity agendas' being implemented? Because of the 'woke brigade', because of the 'woke bandwagon'.

For the uninitiated the term 'woke', when deployed by the right, is a synonym for 'political correctness'. Once again, the radical left and the 'liberal elite' are seen to enter into an unholy union – so concerned are they with the rights of minorities, immigrants – so worried are they by 'unconscious bias' – that they neglect the fundamentals whereby decent Brits 'can live happily in a secure home, work in a good job and send their children to a decent school'.[22] That is why the 'white working class' has been 'written off' – for the liberal elite and the radical left are more concerned with 'politically correct' gesture politics, because they are 'angrier about the "sins" of historical figures rather than trying to make a better life for those who live today'.[23]

It is all rather crude, atavistic stuff. Especially when one considers that a 'liberal elite' completely driven by the 'politically correct', 'woke' agenda of the radical left is yet another fantasy breathed into nebulous life by the right-wing mindset. In fact, those who occupy the centre or centre-left ground of politics in parliament – those who have some policy-making power and might therefore be described both as 'liberal' and 'elite' – more often than not kowtow to the description of the 'white working class' that has become such an accepted staple of the establishment's political vision; a 'white working class' which is inherently racist and nationalistic, and which those of a liberal persuasion feel they have to propitiate by exemplifying patriotism and anti-immigration sentiment, even if they do so somewhat half-heartedly as was the case with Miliband.

For the liberal centre-left, represented by the Labour Party, a new political strategy came to predominate; the votes of the (white) working class would be won – not by increased public spending in response to the crippling austerity the Tories had inflicted – but by pandering to racist sentiment and anti-immigrant feeling in order to shore up 'traditional values' and the community of yore. This became known as 'Blue Labour', but it was a vision to which the Liberal Democrats (the third main political party) also subscribed.

This was, of course, interrupted by the left-wing, anti-austerity programme that came with the election of Jeremy Corbyn to Labour Party leader. But rather than imposing a 'woke', 'politically correct' control over the mechanisms of political power with the collusion of a 'liberal elite', what in fact happened was that the Labour centrists and Conservative right-wingers united in tandem with the mainstream media to systematically torpedo the Corbyn movement, destroying its electoral prospects through a sustained combination of slander and sabotage.

Perhaps even more crucially, the spectacle of Liz Truss ruefully lamenting the way in which the 'white working class' has been left behind manages to paper over, with melancholy nostalgia, the simple fact that it is not the radical left or the 'liberal elite' which has wielded real power in Britain for the last decade. It is the Tory Party – that is, the party that Liz Truss is a leading member of. Her references to 'the woke brigade' and 'political correctness gone mad' once more provide the fantasy outline of a phantom political power while those with a real grip on the political machine get on with the more prosaic job of slashing social spending and squeezing the means of the vast majority in and through the decade long austerity project.

But perhaps the most tragic thing about the ideological vision in which 'a woke brigade' neglects the salt-of-the-earth 'white working class' in favour of immigrants who are eating up the benefits 'indigenous' Britains should receive – is that it helps promote a racist vision of immigration in which foreigners are presented as parasitical and a drain on the economy, when in actual fact, the very opposite is true. If one were, for instance, to go back to 2004 when ten poorer countries joined the EU including Poland, Estonia and Hungary – one can see that the immigrants from these places who came to the UK in the ten years which followed, contributed significantly more to the British economy than the amount they would take out in benefits. According to *The Economist*, £5 billion[24] more in fact. Of course, such a statistic was rarely quoted, either by the majority in the mass media or the political class. Again this was not necessarily part and parcel of a conspiracy of silence.

It was more to do with the fact that the concept of the 'white working class' held a real sway, for it fed into elite prejudices about what the working class actually was, a concentration of under-privilege, seething resentment and ignorance topped off with racist and parochial sensibilities. Senior politicians, of both a Labour and Conservative stripe, often bought into this vision and as a consequence, they bought into the need to propitiate the 'mob'. For that was what the 'white working class' had become – the fear of the mob inculcated and given a modern-day expression.

In the same moment, the evocation of a fantasy 'liberal elite' that had neglected the 'white working class' chimed perfectly with the ideological need of a real elite to divert the population's gaze from the rapacious economic exploitation it was carrying out under the rubric of austerity. And finally, the notion of 'political correctness' or 'wokeness' was needed so as to provide the key motive; the reason why a liberal elite would be so keen to cater to foreigners while neglecting domestics.

Trump, xenophobia and the US 'white working class'

In the United States, a similar political schema has been pulled into focus, particularly during the presidency of Donald Trump. From the outset, Trump appealed to 'nativist' fears which had long since wracked sections of the population; in the nineteenth century, the threat of being swamped by an influx of Chinese labourers was particularly potent in the imagination of many white Americans; in the twentieth century a similar fear was conditioned by the mass immigration that flowed upward from Latin America – the US Empire's so-called 'back yard'. Trump was able to ratchet these fears up to their zenith, even using a rhetoric which bordered on fascist dehumanization of the people who were coming to the country, describing immigrants as an 'infestation'.[25]

And Trump would buttress this kind of inflammatory and sinister language with a more general set of claims about the deleterious effects mass immigration was continuing to have on the United States. He infamously described Mexican immigrants as 'rapists'[26] in the speech which was to launch his presidency. In addition, Trump would promote a series of scare 'statistics'; in 2018, he made the claim that '63,000 Americans were killed by illegal immigrants since 9/11',[27] a claim which was later debunked as hokum. As well, Trump has endeavoured to connect the phenomenon of gangs and gang-warfare in the United States to immigration, as when he 'continuously framed the infamous MS13 Mara Salvatrucha gang as a major "foreign" threat to the safety of Americans' whereas in actual fact 'MS13 originated in Los Angeles … [and] … was a consequence of the U.S. government's "dirty war" in El Salvador during the 1980s and spread to Central America via deportations'.[28]

But it is not only specific information that Trump cites which is often distorted or simply factually wrong. It is also the general picture of immigration he offers up. In actual fact, as the sociologists Laura Finley and Luigi Esposito point out in a comprehensive study, there is evidence to suggest that immigrants commit far less crime than the native-born population in the United States. In reality, 'while the immigrant population increased by 116 per cent from 1980 to 2016, the rate of violent crime fell by 36 per cent during the same period'.[29]

In addition, another major study carried out by the Harvard Sociologist Robert Sampson examined Mexican first-generation immigrants and found that they 'were 45 per cent less likely to commit violence than third-generation Americans, adjusting for individual, family, and neighborhood background. Second-generation immigrants were 22 per cent less likely to commit violence than the third generation.'[30] Sampson's study showed – contrary to Trump's belligerent rhetoric – that in the period from 1995 to 2003 statistics demonstrated that '[i]mmigration thus appeared "protective" against violence' rather than generating it.

But to the phantom spectre of the sinister foreigner, Trump counterposed the figure of the blue-collar worker; patriotic, religious, family-orientated and aspirational – rooted in the work ethic of Protestant individualism, and yet someone about whom there was the whiff of tragedy, for their community, culture, job security and even the physical safety of their families had come under threat from the tsunami of immigration that had been unleashed. As another Harvard Professor of Sociology, Michele Lamont, would note, Trump was cultivating an image of 'the masculinity of white male workers and their role as providers and protectors, one of the lynchpins of their self-worth' before opposing that to the depiction of 'immigrants, Muslims, and refugees as direct threats to the safety and well-being of women and children'.[31]

The question of labour became key to the way Trump portrayed a disenfranchised and neglected 'white working class'. As part of his campaign manifesto for the 2016 election, Trump emphasized how an 'influx of foreign workers holds down salaries, keeps unemployment high and makes it difficult for poor and working Americans … to earn a middle-class wage'.[32] From 2016 to 2018 Trump emphasized over fifteen times in his political speechifying 'how poor trade deals and weak immigration policies have lowered wages for Americans.'[33]

But once again, the reality undermines the ideological vision Trump is endeavouring to raise. Maria E. Enchautegui has shown, for example, that in the United States, the predominant tendency is for immigrant labour to be focused by and large on sectors in the workforce which US-born workers don't generally occupy. So, for instance, the top three occupations of unskilled immigrant workers are 'maids and house cleaners, cooks, and miscellaneous agricultural workers' whereas for US-born unskilled workers the top three jobs are 'cashiers, truck drivers, and janitors and building cleaners.'[34]

In the same vein, those immigrant workers who have a high-school diploma but never passed into higher education tend to be over represented as 'miscellaneous personal appearance workers, such as manicurists (87 per cent immigrant); workers who grade, sort, and classify unprocessed food and other agricultural products (82 per cent); and sewing-machine operators (81 per cent)'. Their US-born counterparts, on the other hand, are most over-represented as 'counter attendants in cafeterias, food concession stands, and coffee shops (86 per cent native workers); hosts and hostesses at restaurants, lounges, and coffee shops (85 per cent); and receptionists and information clerks (81 per cent)'.[35] In other words, rather than competing with one another, the research seems to suggest that – in most cases and in most sectors – the work of immigrants and the work of native workers 'could be complementing each other.'[36]

In reality, the biggest drain on available jobs in the United States comes not from immigrants stealing them away but rather from outsourcing. Stuart Anderson, writing in *Forbes Magazine*, argued that by 2017 nearly 'every major company in America, and many mid-sized companies, already has increased its presence outside the United States.'[37] Angie Mohr writing for Investopia suggests that the amount of jobs moved abroad by the time of 2015 could be estimated to be as high as 3.3 million.[38] A more recent study by the Economic Policy Institute suggests that more than 5 million jobs and 91,000 plants have been outsourced in the United States since 1998.[39] Despite the fact that Trump went on the record to attack such practises as part of the globalism and neoliberalism of the fabled 'liberal elite', nevertheless over '1,800 factories have disappeared during the Trump administration between 2016 and 2018'[40] as a result of outsourcing.

The electricity needed to charge Trump's vision of a fantasy dystopia where immigrants in their hordes are swamping an indigenous 'white working class' was provided by the notion of 'political correctness' itself. When Trump ran for president he put 'political correctness' at the very heart of his campaign. He emphasized that he was to be the 'anti-political correctness president'.[41] Once he was in power, he repeatedly revisited this same theme, describing 'political correctness' as 'a cancer eating away at the body politic' or saying 'political correctness is just absolutely killing us as a country. You can't say anything.'[42]

The notion of not being able to say anything 'for fear of being labelled intolerant or un-enlightened'[43] by a totalitarian culture of 'political correctness gone mad' was incredibly useful for someone like Trump, for every time one of his falsehoods on immigration was challenged, every time his bigotry was placed in the spotlight, every time his corrupt business practises or strategies of tax evasion were alluded to – he could at once take the sting out of the criticisms by suggesting that they were motivated by a 'politically correct' need to silence someone like himself who had the courage to speak out. In this way, rational criticism could be countermanded by an emotive and fiery indignation which suggested how, to even question Trump's credentials, was part and parcel of a broader conspiracy to silence the dissenting voice. For someone like Trump, the need to shift the debate from the terrain of reason to that of a fear-mongering polemic was an absolute that came not only from his own clearly writ intellectual inadequacy, but also because any sober assessment of the facts of his life – his privilege, his great wealth, his utter entitlement – vividly revealed him to be a member of the elite he was so keen to deride.

More important still, however, was the way in which 'political correctness' powered the broader political narrative Trump was promoting. The 'native' (read white) working class could be portrayed as under threat from immigration – and though the claim was both racist and untrue, it could be presented as being put forward by someone who had the gumption to tell it 'how it is' in order to stand up for the 'little man' against a liberal elite whose 'political correctness' had blinded it to the realities on the ground. 'Political correctness' allowed for that sinister alchemy which transforms racism and xenophobia into speaking truth to power – while the demand for equality, the need for social justice and human rights became the means by which a so-called 'politically correct establishment' is able to ride roughshod over the lives and conditions of the 'native' poor and their dwindling communities.

The political realities behind the scenes

But who was this elite that was so concerned with the rights of Muslims and immigrants they were prepared to sacrifice the lives of 'good Americans' on the altar of globalism and cosmopolitanism? In his time as president, Trump would often reference the Democrats, in particular the previous administration headed by Barack Obama with Hillary Clinton as Secretary of State. Trump would connect the Democratic administration with a 'global neoliberalism' which saw industry decimated and the floodgates opened to a tidal wave of immigration. In 2016, during his presidential campaign, he argued that Hillary Clinton, as part and parcel of a 'globalist' network, had made a 'radical call for open borders, meaning anyone in the world can enter the United States without any limit at all'.[44] This was yet another claim which was swiftly and easily debunked by reference to what Clinton had actually said; she had indeed used the phrase 'open borders' but only in the context of the free trade of products rather than the movement of peoples.

But Trump's assault on the facts is even rawer when one considers the actual record the previous administration did have on immigration: in fact, the Obama administration (of which Clinton was one of the leading lights) had deported over three million people from the country during its two terms.[45] Not only does that number exceed the number of deportations carried out by every president previous to Obama *combined* – but in a twist of bitter irony, a comparison of the first term of each, reveals that the Obama administration actually deported more people than Trump's.[46] In fact, it was noted that the 'Obama administration deported 409,849 people in 2012 alone, while the Trump administration has yet to deport more than 260,000 people in a year.'[47] All of which was enough to get Obama satirized as 'The Deporter in Chief'.

The notion, therefore, of a 'politically correct' Democrat administration which is consistently offering succour to foreigners at the expense of 'native' workers is a fiction of the most fantastical sort, and yet, somehow, such a fiction has sustained. And this, in part, was because the myth of 'political correctness gone mad' had become so entrenched; a 2015 poll by Fairleigh Dickinson University found that 68 per cent of Americans believe 'political correctness' is a 'big problem'[48] while a poll taken in the following year by Quinnipiac University during the Clinton-Trump election contest 'found that 51 per cent of respondents believed political correctness is a bigger problem than prejudice'.[49]

Trump's political strategy sought to align a 'liberal elite' with a 'globalist policy' which facilitated open door immigration while at the same time emphasizing the neoliberal tenor of that elite's economic policy. In the case of the Democrats and figures like Clinton and Obama – on the neoliberal nature of their politicking – Trump certainly had a point; the Democratic administration had shored up the big banks, supporting the 'Emergency Economic Stabilization Act of 2008'[50] which was passed by the Republican administration of George W. Bush and which provided a $700 billion bailout to the financial sector from the taxpayer. In addition, Obama had promised to change NAFTA – the notorious neoliberal free trade agreement that had been negotiated in the early 1990s – and yet, in the event, reneged on his pledge.[51] Clinton too supported NAFTA (though flip-flopped somewhat on her position when campaigning as a presidential candidate).[52]

For these reasons, Trump could consistently portray Clinton, Obama and the previous administration as those who sought a 'globalist' economic agenda that intensified free trade by removing the protections offered by local tariffs to indigenous industries. And this chimed well with the notion of Trump as an authentic patriot looking to shore up the rust-belt, blue-collar heartlands against the anonymous and inhuman forces of globalization. Someone who would say 'politically incorrect' things in defence of the white Protestant hard-working American who was now an endangered species, whose culture and livelihood was increasingly diminished before the prosaic forces of the global cash nexus and the anonymous legions of foreigners forever flooding the borders.

However, the anti-capitalist romanticism of Trump's political rhetoric once more masks the social realities. On the issue of NAFA, Trump did indeed abolish it, but he replaced it with new legislation in the form of USMCA – a trade agreement which was, in essence, virtually identical to the neoliberal tone of the previous one, but involved a few minor cosmetic changes.[53] More generally, however, 'while Trump … [has used] … the language of patriotism and nationalism to convey the idea that he is a protector of American workers, he has also followed tactics straight out of the neoliberal playbook by cutting taxes and public expenditures, all of which disproportionately benefit the upper classes.'[54]

Or to say the same, the idea of a 'white working class' in the American context operated in a remarkably similar way to that of the British; that is, it allowed establishment power to continue exploiting the actual working class in the United States in a ruthless and efficient fashion while at the same time displacing class antagonism onto a fantasy setting in which 'a white working class' finds its antithesis in the phantom foreigner and the malign spectre of the 'other'.

But the 'white working class' template also provided a useful tool for disgruntled liberals who had been repelled by the Trump phenomenon, its open racism and its aggressive, vulgar patriotism. When the reins of state were removed from the sleek, manicured hands of professional and smooth-talking liberals such as Barack Obama and Hillary Clinton and delivered to the crass-speaking and gaudy demagogue Trump, many career politicians of a Democrat stripe experienced a sickening sense of disorientation as the etiquette of the political order as they understood it was upended. In trying to rally themselves, trying to comprehend just how this type of cretin could have possibly usurped such a sacred and hallowed position, 'the white working class' provided a very attractive and convenient explanation.

Why did Trump win?

Trump had won because – so the liberal narrative went – his racism and neo-fascist rhetoric had appealed to the forces of the angry, seething, ignorant and poverty-stricken mob; specifically 'The Father-Führer' (Donald Trump) had managed to rally a 'white working class … in thrall to a vicious, selfish culture whose main products are misery and used heroin needles'.[55] A 'white working class' which was as well a drug-addicted and morally bereft 'underclass' made 'to feel good' by Donald Trump's speeches in the same way they are made to feel good by 'OxyContin'.[56]

The liberal narrative could then run as follows: an epoch of rational free speech and liberal individualism personified by figures such as Clinton and Obama was eclipsed by a darker period inaugurated by a proto-fascist demagogue who appealed to the most base and irrational emotions on the human spectrum: racism, xenophobia and unadulterated nationalism. Specifically, a 'white working class' – which had in some way been left behind by deindustrialization, which had not been sufficiently educated – could be mobilized by Trump, spilling over in a wave of patriotic rancour that was swiftly translated into a far-right electoral win as the centre ground collapsed.

And yet, such a romantic, tragic narrative of the failure of the forces of reason to offset the broiling fascism of the mob and the sinister demagogue who conjures it up – helped disguise a very different type of story. For, in actual fact, when one examines the number of votes the Republican Trump received in 2016 one comes to understand that they were only marginally more than those received by the Republican John McCain in his 2008 campaign. In 2008, McCain had won 45.7 per cent[57] of the popular vote in comparison to Trump winning 46.1 per cent in 2016.[58] The real difference came from the other side; in 2008 the Democrat candidate Barack Obama took 52.9 per cent[59] of the popular vote while in 2016 his equivalent, Hillary Clinton, only managed to secure 48.2 per cent.[60] In other words, it was not the case that Trump was boosted into power on the back of a campaign which caused 'the white working class' to vote in its hordes; rather Trump won because millions of people didn't elect to vote in the first place; specifically, they didn't turn out for the Democrats, who, in 2016, experienced a massive drop in votes as compared with 2008.

And there is a highly credible explanation for such a decline. In 2008, Obama had swept into office on the radical promise of change. He was going to overturn the neoliberal free trade agreement of NAFTA. But in the event, that didn't transpire. He was going to challenge the hegemony of the bankers. Instead he gave them his full political support and fortified the bailout package. He was going close down that infamous hothouse of coercion and torture, Guantanamo Bay, but once more he reneged on his promise. He was going to pull the troops out of Iraq, but not only was this not achieved, but in fact Obama – during his two presidential terms – would ramp up the imperial tempo of bombing and the decimation of lives in lands faraway. The years of military strikes in one country after the next: Afghanistan, Iraq, Syria, Libya, Yemen, Somalia and Pakistan. In fact, Barack Obama launched ten times more air strikes in comparison with the George W. Bush presidency which came before.[61]

To say the same: Clinton did not lose to Trump in 2016 because millions more people were mobilized by his neo-fascist message – rather she lost because the previous eight years of Democrat administration revealed so starkly liberal complicity in military mass murder and the shoring up of a financial system that had devastated the lives of millions. As a consequence, the votes of the Democrats fell off like wheels from a rickety wagon. But the narrative of 'the white working class' undoes all of this; it absolves the Democrats of their complicity with the status quo, reinventing them as the last bastions of humanitarianism mounting a lonely and noble vigil before the encroaching darkness of fascist barbarism.

And so the threat to society from a rapacious financial system and an unregulated market is replaced with the much more palpable and dramatic threat of the ignorant mob, flaming torches in tow, primed to burn down the edifice of civilization itself. The 'white working class' once again becomes a placeholder for patrician contempt and prejudice towards the majority of the population, and for the professional politician and Democratic Party functionary, the notion that the uneducated masses can be blamed for the rise of a grotesque like Trump is a more alluring prospect than the prosaic examination of your own political resume and its record of fidelity and service to the political and financial powers-that-be.

But was there any sense in which Trump's votes in 2016 were drawn from predominantly working-class groups? Again the statistical analysis reveals a different image from the one which has been purveyed by much of the mainstream media. A 2016 NBC survey showed that 'only a third of Trump supporters had household incomes at or below the national median of about $50,000. Another third made $50,000 to $100,000, and another third made $100,000 or more, and that was true even when we limited the analysis to only non-Hispanic whites.'[62] If one assumes that working-class jobs tend to fall at the lower end of the economic spectrum, then one has to conclude that the vast majority of Trump supporters in the run-up to the 2016 election were simply not of the working class. In the same vein, the biggest survey to take the measure of the 2016 election carried out by the American National Election Study revealed that, among 'people who said they voted for Trump in the general election, 35 per cent had household incomes under $50,000 per year.'[63]

The issue, it seems, is that the definition of 'working class' some of the pollsters utilize is sometimes vague and imprecise – often, for example, education is made into the defining criterion and the working class is described as those 'people who don't have college degrees.'[64] This allows for the definition to encompass not simply those who are workers and are employed by a company on the basis of a wage-labour contract – but also many who might be self-employed, who might have small businesses such as garages, small shops or those who own taxis or market stalls.

In early 2020, after Trump refused to accept the results of his election loss to the Democrat candidate Joe Biden, a rabble of Trump supporters was roused to such heights of stormy indignation, they were able to amass in Washington and storm the citadel of political power, Capitol Hill. The chaotic scenes which ensued reverberated around the world and were portrayed by many in the TV and print media as once again exemplifying Trump's deadly appeal to the disgruntled 'white working class' – the modern-day-mob. And yet, as soon as the demographic of the rioters was analysed in any detail, a different picture began to emerge.

In fact, those who partook in the riot were predominantly 'business owners, CEOs, state legislators, police officers, active and retired service members, real-estate brokers, stay-at-home dads' along with those politicos who were active members of white supremacist organizations such as 'the Proud Boys'.[65] As in the case of the Brexit movement in the UK, the racism and extreme nationalism were powered not by a 'white working class' but by a 'middling layer' of mainly lower-middle-class people in alignment with a section of the elite and its representative (Johnson/Trump) who had chosen to promote a more 'isolationist' and 'nativist' agenda as the fulcrum to launch their own political power.

As Adam Serwer points out, the riot on Capitol Hill, which Trump helped incite, was not born from the economic desperation of impoverished people but rather from the type of entitlement – syphoned through a paradigm of race-hate – which comes from 'respectable people' who believe 'they had been unjustly stripped of their inviolable right to rule'.[66] And as Serwer astutely recognizes, the notion that this rioting was yet another product of the febrile mob mentality of 'the white working class' plays into 'the belief that only impoverished people engage in political violence – particularly right-wing political violence', a belief which is itself 'a misconception often cultivated by the very elites who benefit from that violence'.[67]

The neoliberal model

In the last forty years, we have seen the ascension of the neoliberal economic model precisely at the expense of industries, working-class power and organization, and public ownership. The influence of financial capital has grown exponentially, facilitating the global economic crash, but since that time – despite the bailouts, despite the devastation wreaked on the lives of billions – the financial elite have grown more audacious, more ruthless still. A study by the Institute for Public Policy Research think tank found that the austerity measures which the Tory government had introduced in the UK meant that from 2012 onward, 130,000 people lost their lives. Most damning of all that same study concluded that those 130,000 deaths were actually 'preventable'[68] – that is to say, if the austerity measures hadn't depleted the public health sector then those people would in all likelihood still be alive.

At this point it is worth posing the following question: What would have happened if – instead of targeting the poorest in society and slashing healthcare and social security, the Tory government had focused on the rich, by increasing corporation tax, bringing it in line with the European average and covering the greater portion of the debt that way? The real question then becomes – how many CEOs of super corporations or heads of finance would have fallen by the wayside if they had endured a rise in tax on their billions of, say, even a meagre 6 per cent? How many of their numbers would have committed suicide in abject desperation at earning only 94 million instead of 100 million? How many of them would have wasted away? How many of them would have suffered from severe ill health? How many would have died from disease as a result? I would hazard a guess that such a number would probably be around the zero mark.

And that's the true issue here. The government, the apparatus of state, which introduced austerity measures, knew in advance that these would lead to deaths across the board. But they were the deaths of predominantly poor people, and therefore, lives which could be written off in the first place. And yet, to accomplish such a cold and calculated experiment in human suffering, a complex ideological rationale was required.

And here we see how a key triangulation became ever more *de rigueur*: the working class which was the primary victim of austerity economics was increasingly described as a 'white working class', a parasitical entity that required the labour 'discipline' it was being subject to. Simultaneously the economic picture of society was radically reconfigured; by assigning the prefix 'white' – by racializing the working class in this way – the issue of its exploitation could be transformed from the austerity measures the elite were inflicting on it, to the jobs and resources which were supposedly being eaten up by foreigners like a wheat field by locusts.

At which point the triangulation was brought to fruition: to the image of the traditional white worker and foreign interloper was added a 'liberal elite' and its overwhelming sense of 'political correctness', a 'political correctness' that provided the motive power whereby the white worker could be sacrificed to the immigrant, the national spirit to the faceless forces of internationalism, local communities to be subsumed under 'globalism'. By raising the spectre of a 'liberal elite' suffused with 'political correctness', determined to neglect and malign the 'white working class' – the real elites could get on with the rather more banal and everyday business of decimating the actual working classes in and through their austerity programmes.

And for those who argued that the devastation and deaths bequeathed to the population were the responsibility of that same elite, that the NHS was actually enriched by foreign labour rather than being depleted by it; for those who critiqued the climate of racism and xenophobia which the Tories had so systematically cultivated, and for those who endeavoured to show solidarity with its victims – well that was the easiest thing of all. They could be dismissed as 'liberal luvvies' or 'lefty-loons'. And as for their criticism of the murderous nature of establishment power? It simply didn't count. It was, after all, nothing more than 'political correctness gone mad'.

Conclusion

Historical background

In the nineteenth century the existence of the working classes in much of Western Europe was a hard one. The working days of those in the newly developed industrial hubs were long and gruelling, with meagre financial compensation provided for the backbreaking labour required. Slums grew up around the industrial centres, and the steam, smog and poverty of the swelling cities could be unbearable, as writers like Dickens so indelibly and tragically recorded.

And yet, as the century rolled on, some things began to change for the better. The impetus to technology and science provided by the Industrial Revolution meant that it was possible to identify diseases at the bacterial level and this, alongside the creation of more modern sewage systems, put an end to the cholera epidemics that had plagued the cities in the middle part of the century. The ability to mass-produce food on an industrial scale also meant that a more varied diet was accessible to large numbers of the general population.

Perhaps more importantly still, the nineteenth century saw the first great movements of an industrial working class that was organizing independently and developing its own political programmes: the Chartist movement which sprang up in England towards the end of the 1830s, the first Trade Union Congress which was declared in 1868 in Manchester – while in Germany, in 1848, Marx and Engels published their famous *The Manifesto of the Communist Party*, a proclamation of workers' power at a time where revolution was erupting across Europe more broadly. All of this helped to ensure that workers were living longer, for in many cases they were able to successfully push for the limiting or abolition of child labour, the shortening of the working day, the introduction of health insurance, the earliest pension systems and increased representation in the political sphere in and through parliamentary reform leading to the eventual achievement of universal suffrage.

These great working-class movements – their visibility and their militancy – must have felt to the elites of the day much the way something like the Black Lives Matter movement feels to those in our own times. The sense that people from below are more and more asserting their own rights and power in a bid to overturn the caveats and expectations of the old political order. The anxiety which was growing on the part of the middle classes and the aristocracy of old to the development of a more militant working class was expressed in numerous ways; the feeling of being overwhelmed by the hordes, the 'great unwashed'. And this sense of being swamped by sheer numbers was given a veneer of theoretical respectability by thinkers such as Malthus who provided academic credence to the notion that society would collapse under the heaving strain of the multiplying masses. The same kind of logic, incidentally, that is upheld by many in the anti-immigration brigade today.

But perhaps the most eloquent and suggestive purveyor of ruling-class sensibility towards the eruptions from below that had wracked the nineteenth century was Friedrich Nietzsche. Nietzsche had developed a theory of history, romantic, violent and disturbing – a type of gothic fairy tale – according to which, in the time of the distant past, there were the rulers and the ruled and never the twain would meet. The rulers were part of a bloody aristocracy that had no compunctions about submitting those they ruled to the most abject and violent modes of domination, they had no qualms about reducing the bovine and passive masses to the level of slaves in pursuit of their own brutal self-interest. In unleashing such naked forms of domination, they also unleashed the 'aesthetic' spirit of a minority; those in power could now accomplish great deeds, write great epics, generate great art and architecture – straddling the world and stamping it with their own creativity, vivaciousness and *joie de vivre*.

And yet, somewhere along the line, things began to change. The age of heroes was elided into the age of bureaucrats. Courage became careerism.

And the creative spirit of the human species began to wither and die. For Nietzsche, the change occurred with what he described as the rise of the 'slave' or 'herd' morality and this was expressed in and through the ideologies of Judaism, Christianity, socialism and democracy. For Nietzsche, these ideologies acted as great levellers; that is, they preached an abstract equality where everyone is the same before God or the state, and in so doing they nullified the individuality of the 'noble' spirit which was creative precisely because it was unequal, precisely because it was able to differentiate itself and rise above the ordinary mainstay of the majority of human beings. These 'slave' ideologies, then, reduced everyone to the level of the masses, dissolving the creative and world-historic individual in a grey and monotone equality, and cutting off the true source of human progress from itself.

But in order for the masses to be able to impose their own power, to perpetuate 'slave morality', Nietzsche noted, something more was necessary. Specifically, the masses had to 'infect' the masters with these doctrines of equalization. This process began with the Christianization of the Roman state, and in his own century Nietzche saw the 'democratic movement' as the 'heir to Christianity', a movement which culminated in the introduction of universal male suffrage in 1867. For Nietzsche such a concession was a result of the fact that the rulers themselves had lost their way, had in some way become 'effeminized' such that they had relinquished the 'will to power' which ruling requires, capitulating to the passive-aggressive, insidious demands of a 'herd' that sought to reduce the capabilities of the higher human individual to the stagnant and mediocre standard of the mass.

What is 'radical' about Nietzsche's philosophy here is that he is doing something which has not been done before. In the past, defences of any given social order had worked along the following lines: thinkers had recognized the rule of the elite in that particular society and tended to justify it in naturalistic terms. For example, Aristotle defended the 'right' of the Greeks of Antiquity to own slaves by arguing that some people were slaves by nature – a slave was 'anyone who, while being human, is by nature not his own but of someone else'.[1] Sometimes the aura of legitimacy was bestowed on the powerful by God Himself; supporters of James I, for instance, argued that the absolute monarch had been appointed in his rule by 'divine right'.

But what Nietzsche does is radically different. Rather than simply looking for some external authority – natural or divine – to legitimize the rulers of his own epoch, he instead inverts the relation of ruler and ruled more generally. He raises a topsy-turvy, upside-down vision of the world in which those who are least powerful, and struggling to gain representation and rights, are in fact the secret dictators whose morality has come to infuse and corrupt the whole political system. Those who were once hugely powerful by virtue of their aristocratic traditions and a wolfish will-to-power have been rendered low by the sneaky wiles of the mass – their strength and their creative freedoms drained from them thereby.

Thus the people at the top – the wealthy, the great landowners, the aristocrats, the industrial barons, the elite more generally – become defanged and helpless, decadent and disorientated, before the forces from below that have infiltrated the political system, rendering them quiescent before the 'abstract equality' of the various manifestations of 'slave morality'. Only one other thing remains to be added; for those at the bottom to achieve this, for them to usurp the power of the 'masters' there must be a section of the ruling elite which actively collaborates with the forces from below, which adopts the mantle of 'slave morality' in whatever ideological guise, and which pushes through the increasing democratization of society despite all its dangers and absurdities, despite the threat it poses to a human development that, in more traditional and venerable times, had proceeded unbound.

The political correctness gone mad narrative today

Nietzsche never used the phrase, but the complicit element which he describes – that section of the rulers which actively promotes 'slave morality' and thus works to increase the democratic power of the masses – could well have been described as 'the liberal elite'. And when we look at what the 'political correctness gone mad' thesis actually involves, we discover it is a form of 'slave morality' as Nietzsche understood it. For it operates along remarkably similar lines. Not only does 'political correctness' infiltrate the 'liberal elite' and thereby contaminate a section of the rich and powerful with the 'slave morality' of those at the bottom (workers, repressed minorities, poor immigrants, trans people and so on). But, as with Nietzsche, it is often said to achieve this through the endeavour to impose a template of 'abstract equality' on society more broadly, thus annulling the real differences between human beings which make progress possible. Writing on the 'politically correct worldview', the academic Manuel Doria argues it involves 'the denial of the existence of significant mental differences in between socially oppressed groups and their respective groups of oppressors'[2] – or to say the same, it involves the endeavour to reduce everyone to the dull, banal equality of those at the bottom which Nietzsche so eloquently described.

Thus, anti-politically correct figures often attack 'political correctness' on precisely this basis. Lawrence Summers, a career economist and former president of Harvard University, argued that men tend to outperform women in science and maths, not because of differences in opportunity wrought by different social standards, but rather through the biological differences which exist between the sexes: 'Research in behavioural genetics is showing that things people previously attributed to socialisation weren't due to socialisation after all'.[3]

In other words, social inequality between the sexes is innate, and the fact that men find themselves more frequently in better positions in academia is simply the natural and inevitable consequence of this. Indeed, during Summer's presidency of the university, the number of tenured positions offered to women fell from 36 per cent to 13 per cent[4] – though whether that was to do with the innate intellectual 'inferiority' of women per se, or whether it had to do with the fact that the people making the hiring decisions tended to be men like Summers with those kinds of beliefs, can only be left to the discretion of the reader to decide.

In any event, Summers went on to have a lucrative career working as a visiting professor for Harvard, a hedge fund manager, a special advisor to the Obama presidency, a member of the board of a multi-million dollar financial company and a leading member of the Bilderberg group among others. Naturally, in the same period, he spent a good deal of time giving interviews to some of the world's biggest news outlets and writing articles for some of the world's most prestigious magazines on just how the 'creeping totalitarianism' of 'absurd "political correctness"'[5] was more and more stifling the opportunities and voices of men such as himself.

Perhaps one of the most strident voices raised against 'political correctness' is that of Jordan Peterson – a Canadian professor who combines a set of atavistic far-right political positions with the kind of trite psychology of the self-help manual. Like Summers, Peterson too wants to demonstrate that there are certain innate differences between men and women which inexorably determine the nature of the social relationships that open up between them. So, for instance, Peterson argues that 'boys' interests tilt towards things' while 'girls' interests tilt toward people' and this is strongly determined by 'biological factors'.[6]

Because women are more inclined towards people, they naturally make for better carers, whereas men are less passive and more acquisitive, determined to seize control of the things they covet. For this reason, men tend to get paid more, get promoted, rise higher in the hierarchy because they are built to be more demanding and more aggressive, and are naturally able to win through to the things they desire. Indeed for a woman to do well career-wise, Peterson avers, 'masculine traits are going to be helpful'.[7]

One can see exactly how innate templates of 'manhood' and 'womanhood' allow real-world disparities and injustices such as the gender pay gap to be normalized, all under the rubric of attacking the abstract equality of 'political correctness'. In a somewhat similar vein, the pseudo-Marxist Slavoj Žižek describes the refugee crisis in Europe. He argues that, instead of 'prohibiting any critique of Islam as a case of "Islamophobia"', people should recognize a fundamental difference between 'Islamic' culture and the culture of the First World countries Muslims find themselves journeying to: 'It is a simple fact that most of the refugees come from a culture that is incompatible with Western European notions of human rights.'[8] Of course, what Žižek reproduces here is little more than vulgar racism – the archaic and fearful depiction of Muslims as unlettered savages who are inherently incapable of rising to the norms and etiquettes of the civilized life. Elsewhere he wonders rhetorically: 'Should we tolerate migrants who prevent their children from going to state schools; who force their women to dress and behave in a certain way; who arrange their children's marriage; who discriminate against homosexuals?'[9] Again, these negative features are inscribed into the category of 'Islam' as a whole.

And such a racist critique also doubles as a critique of 'political correctness' too: in Žižek's account it is the left and the well-to-do liberals – 'the European left' – who refuse to acknowledge 'the differences between different sets of values';[10] that is, they impose an abstract and 'politically correct' template of equality on two profoundly unequal and antagonistic cultural forms – that of 'Islam' and 'Western modernity'. Furthermore, like so many of his right-wing counterparts, Žižek too has come to wax lyrical about 'political correctness' in the most ominous of tones; like them – he describes it as a 'modern totalitarianism'.[11]

And yet, where does the danger of real totalitarianism lie? If all the 'politically correct luvvies' are delusional, if there can be no genuine equilibrium between 'cultures', if the lives of Muslims are fundamentally incompatible with 'Western values', then how do 'we' treat the Muslims in our midst? If they cannot reconcile themselves to the liberal values of an 'enlightened' modernity, then surely their behaviour must be compelled in accordance with those values from without. Indeed this is the conclusion many liberal commentators as well as those on the right have increasingly drawn.

Consider, for example, the man of *belles-lettres*, the radical 'humanist', liberal 'progressive' and renowned author and aesthete, Martin Amis. In his salubrious, lofty and rich patrician drawl, he regularly pontificates on the backwardness of Islam claiming 'some societies are just more evolved than others' and that 'in the West we have the most evolved society in the world and we are not blowing people up'.[12] Such sophisticated political and cultural analysis is supplemented by a solution to the problem of the barbaric Muslims: 'The Muslim community will have to suffer until it gets its house in order. What sort of suffering? Not letting them travel. Deportation – further down the road. Curtailing of freedoms. Strip-searching people who look like they're from the Middle East or from Pakistan … Discriminatory stuff, until it hurts the whole community and they start getting tough with their children'.[13]

The political correctness gone mad narrative and fascist ideology

Amis's comments demonstrate how easily a critique of a 'political correctness' and its equalizing tenets which absolve the 'real' differences between one group and another – grow into something more sinister, a call to arms, a licence for repression and worse. Behind the liberal facade, behind Amis's undoubted eloquence as a writer and orator, there is something darker and more primitive at work. That call for 'deportation … further down the line' – not based on an appraisal of a crime committed by any given individual, but rather the exhortation to punish a 'race' *qua* 'race'. In his desire to make sure uppity minorities know their place, Amis begins to wander into darker terrains – begins to stray in the direction of some form of ethnic cleansing; his exhortation to make a whole ethnic group 'suffer' helps evoke the sinister aroma of some of the darkest episodes from our historical past.

Other commentators, who have styled themselves as martyrs of free speech prepared to tell the truth to a 'politically correct liberal establishment' often reveal themselves in similar terms. Katie Hopkins – a notorious shock-jock and right-wing crank who has devoted a lucrative media career to attacking 'political correctness gone mad' – confronted by the issue of desperate refugees risking their lives to cross the Mediterranean Sea (and often drowning in the process) – chose to describe such people as 'cockroaches'. In addition, she argued, the responsible thing for European states to do would be to greet their plight by deploying 'gunships', because these people weren't quite people at all; instead, they were 'feral humans' who spread 'like Noravirus'.[14]

The most visible example of someone using a fascist rhetoric as a way of attacking those at the bottom, however, was the self-styled 'anti-political correctness' president Donald Trump. From the start of his presidential campaign, Trump pivoted his political platform on the idea of nullifying the type of 'politically correct' programme that was supposedly sacrificing white Christian Americans to the needs of the foreigner or the Muslim. In so doing, however, in endeavouring to restore the 'rights' of white Protestant America – Trump was required to demonize the 'other' in order to 'justify' the rage and fury he was endeavouring to channel.

Not only were Mexican immigrants described as 'rapists', for instance, but more than that, illegal immigrants were described in subhuman terms, as infestations – 'illegal immigrants, no matter how bad they may be … pour into and infest our Country'.[15] Trump exhorted four congress women of colour to 'go back' to 'help fix the totally broken and crime-infested places from which they came',[16] not even referencing the fact that three of those women were actually American-born and one had moved to the United States when she was just a child. Clearly in Trump's book, a darker skin tone denotes 'otherness' whatever the place of birth, and to this otherness is attached a key aspect of dehumanization – 'crime infested places from which they came'. The use of the word 'infestation' is neither coincidental nor benign; as the writer Jamil Smith reflects, '[w]hen Trump speaks of immigrants "infesting" America, he speaks in the language of genocide, not governance. By likening people to insects or vermin, even if he considers them criminals, he provides himself license to be an exterminator'.[17]

Of course, while not everyone who thinks society is run on a 'politically correct' basis by a 'liberal elite' is a fascist or has fascist sympathies, there is a sense in which the narrative of 'political correctness gone mad' – driven to its logical conclusion – tends to yield a fascist-type solution. After all, if there is no point at which a given minority – because of their innate and inherent difference – can ever be 'equalized'; that is to say, can never be integrated into society without destroying the capacity of that society to successfully regulate the best interests of its 'own' citizens – then surely those alien and 'other' elements must be controlled by an external application of force and – in the interests of a more healthy society – eventually purged from the body politic. It is worth noting here that in Nietzsche's original 'anti-equality' project, the pull towards a more fascist solution was likewise pronounced: 'That party of life which takes in hand the greatest of all tasks, the higher breeding of humanity, together with the remorseless extermination of all degenerate and parasitic elements, will again make possible on earth that superfluity of life out of which the Dionysian condition must again proceed'.[18]

Both the Nietzschean prospectus and the modern-day conception of 'political correctness gone mad' involve the same central guiding thread: that is, they seek to argue that social differences in terms of political power and exploitation are inherent features of any successful social order, and the endeavour to try and challenge this in and through social movements or ideologies that hope to create a more egalitarian society results in a deeper and more insidious corruption of that same social order. In the words of the anti-political correctness guru Jordan Peterson, 'inequality and hierarchy give life its purpose'.[19] And yet, at the same time, there is a vital difference between the Nietzschean philosophy and any notion of 'political correctness' as it is posed today.

Specifically, Nietzsche's attack on social equality was posed from the point of view of an elite and the world historic figure of the *Übermensch*; the lower orders needed to be submitted entirely to the will of the upper class minority. But what makes the philosophy of 'political correctness' so effective is that, while it endeavours to fortify 'inequality and hierarchy' in order to guard the privileges of the elite and combat protest movements from below – nevertheless, its protagonists achieve this by claiming to be acting in the interests of 'ordinary people'. It's understood that Trump is a billionaire, that he rocks the kind of decor which would have made Marie Antoinette blush, that he has a history of exploiting workers, that his shoddy business practises have ensured hazardous conditions, that he inherited vast amounts of wealth, and that his father stimulated his first business venture with a loan which ran into the millions. It is difficult to imagine someone with less in common with a blue collar worker from the rustbelt.

And yet, by presenting himself as a person who is fighting against 'political correctness', Trump is not only better able to legitimize the racism directed towards poverty-stricken immigrants, but also to do this in conjunction with 'protecting' the interests of 'ordinary' Americans. Trump himself, in this creative political vision, is transformed from a billionaire capitalist and a president who consistently went to bat for the elite by reducing taxes on the most wealthy – to a figure welded to the post-industrial heartlands and the plight of the all-American blue-collar underdog, desperately trying to recapture the spirit and culture of a vanishing world. Likewise, when right-wing journalists attack the 'political correctness' (read basic human empathy) which involves recognizing trans women as women, they can couch their transphobia as part and parcel of a struggle to protect 'ordinary' or 'real' women.

Likewise the endeavour to demonize and 'other' Muslims – is achieved not simply from the standpoint of the elites, but from the notion that the racist oppression of this poor minority is key to protecting poor white girls from sexual abuse. Or the attack on movements which hope to improve the rights and conditions of women such as Me Too is achieved by conjuring up the image of workplaces where 'ordinary' men and women can no longer form romantic attachments because every aspect of their behaviour is being policed by a totalitarian series of 'politically correct' rules. While the critique of 'political correctness' took on the idea, bequeathed by Nietzsche, that social equality is something stifling and repressive – it posed this critique not in the interests of the elite 'masters' in the way Nietzsche had done, but in the interests of 'ordinary people' themselves. And this is what makes it such a resilient and powerful political ideology – it disguises the fact that it is really supporting the elite by claiming it is fighting for the interests of the 'ordinary' majority.

It's just good common sense

Which brings us to the final aspect of 'political correctness gone mad'. And that's the notion of 'common sense'. According to the 'political correctness gone mad' narrative, a so-called 'liberal elite' are always imposing 'politically correct' mandates on the population at large, but one of the things that helps ordinary people to resist such 'political correctness' is because they have a good degree of common sense, a common sense that is able to recognize, in plain and simple terms, the absurdity of what the 'politically correct' line entails. Just as the 'liberal elite' are opposed to 'ordinary people', so too do we get the opposition between 'political correctness gone mad' and good, down-to-earth common sense. The 'liberal elite' lack common sense because they have been abstracted from the simple, practical problems of everyday life by the fact of their material privilege; living in their ivory towers, they remain untouched by the problems of the ordinary world. That is why, despite all their academic qualifications (for example), they don't have the type of life experience which would allow them to understand the way the 'real world' actually operates.

Common sense – as opposed to abstruse intellectual analysis – looks at problems with an eye to breaking them down into their basic components and coming up with a simple and practical solution. The difficulty is that such thinking has certain untraversable limits. So, for example, when one sees a wild dog in the streets, slavering and barking, our common sense is rather useful in letting us know that petting it probably wouldn't be the best idea. Or if one scalds one's hand on something hot, our common sense might usefully inform us that the best thing might be to put the hand under the cold water tap.

And yet, common sense would not prove so useful for diagnosing liver cancer. For that, we would need a form of scientific knowledge that was capable of going to the root of the problem, of penetrating the appearance of phenomena and uncovering (in this case at the microscopic level) the fundamental essence. Not only is common sense incapable of plumbing these deeper realities, but more importantly, the endeavour to use it this way can often yield fallacious results. So, for instance, in 2010, the Conservative-Liberal coalition implemented the set of austerity measures that utilized taxpayer bail outs to prop up the failing financial sector. And as Sophia Hatzisavvidou points out, such a 'process was supported by the circulation of a rhetoric that argued for austerity as a form of conventional wisdom or common sense.'[20] The previous administration (a 'liberal elite') had lost all connection to the 'real world'; thus the Conservatives were able to contrast themselves – as a common sense 'government of thrift' – with those who came before, 'Labour's spendaholic government.'[21]

Such a gambit harkened back to the days of Margaret Thatcher. She too would couch neoliberal spending measures in the ordinary refrain of good common sense, she compared her own cuts of social services to a dutiful housewife saving money, balancing the budget and staying solvent: 'I can't help reflecting that it's taken a Government headed by a housewife with experience of running a family to balance the books for the first time in 20 years.'[22]

In reality, however, any national economy is a considerably more complex and paradoxical affair. For if a single household decides to cut back on its spending by 15 per cent, such a reduction won't affect the external incomes of any of the household members. If a government cuts the national budget by the same amount, employment and/or wages fall in the public sector, which means that those self-same people – nurses, police, teachers – end up spending less in the economy more generally, thereby harming businesses which are not directly under the auspices of government investment. The so-called 'multiplier' effect means – all things being equal – such cuts can, ultimately, result in the type of reduction in gross domestic product which comes from a decrease in demand; and, therefore, the government itself can find the overall pool of taxable income reduced.

In other words, cutting down household spending doesn't reduce the wages of those employed outside the house; but by 'cutting its spending the government also ends up reducing its own income'.[23] Or to say the same, a reduction of spending on the household level can have precisely the opposite effect of a reduction of spending at the level of the economy as a whole. This is because of the way the broader categories of the state, state workers, the private sector and consumers more generally, are fused in social and symbiotic relationships of investment, consumption, waged-labour and taxation.

Applying the metaphor of a householder managing domestic finances, therefore, allows the complex and contradictory network of social and class relationships which underwrite the economy to be reimagined as a zero sum paradigm of a generic amount of money coming in and money going out. This, in turn, allows the state to rationalize measures of austerity – slashing to the state expenditure and social welfare – as coming under the rubric of the good commonsensical need to be careful with one's finances in the most simple and practical of fashions.

And so, the austerity measures of 2010 – that is, the slashing of social welfare and harder taxation policies against the poor majority in order to relieve the debt burden of high-finance – become reimagined as the tale of a government, having fallen on hard times, trying to be that bit more careful with the purse strings and needing to balance the books. A policy in the interests of a tiny minority of the most wealthy is repackaged as a series of measures which benefits society more broadly as we all work together to keep our heads above water. And the 'common sense' component is integral to this, for it speaks to a mode of conceiving the world that arises from everyday life as experienced by ordinary people – that is, people who experience the struggle to balance their household finances. By deploying notions of 'common sense', therefore, the political elite can hope to pull a section of the population into the type of ideology which in reality only benefits themselves.

Something similar is true of the immigration debate. So right-wing demagogue Nigel Farage, for example, uses the concept of 'common sense' to downplay the racism and xenophobia he has spent decades perpetuating. In his account of immigration, everything is simplified to the point of a zero-sum paradigm: there is a given amount of space and resources, and extensive immigration provides a drain on these. There are only so many jobs to go round. For this reason, the tenor of his anti-immigration stance can be repurposed as a 'non-racist' and purely commonsensical proposition: 'Getting immigration right isn't racist, it is common sense.'[24] And this is a highly effective way of smuggling racist views in, of making them more palatable and respectable, because they are cossetted behind the guise of plain and simple commonsensical 'facts'.

And yet, we know that immigration doesn't work in a purely black and white way. There is not a single sum quota of jobs which exists in an economy indefinitely. Sometimes an increase in immigration allows more jobs to be created. And the idea of resources is less than static too. There is not, by nature, a fixed quanta of houses or utilities to be allocated; the government can invest more, should it choose, in these areas; likewise growth can be stimulated or reduced depending on rises or dips in the economy more broadly. But what we do know is that the effects mass immigration has on a nation tend to be contrary to common-sense thinking. Indeed the immigrants from the ten poorer countries, such as Poland, Estonia and Hungary who had joined the EU in 2004, and who had migrated to Britain in the ten years which followed – actually contributed significantly more to the UK economy than they had taken out in benefits. Five billion pounds more to be exact.[25]

Common sense is often presented as a type of 'antidote' to 'political correctness gone mad', and thus helps support the attack on social movements which are seen to be 'politically correct' in their endeavour to update and equalize the social conditions of a given oppressed minority. So, for example, when the Me Too movement hit, one of the ways in which it was countered was to suggest that it was creating an atmosphere of 'politically correct totalitarianism' in the workplace. Liberal politicians were, so the narrative ran, increasingly 'compelled' by 'Feminazis' into enacting 'politically correct laws', laws which would police gender relationships in the workplace so that it is no longer possible for people to initiate romantic relationships based on a general commonsensical understanding of physical boundaries. Instead, men become absolutely terrified of being sued by a female colleague just for the fact of having looked at her the wrong way. What should be organic, spontaneous and joyful in the human experience is thus warped into a fixed and rigid set of 'politically correct' prohibitions.

The common sense narrative is also deployed against the autonomy of trans people. It is, so the argument goes, obvious that men have dangly bits and lots of testosterone, while women have wombs and estrogen and never the twain shall meet – that much is just good common sense. In reality, however, such commonsensical thinking not only serves to blur the science which reveals just how the biologies of men and women can bleed into one another (intersex conditions for example) but perhaps more importantly, it belies the essence of human beings as social beings, as creatures whose rich social identities are so much more than the sum of their biological parts.

In practice, of course, militating against laws which hope to address sexual harassment in the workplace – by arguing work relationships should not be regulated for they are just a matter of good 'common sense' – provides an effective means to inscribe the power of wealthy, typically male bosses against their junior and less powerful underlings. Likewise, the warning against immigration which is articulated in a common sense refrain – 'there are only so many jobs, only so many houses' – relieves the government of its responsibility for creating more jobs, for building better houses, and helps fortify racism and suspicion towards immigrants. Likewise, the commonsensical distinction, wholly grounded in 'biology', between what a man is and what a woman is – ultimately serves as a justification for the mistreatment of a vulnerable minority (trans people) and also works to bolster and reinforce traditional gender roles that tend to enshrine the power of men over women. And so on.

In all these instances, the language of common sense hopes to pull ordinary people into a debate, suggesting that the absurdities of 'political correctness' have become so entrenched that the very possibility of living an everyday life is threatened; you can't ask a woman out at work anymore because you risk being fired or even prosecuted; you can't see your local GP when you need to because the liberal elite have gifted your appointment to an asylum seeker; your daughter can no longer be Cinderella in the school play because the 'politically-correct' school governors have decreed that this role must go to a trans girl. But behind this smokescreen – behind these phantoms of 'political correctness gone mad' – what you nearly always find is that it is the interests of the elite or the powerful who are really being served, once one asks who actually benefits.

Are there genuine occurrences of 'political correctness gone mad' which are particularly frustrating or damaging to everyday people as we go about our lives? From my research for this book, I would have to say yes. There are certainly occasions where people – often out of a genuine need to protest the inequality and injustice of the modern world – do so in an absurd and ridiculous fashion. Take, for example, the university researchers who felt it was important to fight for the acceptance of those people who 'identify as real vampires'[26] or the professor who argued that the use of small chairs in pre-school was 'gendered', 'problematic' and 'disempowering'.[27]

Sometimes the absurd meets the trivial in terms of a rather fetishized focus on undoing 'inequalities' in language rather than speaking to the deeper social relationships of exploitation such language reflects. So, for instance, an NHS hospital consultant was chastised by the parents of one of his patients in the form of an official complaint for using the word 'manfully' as a stand in to suggest 'courage' or 'responsibility'.[28] And while much of this stuff is silly but harmless, there are instances which do real damage. On the issue of cancel culture, there was the recent case of Emmanuel Cafferty, a San Diego Gas & Electric company employee, who was fired for supposedly having made a white supremacist hand gesture when he was pulled up in his truck at a traffic light.

In actual fact, Cafferty had just been dangling his hand out of his truck absent-mindedly, and the 'gesture', which another driver had recorded, had been purely coincidental. In addition, Cafferty is Mexican on his mother's side, so it is difficult to imagine him taking part in the behaviour (promoting white supremacy) of which he had been accused. Nonetheless, the accusation against him (levelled by a white man incidentally) at once blew up – perhaps because it had occurred in the incredibly fraught and angry atmosphere following the murder of George Floyd in 2020. People went onto Twitter to condemn Cafferty in a deluge of outrage and anger which soon took on a life of its own, and eventually led to Cafferty's employers taking the decision to fire him. Cafferty was eventually able to get his own side of the story out, to draw attention to the fact of his own ethnicity, and his initial accuser – when pressed – admitted he might have misinterpreted[29] the gesture he thought he had seen Cafferty make.

Unfortunately, by this time, the damage was done. At the time of writing, San Diego Gas & Electric company have refused to reinstate Cafferty. The damage done to his life as a result of the Twitter storm has been considerable. And he is currently in the process of suing his old employers for damages.

At about the same time, there was also the case of Majdi Wadi.[30] Wadi, a local Minneapolis businessman, ran the 'Holy Land' enterprise, a series of stores and delis. In the aftermath of the George Floyd killing, a series of social media posts emerged that had been made by Wadi's teenage daughter from the period 2012–16. These posts contained anti-Black, anti-Semitic and anti-LGBT sentiments. But although Majdi Wadi was not aware of the posts until they were highlighted in 2020, and although he dismissed his daughter from his employ as a result, nevertheless he experienced a Twitter backlash which would ultimately cost his business millions of dollars in contracts and he was evicted from one of his locations too.

A right-wing conspiracy theory

But while there are no doubts these type of incidents can and do occur, they are also very few and far between. And this latter point is significant. Those ideologues who argue against 'political correctness gone mad' do not simply do so on the basis of this or that example. They go further. They put forward a more general theory about the way in which society is being run; that is, they endeavour to argue that 'political correctness' has become the norm; that it has established an iron-like grip on the mechanisms of state and culture more broadly. They repeatedly describe it as a modern form of 'totalitarianism' that has either already taken control or is on the verge of doing so, an opinion which can unite both right wingers and centrist liberals.

So, for example, the right winger Jordan Peterson argues that PC culture and its 'identity politics' lead to 'totalitarian oppression'[31] while the British liberal, TV personality and raconteur Stephen Fry also describes 'political correctness' as the latest in a long line of totalitarian forms: 'I mean you've only got to read Darkness at Noon to see this at its most extreme. It always starts off with an ideal and a hopeful goal – equality of societies, how communism began, the French Revolution, equality, fraternity, liberty, all those wonderful things.'[32]

Fry then makes the comparison even more explicit – 'The French Revolution ended up with the Committee of General Security, which had a law passed. It said you could take a piece of paper saying something like "Citoyen de Roque is an enemy of the Revolution," put it on the central square on a post, and that person would be arrested. It's basically the same as tweeting it.'[33] Mr Fry uttered these words in 2018. At the time of writing (late 2021) I have made a quick perusal of Mr Fry's twitter account and can relay he has some 12.4 million followers. To my knowledge, he has yet to be guillotined.

But beyond the complete absurdity of Fry's comparison, beyond the sheer historical illiteracy of it (the idea that the French Revolution's descent into dictatorship was a product of a culture of denunciation in abstraction rather than the fact that the new regime was locked into a civil war and an existential struggle to stave off foreign invasion) – there are nevertheless the same points of contact. Like Peterson (and Nietzsche before them though he expressed it in a different terminology) Fry defines 'political correctness' as a push to 'equality of societies' which ultimately ends up supressing the truly human, the creative and above all the individual. In addition, what is interesting about Fry's analysis is that it reflects an important modification of the thesis of 'political correctness gone mad' that has taken place in the last decade. Or to say the same, the thesis has been more and more focussed on the role of social media like Twitter.

Now that's partly because there is a lot of bullying and nastiness on fora like Twitter – though it comes from large numbers of people on both the left and right of the political spectrum. But more significantly, it is because – despite all its faults – social media and the internet more broadly has formed a locus point whereby the possibility of creating a more equal playing field is given. As the journalist Shamira Ibrahim says of social media, it is 'one of the few spaces that exists for collective feedback and where organizing movements that threaten [conservatives'] social standing have begun'.[34] The Me Too movement was started in 2006 but it was only in the time of social media that it was able to achieve such sweeping global significance, as when millions of people shared their experiences on Facebook, Twitter and other forums deploying the #MeToo.

In the case of Black Lives Matter also – the campaign began with social media. In 2013, a Facebook post employed the caption 'Black Lives Matter' in response to the slaying of the unarmed Black teenager Trayvon Martin and the acquittal of his killer, George Zimmermann. But the movement exploded after the killing of George Floyd in 2020 and part of that was due to the way people on social media could share the footage of his murder such that within hours it had spread around the world. Petitions calling for action, outraged articles written by citizen journalists, people in different cities and different countries coordinating protests – all achieved through the use of online networks and social media sites.

All of this spoke to a great sea change. As the podcaster and journalist Michael Hobbes points out, 'American media was controlled by a tiny number of gatekeepers. Count up all the top editors of all the national news outlets in the pre-internet era and you would have gotten a shockingly small number. If that tiny – and overwhelmingly white, male, straight and cis-group of editors decided that an opinion was not worthy of being heard, it wasn't.'[35] The intensification of the 'political correctness gone mad' narrative – the extension of it to a moral panic surrounding something called 'cancel culture' – took place during a period when we had 'shifted from a media environment defined by a small group of gatekeepers to one with no gatekeepers at all';[36] when social movements like Me Too and Black Lives Matter were passing across the panorama like great storms, illuminating chasms of inequality and injustice with their flashing lightening.

I doubt very much, by the way, that someone like Stephen Fry, a public intellectual and humanist, would have much truck with sex predator Harvey Weinstein or with the murderer of George Floyd, Derick Chauvin. In fact,

I believe he would loathe such people and their crimes. But the tremendous outbreaks of social struggle which these horrific events precipitate, shake to the core the foundations on which people like Fry have not just based their careers, but also based their existence; a world in which predominantly wealthy, upper-class white men such as themselves have had unadulterated access to the means of information via 'an old boy's network' of elite privilege – a world in which their voices have consistently been amplified and fortified through the conduits of the biggest TV channels, the most prestigious media outlets.

They have never really known any other state of being and, consequently, it is difficult for them to imagine one. When movements explode from below, when more and more ordinary people flood onto a virtual world, mobilizing the social media that allows them not only to assert their own interests in the public realm, but also to challenge the discrepancies and disparities in the prevailing social order – for the privileged and powerful this must inevitably appear in the guise of a menacing authoritarianism, a 'totalitarian conspiracy' which strikes out at the set of verities and stabilities (read inequalities) that the foundations of their lives have been grounded on. That they themselves hold dear.

And that is what the narrative of 'political correctness gone mad' truly represents. It is a conspiracy theory of a sort, birthed by ruling elites in order to counter the spectre of change. Employing a Nietzschean prospectus, it describes how the struggle for broader equalities has produced a deformation in human life – and in so doing raises a vision of a fantastical and topsy-turvy world in which those who suffer most from inequality and discrimination are the most powerful, the most monstrous; while at the same time, those who enjoy power and privilege now reappear as the victims – as the repressed who are perpetually on the verge of being silenced, criminalized and extinguished by the madness of 'political correctness' and its insipid and tyrannical march toward equality.

Of course it is a chimera, and an absurd one at that. It does not require too deep an investigation into someone like Donald Trump – the details of his life, the privilege he was born into, the media coverage as a billionaire business baron he enjoyed, his stint as a reality TV celebrity before being catapulted into the highest office in the world – it doesn't take a great deal of rational thinking to figure out that this man is not a victim of some kind of radical authoritarianism and has never been in danger of having his voice silenced.

Likewise, on a smaller scale, it does not take a great deal of research to understand that the majority of poor immigrants *do* work, often doing the most undesirable jobs for the most meagre forms of compensation; and furthermore that they tend to contribute a significantly larger amount to the state than they take out in benefits. Or, for instance, that the number of men who escape prosecution, having been accused of rape is incredibly high, while the number of women who falsely accuse men of that same crime is incredibly low. It is not the case that vast numbers of embittered, vengeful women are sending good god-fearing men into prison in their droves by crying rape, or that immigrants are everywhere living in mansions subbed by the largesse of a woolly liberal state.

It doesn't take a great deal of research to acquaint oneself with the statistics regarding these issues, statistics which provide an unequivocal picture of which side of a given set of social relations power truly lies. And yet, it is here that the narrative of 'political correctness gone mad' once again comes into its own, because it is able to invert the picture; it is able to reflect back contraries in the strange and surreal mirror of its ideology. A person providing a statistical refutation of the claim that the state indiscriminately favours poor immigrants can simply be rejected by the acolytes of 'its political correctness gone mad' as someone who is out-of-touch with the realities of direct and immediate experience. Often the use of statistics and a deeper intellectual analysis is recast – by the narrative of 'political correctness gone mad' – as an activity carried out by ivory tower academics and liberal elites who bandy about facts and figures but have no idea of the living flesh-and-blood experience of the ordinary people who endure the consequences of their 'politically correct' mandates. After all, he or she can throw up all the facts and figures they want, but I bet in their posh Islington suburb they've never had to live next door to a group of … shock, horror … *Romanian immigrants!*[37]

In this way, the 'political correctness gone mad' narrative inoculates itself against rational and factual refutation by reverting to notions of the 'everyday experience' supposedly had by 'ordinary people' – and it is here that the concept of 'common sense' ties everything together. Not only does 'common sense' allow for a form of irrationalism which tends to privilege experiential anecdotes and sensationalist tabloid horror stories over genuine sociological investigation and statistical fact – it also allows such an opposition to be framed as that between ordinary people and a liberal elite, a liberal elite that lacks common sense and whose 'politically correct' mandates are threatening the culture and the existence of the majority.

There is one final thing worth noting about the 'political correctness gone mad' narrative. Although it purports to be taking the side of 'ordinary people' against a 'liberal elite' – one better apprehends the true nature of its agenda when one considers how it always requires a stratagem of divide and rule; that is, it always promises to uplift one section of the poor or oppressed by seeking to disparage another. So, for example, it might claim to be protecting the working class – but only in the context of an attack on immigrant labour, or the rights of 'real' women – but only against those of trans women, or the status of 'indigenous' whites – but only against Black people, and so on. In this way, it is capable of presenting what is a perpetual and ruthless process – that is, the struggle of elites in society to resist the push from below for greater equality on the part of the repressed majority – as a struggle that is supposedly enacted in 'favour' of one section of that majority against another.

The 'political correctness gone mad' narrative creates a fantasy vision of the world, driven by a conspiracy theory in which 'the liberal elite' becomes the prime mover over and against 'ordinary people'. In so doing, it manages to reconfigure interests of the wealthy as those of ordinary people; it achieves a strange, spectral magic by which the most powerful in society become the most persecuted, and the oppressed become the oppressors. But, ultimately, such a pernicious and ethereal illusion is chased away and evaporated by those who are most ardent, most desperate to sell it to you. What the attack on 'political correctness gone mad' ultimately demands, in the words of one of its most strident protagonists, is the acceptance of a society in which 'inequality and hierarchy' are unchangeable and immutable features to the extent that they 'give life its purpose'.[38] And in such a society, the needs and privileges of the wealthy and the powerful must remain sacrosanct and forever untouched.

Notes

Chapter 1

1   Soeren Kern, 'How "political correctness" is transforming british education', *Gatestone Institute International Policy Council* 16 July 2012: https://www.gatestoneinstitute. org/3170/british-education-political-correctness

2   Chris Johnson, 'Primary school cancels nativity play because it interferes with Muslim festival of Eid', *The Daily Mail* 4 December 2008: https://www.dailymail.co.uk/news/ article-1091594/Primary-school-cancels-nativity-play-interferes-Muslim-festival-Eid. html

3   George Fanning, 'Nottingham school cancels christmas to make way for Islam', *The British National Party* 4 December 2008: http://web.archive.org/ web/20081205121602/http://bnp.org.uk/2008/12/nottingham-school-cancels- christmas-to-make-way-for-islam/

4   Greenwood Primary School staff cited in The Christian Institute, 'Christmas play moved in favour of Muslim festival', 5 December 2008: https://www.christian.org.uk/ news/school-moves-nativity-in-favour-of-muslim-festival/

5   Louise Eccles, 'Early Learning Centre bans toy pig from farmyard set for fear of offending Muslims (but keeps sty and oink noise)', *The Daily Mail* 16 November 2010: https://www.dailymail.co.uk/news/article-1329897/Early-Learning-Centre-toy-pig- banned-farm-set-avoid-offending-Muslims.html

6   Ibid.

7   ELC cited in 'Early Learning Centre toy pig banned', *Metro* 16 November 2010: https://metro.co.uk/2010/11/16/early-learning-centre-toy-pig-banned-581622/

8   Laura Clark, 'New curriculum will 'make every lesson politically correct', *The Daily Mail* 25 January 2007: https://www.dailymail.co.uk/news/article-431316/New- curriculum-make-lesson-politically-correct.html

9   Douglas Carswell cited in Laura Clark, 'New curriculum will 'make every lesson politically correct", *The Daily Mail* 25 January 2007: https://www.dailymail.co.uk/ news/article-431316/New-curriculum-make-lesson-politically-correct.html

10   Nicole Krauss, *The History of Love* (Penguin Books, Great Britain: 2006), p. 11.

11   Sarah Champion, 'British Pakistani men ARE raping and exploiting white girls …
     and it's time we faced up to it', *The Sun* 10 August 2017: https://www.thesun.co.uk/
     news/4218648/british-pakistani-men-raping-exploiting-white-girls/

12   Roger Scruton, 'Why did british police ignore pakistani gangs abusing 1,400
     rotherham children? "political correctness"', *Forbes* 30 August 2014: https://www.
     forbes.com/sites/rogerscruton/2014/08/30/why-did-british-police-ignore-pakistani-
     gangs-raping-rotherham-children-political-correctness/?sh=38394703754a

13   Ibid.

14   Ibid.

15   Ibid.

16   Vikram Dodd, 'Is child grooming and sexual abuse a race issue?', *The Guardian*
     14 May 2013: https://www.theguardian.com/uk/2013/may/14/child-grooming-sexual-
     abuse-race

17   Donald Trump cited in Julie Carrie Wong, 'Trump referred to immigrant "invasion"
     in 2,000 Facebook ads', *The Guardian* 5 August 2019: https://www.theguardian.com/
     us-news/2019/aug/05/trump-internet-facebook-ads-racism-immigrant-invasion

18   Christopher Hitchens, 'Martin Amis is no racist', *The Guardian* 21 November 2007:
     https://www.theguardian.com/uk/2007/nov/21/race.religion

19   Vikram Dodd, 'Is child grooming and sexual abuse a race issue?', *The Guardian*
     14 May 2013: https://www.theguardian.com/uk/2013/may/14/child-grooming-sexual-
     abuse-race

20   'What do we know about the ethnicity of people involved in sexual offences against
     children?' *Full Fact* 6 September 2017: https://fullfact.org/crime/what-do-we-know-
     about-ethnicity-people-involved-sexual-offences-against-children/

21   Jamie Grierson, 'Most child sexual abuse gangs made up of white men, Home
     Office report says', *The Guardian* 15 December 2020: https://www.theguardian.com/
     politics/2020/dec/15/child-sexual-abuse-gangs-white-men-home-office-report

22   Roger Scruton, 'Why did british police ignore pakistani gangs abusing 1,400
     rotherham children? political correctness', *Forbes* 30 August 2014: https://www.forbes.
     com/sites/rogerscruton/2014/08/30/why-did-british-police-ignore-pakistani-gangs-
     raping-rotherham-children-political-correctness/?sh=38394703754a

23   Cited in Andrew Norfolk, 'Rotherham police chief: we ignored sex abuse of children',
     The Times 18 January 2020: https://www.thetimes.co.uk/article/police-chief-we-
     ignored-sex-abuse-of-children-hgrhc358v

24   Theresa May cited in Mark Tran, 'May blames "institutionalised "political
     correctness"" for Rotherham scandal', *The Guardian* 2 September 2014: https://
     www.theguardian.com/uk-news/2014/sep/02/theresa-may-political-correctness-
     rotherham-abuse

25 Lizzie Dearden 'Only 1.7% of reported rapes prosecuted in England and Wales, new figures show', *The Independent* 17 September 2019: https://www.independent.co.uk/news/uk/crime/rape-prosecution-england-wales-victims-court-cps-police-a8885961.html

26 South Yorkshire Crime Commissioner cited in Martin Evans, '"Police treated Rotherham sex abuse victims as prostitutes", crime commissioner admits', *The Telegraph* 5 May 2015: https://www.telegraph.co.uk/news/uknews/crime/11583147/Police-treated-Rotherham-sex-abuse-victims-as-prostitutes-crime-commissioner-admits.html

27 Cited in Diane Abbot, 'Class and misogyny – not "political correctness" – explain Rotherham's abuse scandal', *The Spectator* 6 September 2014: https://www.spectator.co.uk/article/class-and-misogyny-not-political-correctness-explain-rotherham-s-abuse-scandal

28 Cited in Suzanne Moore, 'Poor children are seen as worthless, as Rotherham's abuse scandal shows', *The Guardian* 27 August 2014: https://www.theguardian.com/commentisfree/2014/aug/27/poor-children-seen-as-worthless-rotherham-abuse-scandal

29 Cited in Olivia Goodhill, 'A Rotherham abuse survivor speaks out', *The Telegraph* 7 June 2015: https://s.telegraph.co.uk/graphics/projects/rotherham/index.html

30 Professor Alexis Jay cited in 'Rotherham child sexual exploitation report: At a glance', *BBC News* 26 Agust 2015: https://www.bbc.co.uk/news/uk-28942986

31 Lizzie Dearden, 'Third of British people wrongly believe there are Muslim "no-go areas" in UK governed by sharia law', *The Independent* 17 October 2018: https://www.independent.co.uk/news/uk/home-news/uk-no-go-zones-muslim-sharia-law-third-poll-hope-not-hate-far-right-economic-inequality-a8588226.html

32 Sue Reid, 'As Islamic extremists declare Britain's first Sharia law zone, the worrying social and moral implications', *The Daily Mail* 29 July 2011: https://www.dailymail.co.uk/news/article-2020382/You-entering-Sharia-law-Britain-As-Islamic-extremists-declare-Sharia-law-zone-London-suburb-worrying-social-moral-implications.html

33 Melanie Phillips, 'Another no-go area in Londonistan', *The Daily Mail* 31 October 2011: https://phillipsblog.dailymail.co.uk/2011/10/another-no-go-area-in-londonistan.html

34 Dan Kaszeta, 'Debunking maps of alleged "Islamic No Go Zones" in London', *bellingcat* 9 November 2018: https://www.bellingcat.com/news/uk-and-europe/2018/11/09/debunking-maps-alleged-islamic-no-go-zones-london-2/

35 Cited in 'Fox news in ofcom breach for birmingham "Muslim only" claim' *BBC News* 21 September 2015: https://www.bbc.co.uk/news/uk-england-birmingham-34317107

36 Hamed Chapman, 'Record 18 Muslim MPs elected, majority women', *The Muslim News* 27 December 2019: http://muslimnews.co.uk/newspaper/top-stories/record-18-muslim-mps-elected-majority-women/

37	Rayhan Uddin, 'Widespread experiences and perceptions of Islamophobia in UK Labour, report reveals', *Middle-Eastern Eye* 14 November 2020: https://www.middleeasteye.net/news/labour-party-islamophobia-report-reveals:

38	Joe Evans, 'Keir Starmer hit by "exodus" of Labour members led by Jeremy Corbyn supporters', *The Week* 23 November 2020: https://www.theweek.co.uk/108737/labour-sees-exodus-in-protest-keir-starmer-jeremy-corbyn-suspension

39	'Muslim population in the UK', *Office for National Statistics* 2 August 2018: https://www.ons.gov.uk/aboutus/transparencyandgovernance/freedomofinformationfoi/muslimpopulationintheuk/

40	Alina Khan, 'UK: "One in four" Muslims experience Islamophobia in Labour Party', *Al Jazeera* 14 November 2020: https://www.aljazeera.com/news/2020/11/14/hold-one-in-four-muslims-experience-islamophobia-in-labour-party

41	Adam Rasmi, 'Fewer than 160,000 people will select the next UK prime minister. Who are they?', *Quartz* 19 June 2019: https://qz.com/1644202/who-are-the-160000-conservatives-picking-the-next-uk-prime-minister/

42	Rachel Wearmouth, 'Baroness Warsi: I Cannot Encourage Young Muslims To Join "Islamophobic" Tory Party', *The Huffington Post* 3 June 2019: https://www.huffingtonpost.co.uk/entry/baroness-warsi-i-cannot-tell-young-muslims-to-join-islamophobic-tory-party_uk_5c7ea8f7e4b020b54d7f408e?guccounter=1&guce_referrer=aHR0cHM6Ly93d3cuZ29vZ2xlLmNvbS8&guce_referrer_sig=AQAAAHvNCnPTibU47pAfl_EaSwDg-Ib6WYjg-VHcBHqKIH71W80-bLQHcJnqWGsSwVId3vX654CxIA5-ZOdvrStsGfQTkydg94AzdIBKCp4Qr9EGMvySfPydqbSiM5OD0CH6yLHbCeOLYYu2mgyCFVZomK53zBUJRd_y6qCx541GgZDs

43	'The deep roots of Islamophobia in the conservative party', *Hope Not Hate* 30 September 2020: https://www.hopenothate.org.uk/2020/09/30/the-deep-roots-of-islamophobia-in-the-conservative-party/

44	Press Release, 'MCB submits new dossier of Conservative Islamophobia to EHRC, with evidence of over 300 individuals', *The Muslim Council of Great Britain* 5 March 2020: https://mcb.org.uk/press-releases/mcb-submits-new-dossier-of-conservative-islamophobia-to-ehrc-with-evidence-of-over-300-individuals/

45	Lizzie Dearden, 'Islamophobic incidents rose 375% after Boris Johnson compared Muslim women to "letterboxes", figures show', *The Independent* 2 September 2019: https://www.independent.co.uk/news/uk/home-news/boris-johnson-muslim-women-letterboxes-burqa-islamphobia-rise-a9088476.html

46	Cited in Paul Revoir, 'Yes, we are biased on religion and politics, admit BBC executives', *The Daily Mail* 22 October 2006: https://www.dailymail.co.uk/news/article-411977/Yes-biased-religion-politics-admit-BBC-executives.html

47	Richard Littlejohn, 'We're all going to hell in a hijab', *The Daily Mail* 12 April 2016: https://www.dailymail.co.uk/debate/article-3534997/We-going-hell-hijab-RICHARD-LITTLEJOHN-says-time-head-sand-politicians-heed-Trevor-Phillips-s-comments-Muslim-attitudes.html

48 John Cleese and Bill Maher cited in Annabel Grossman, 'John Cleese says you can't make jokes about Muslims – because "they'll kill you"', *The Daily Mail* 27 November 2014: https://www.dailymail.co.uk/news/article-2851888/John-Cleese-blasts-political-correctness-protecting-select-groups-ridicule.html

49 Allison Little, 'Europe tells Britain: Don't say "Muslims"', *The Daily Express* 5 July 2007: https://www.express.co.uk/news/uk/12236/Europe-tells-Britain-Don-t-say-Muslims

50 Amy Watson, 'Leading newspapers ranked by print and digital reach in the United Kingdom 2019–2020', *Statista* 3 February 2021: https://www.statista.com/statistics/246077/reach-of-selected-national-newspapers-in-the-uk/

51 Ibid.

52 Jim Waterson, 'Most UK news coverage of Muslims is negative, major study finds', *The Guardian* 9 July 2019: Most UK news coverage of Muslims is negative, major study finds.

53 Ibid.

54 Jennifer Philippa Eggert, 'The "Real Housewives of ISIS" sketch: When funny is harmful', *LSE Blog* 16 January 2017: https://blogs.lse.ac.uk/gender/2017/01/16/the-real-housewives-of-isis-sketch-when-funny-is-harmful/

55 Nigel Farage cited in Harriet Alexander, 'Nigel Farage says London blighted by "wholly Muslim areas" as he defends Donald Trump's response to the attack', *The Telegraph* 4 June 2017: https://www.telegraph.co.uk/news/2017/06/04/nigel-farage-says-london-blighted-wholly-muslim-areas-defends/

56 Ken Clarke cited in 'Ken Clarke calls for full Veil Ban in courts', *Sky News* 3 November 2013: https://news.sky.com/story/ken-clarke-calls-for-full-veil-ban-in-courts-10429472

57 'Calls for inquiry as figures show 27% of London's prisoners are Muslim', *Evening Standard* 28 March 2014: https://www.standard.co.uk/news/uk/calls-for-inquiry-as-figures-show-27-of-london-s-prisoners-are-muslim-9221167.html

58 Suhaiymah Manzoor-Khan, 'Let me take a wild guess as to why Muslims are overrepresented in prison', *The Independent* 9 September 2017: https://www.independent.co.uk/voices/lammy-review-prisons-bame-islamophobia-rehabilitation-discrimination-a7937746.html

59 Dan Sabbagh, Detention of Muslims at UK ports and airports 'structural Islamophobia', *The Guardian* 20 August 2019: https://www.theguardian.com/news/2019/aug/20/detention-of-muslims-at-uk-ports-and-airports-structural-islamophobia

60 Julien Hargreaves 'Police stop and search within British muslim communities: Evidence from the crime survey 2006–11', *The British Journal of Criminology*, 58(6) (November 2018), 1281–302: https://doi.org/10.1093/bjc/azy013

61 'Terrorism 2002/2005', U.S. Department of Justice-Federal Bureau of Investigation: https://www.fbi.gov/stats-services/publications/terrorism-2002-2005

62	Robert O'Harrow Jr., Andrew Ba Tran and Derek Hawkins, 'The rise of domestic extremism in America', *The Washington Post* 12 April 2021: https://www.washingtonpost.com/investigations/interactive/2021/domestic-terrorism-data/

63	Ibid.

64	Mona Chalabi, 'Terror attacks by Muslims receive 357% more press attention, study finds', *The Guardian* 20 July 2018: https://www.theguardian.com/us-news/2018/jul/20/muslim-terror-attacks-press-coverage-study

65	Annalisa Merelli, '"Lone wolf" vs "terrorist": the vocabulary of mass shootings', *Quartz* 2 October 2017: https://qz.com/1092042/las-vegas-shooting-terrorist-vs-lone-wolf/

66	*The New York Times* cited in Annalisa Merelli, '"Lone wolf" vs "terrorist": the vocabulary of mass shootings', *Quartz* 2 October 2017: https://qz.com/1092042/las-vegas-shooting-terrorist-vs-lone-wolf/

67	Clark County sheriff Joe Lombardo cited in Annalisa Merelli, '"Lone wolf" vs "terrorist": the vocabulary of mass shootings', *Quartz* 2 October 2017: https://qz.com/1092042/las-vegas-shooting-terrorist-vs-lone-wolf/

68	Rudy Giuliani cited in Daily Mail reporter, 'Giuliani says "culture of political correctness" is preventing government from stopping home-grown terrorism like Boston bombings', *The Daily Mail* 11 July 2013: https://www.dailymail.co.uk/news/article-2360037/Giuliani-says-culture-political-correctness-preventing-government-stopping-home-grown-terrorism-like-Boston-bombings.html

69	Sir Francis Galton, *Inquiries into Human Faculty and Its Development* (Macmillan, London: 1883), p. 24.

70	Even within the context of the poem itself, however, you feel that the author isn't completely blind to the particular type of hogwash he is endeavouring to sell; Kipling lets slip an acknowledgment of the fact that the 'white man's burden' is slightly more militaristic and less benign than one would hope with the rather slippery and Orwellian phrase 'Take up the White Man's burden – *The Savage Wars of Peace*'.

71	John R. Bradley, 'The terrifying truth behind the so-called Arab Spring', *The Daily Mail* 20 December 2011: https://www.dailymail.co.uk/news/article-2076355/Arab-Spring-The-terrifying-truth-revolution.html

72	Andrew Alexander, 'Democracy is not the same as freedom', *The Daily Mail* 2 March 2011: https://www.dailymail.co.uk/debate/article-1362032/Middle-East-protests-Democracy-freedom-David-Cameron.html

73	Andrew Green, 'Why Western democracy can never work in the Middle East', *The Telegraph* 16 August 2014: https://www.telegraph.co.uk/news/worldnews/middleeast/11037173/Why-Western-democracy-can-never-work-in-the-Middle-East.html

74 'Ten years on: The financial crisis in numbers', *This Week* 7 August 2017: https://www. theweek.co.uk/87574/ten-years-on-the-financial-crisis-in-numbers

75 Owen Jones, 'It's socialism for the rich and capitalism for the rest of us in Britain', *The Guardian* 29 August 2014: https://www.theguardian.com/books/2014/aug/29/ socialism-for-the-rich

76 Owen Jones, 'Benefits Street: A healthy media would stand up to the powerful and wealthy. Ours targets the poor and voiceless', *The Independent* 8 January 2014: https:// www.independent.co.uk/voices/comment/benefits-street-healthy-media-would-stand-powerful-and-wealthy-ours-targets-poor-and-voiceless-9046773.html

77 Tony McKenna, 'The Jeremy Kyle Factor', *Counterpunch* 28 May 2019: https://www. counterpunch.org/2019/05/28/the-jeremy-kyle-factor/

78 Sue Reid, 'The truth about polygamy: A special investigation into how Muslim men can exploit the benefits system', *The Daily Mail* 24 September 2011: https://www. dailymail.co.uk/news/article-2041244/Polygamy-Investigation-Muslim-men-exploit-UK-benefits-system.html

79 Lucy Mae Beers, 'No veiled threat: Millionaire Muslim fraud to be EVICTED from housing commission flat she lived in for 15 years – despite buying two homes with her husband's million-dollar business', *The Daily Mail* 23 February 2017: https:// www.dailymail.co.uk/news/article-4251416/Muslim-frauds-EVICTED-housing-commission-flat.html

Chapter 2

1 Cited in Amelia Gentleman and Holly Watt, '"It was like tending to a disgusting baby": life as a Harvey Weinstein employee', *The Guardian* 29 September 2019: https:// www.theguardian.com/film/2018/sep/29/harvey-weinstein-three-former-employees-on-working-for-him

2 Ibid.

3 Ibid.

4 Ibid.

5 Rebecca Traister cited in Gabrielle Bruney, 'Hulu's untouchable illustrates just how Harvey Weinstein operated in plain sight', *Esquire* 3 September 2019: https://www. esquire.com/entertainment/a28892646/hulu-untouchable-harvey-weinstein/

6 Amelia Gentleman and Holly Watt, '"It was like tending to a disgusting baby": life as a Harvey Weinstein employee', *The Guardian* 29 September 2019: https://www. theguardian.com/film/2018/sep/29/harvey-weinstein-three-former-employees-on-working-for-him

7   Jennifer Aniston cited in Melissa Mitas, 'What Jennifer Aniston says about her interactions with Harvey Weinstein', *Showbiz Cheat Sheet* 12 October 2019: https://www.cheatsheet.com/entertainment/what-jennifer-aniston-says-about-her-interactions-with-harvey-weinstein.html/

8   Katherine Kendell cited in Mark Townsend, 'Weinstein accuser says she was scared to go public with harassment claim', *The Guardian* 21 October 2017: https://www.theguardian.com/film/2017/oct/21/harvey-weinstein-katherine-kendall-accusations-swingers-actress

9   Cited in Lauren Aratani, 'Harvey Weinstein bewildered as women he abused have their say', *The Guardian* 11 March 2020: https://www.theguardian.com/world/2020/mar/11/harvey-weinstein-bewildered-as-women-he-abused-have-their-say

10   Jim Ransom, 'Harvey Weinstein's stunning downfall: 23 years in Prison', *The New York Times* 11 March 2020: https://www.nytimes.com/2020/03/11/nyregion/harvey-weinstein-sentencing.html

11   Katherine Kendell cited in Anna North, 'How Harvey Weinstein's first accusers paved the way for more', *Vox* 12 October 2017: https://www.vox.com/identities/2017/10/12/16459000/harvey-weinsteins-assault-accusers

12   Tarana Burke cited in Leah Fessler, 'Tarana Burke, creator of Me Too, believes you don't have to sacrifice everything for a cause', *Quartz at Work* 6 February 2018: https://qz.com/work/1193569/me-too-movement-creator-tarana-burke-says-you-dont-have-to-sacrifice-everything-for-a-cause/

13   Mary Pflum, 'A year ago, Alyssa Milano started a conversation about #MeToo. These women replied', *NBC News* 15 October 2018: https://www.nbcnews.com/news/us-news/year-ago-alyssa-milano-started-conversation-about-metoo-these-women-n920246

14   Amanda Yennie cited in Mary Pflum, 'A year ago, Alyssa Milano started a conversation about #MeToo. These women replied', *NBC News* 15 October 2018: https://www.nbcnews.com/news/us-news/year-ago-alyssa-milano-started-conversation-about-metoo-these-women-n920246

15   Nora Yolles Young cited in Mary Pflum, 'A year ago, Alyssa Milano started a conversation about #MeToo. These women replied', *NBC News* 15 October 2018: https://www.nbcnews.com/news/us-news/year-ago-alyssa-milano-started-conversation-about-metoo-these-women-n920246

16   Cassandra Santiago and Doug Criss, 'An activist, a little girl and the heartbreaking origin of "Me too"', *CNN* 17 October 2017: https://edition.cnn.com/2017/10/17/us/me-too-tarana-burke-origin-trnd/index.html

17   Moira Donegan, 'How #MeToo revealed the central rift within feminism today', *The Guardian* 11 May 2018: https://www.theguardian.com/news/2018/may/11/how-metoo-revealed-the-central-rift-within-feminism-social-individualist

18 M.C. Garibotti and C.M. Hopp, 'Substitution activism: The impact of #MeToo in argentina', in B. Fileborn and R. Loney-Howes (eds), *#MeToo and the Politics of Social Charge* (Palgrave Macmillan, Cham: 2019). https://doi.org/10.1007/978-3-030-15213-0_12

19 Devex Editor, 'What #MeToo has meant around the world', *Devex* 26 November 2018: https://www.devex.com/news/what-metoo-has-meant-around-the-world-93871

20 Brendan O'Niell, 'The forgotten victims of #MeToo', *Spiked* 20 February 2018: https://www.spiked-online.com/2018/02/20/the-forgotten-victims-of-metoo/

21 Joanna Williams, 'Telford girls: the wrong kind of victims', *Spiked* 13 March 2018: https://www.spiked-online.com/2018/03/13/telford-girls-the-wrong-kind-of-victims/

22 Alianza Nacional de Campesinas, 'The sexist reality we know far too well', *Socialist Worker* 17 November 2017: https://socialistworker.org/2017/11/14/the-sexist-reality-we-know-far-too-well

23 Epstein Becker Green, 'California enacts numerous changes to sexual harassment and other laws affecting the workplace', *JD Supra* 18 October 2018: https://www.jdsupra.com/legalnews/california-enacts-numerous-changes-to-39823/

24 Jan Ransom, 'Harvey Weinstein's stunning downfall: 23 years in prison', *The New York Times* 11 March 2020: https://www.nytimes.com/2020/03/11/nyregion/harvey-weinstein-sentencing.html

25 Hadley Freeman, 'What does Hollywood's reverence for child rapist Roman Polanski tell us?', *The Guardian* 30 January 2018: https://www.theguardian.com/film/2018/jan/30/hollywood-reverence-child-rapist-roman-polanski-convicted-40-years-on-run

26 Harvey Weinstein, 'Polanski has served his time and must be freed', *The Independent* 13 November 2017: https://www.independent.co.uk/voices/commentators/harvey-weinstein-polanski-has-served-his-time-and-must-be-freed-1794699.html

27 Luke Morgan Britton, 'Kate Winslet criticised after defending working with Woody Allen and Roman Polanski', *NME* 8 September 2017: https://www.nme.com/news/kate-winslet-woody-allen-roman-polanski-2135644

28 Kate Winslet cited in Matt Fernandez, 'Kate Winslet admits she has 'Bitter Regrets' over working with certain 'Men of Power', *Variety* 29 January 2018: https://variety.com/2018/film/news/kate-winslet-regret-woody-allen-roman-polanski-1202680173/

29 Isabelle Hupert cited in 'Isabelle Huppert réagit au cas Polanski: 'Le lynchage est une forme de pornographie', *Gala* 2 March 2020.

30 Woody Allen cited in Kyle Swenson, 'Woody Allen, of course, warns of "witch hunt atmosphere" following Harvey Weinstein scandal', *The Washington Post* 16 October 2017: https://www.washingtonpost.com/news/morning-mix/wp/2017/10/16/woody-allen-of-course-warns-of-witch-hunt-atmosphere-following-harvey-weinstein-scandal/

31 Terry Gillingham cited in Edward Helmore, 'Terry Gilliam faces backlash after labeling #MeToo a "witch-hunt"', *The Guardian* 4 January 2020: https://www.theguardian.com/film/2020/jan/04/terry-gilliam-metoo-witch-hunt-backlash

32 Ibid.

33 Ibid.

34 Ibid.

35 Cathy Young, 'Is "Weinsteining" getting out of hand', *The LA Times* 1 November 2017: https://www.latimes.com/opinion/op-ed/la-oe-young-weinsteining-goes-too-far-20171101-story.html

36 Claire Berlinski, 'We're on a sexual warlock hunt', *USA Today* 7 December 2017: https://www.google.com/search?q=%2C+%E2%80%9CWe%E2%80%99re+on+a+Sexual+Harassment+Warlock+Hunt.%E2%80%9D&oq=%2C+%E2%80%9CWe%E2%80%99re+on+a+Sexual+Harassment+Warlock+Hunt.%E2%80%9D&aqs=chrome..69i57.424j0j7&sourceid=chrome&ie=UTF-8

37 Henry Olsen, 'McCarthyism is back, but this time it's woke', *The Washington Post* 15 July 2020: https://www.washingtonpost.com/opinions/2020/07/15/mccarthyism-is-back-this-time-its-woke/?fbclid=IwAR0FEt5JfHHjiwuGMRvLaMxK719nuw7kUb8HWHteBgQ4zglOdlGbrHN_57s

38 Jane Merrick, 'The Michael Le Vell verdict is in, but all the lessons are still to learn', *The Independent* 13 September 2013.

39 'Violence against women: an EU-wide survey. Main results report' European Union Agency for Human Rights 3 March 2014: https://fra.europa.eu/en/publication/2014/violence-against-women-eu-wide-survey-main-results-report

40 Lisa Lazard, 'Here's the truth about false accusations of sexual violence', *The Conversation* 24 November 2017: https://theconversation.com/heres-the-truth-about-false-accusations-of-sexual-violence-88049

41 Alexandra Topping and Caelainn Barr, 'Rape convictions fall to record low in England and Wales', *The Guardian* 30 July 2020: https://www.theguardian.com/society/2020/jul/30/convictions-fall-record-low-england-wales-prosecutions

42 Cited in Liv Moloney, 'Is rape the perfect crime?', *Sky News*: https://news.sky.com/story/99-of-rapes-reported-to-police-in-england-and-wales-do-not-result-in-legal-proceedings-why-12104130

43 Ibid.

44 Andrew Van Dam, 'Less than 1% of rapes lead to felony convictions. At least 89% of victims face emotional and physical consequences', *The Washington Post* 6 October 2018: http://newsdiffs.org/diff/1887376/1887394/https%3A/www.washingtonpost.com/business/wonkblog/less-than-1-percent-of-rapes-lead-to-felony-convictions-at-least-89-percent-of-victims-face-emotional-and-physical-consequences/2018/10/06/cf9e6559-8f1d-492f-8454-ebd3376e578b_story.html

45   Bill Sorem, 'Most sexual assaults go unreported, unsolved, unpunished', *The Uptake* 14 September 2018: https://theuptake.org/2018/09/14/most-sexual-assaults-go-unreported-unsolved-unpunished/

46   Maureen Mullarkey, 'Why criminalizing sexual harassment fosters witch hunts', *The Federalist* 15 December 2017: https://thefederalist.com/2017/12/15/criminalizing-sexual; Owen Bocott, 'Police in England and Wales dropping rape inquiries when victims refuse to hand in phones', *The Guardian* 29 April 2019: https://www.theguardian.com/society/2019/apr/29/why-might-rape-victims-refuse-to-give-phones-to-police-harassment-fosters-witch-hunts/

47   Owen Bocott, 'Police in England and Wales dropping rape inquiries when victims refuse to hand in phones', *The Guardian* 29 April 2019: https://www.theguardian.com/society/2019/apr/29/why-might-rape-victims-refuse-to-give-phones-to-police

48   Steven Morris and Alexandra Topping, 'Ched Evans: footballer found not guilty of rape in retrial', *The Guardian* 14 October 2016: https://www.theguardian.com/football/2016/oct/14/footballer-ched-evans-cleared-of-in-retrial

49   Moira Donegan, '"Who will protect you from rape without police?" Here's my answer to that question', *The Guardian* 17 June 2020: https://www.theguardian.com/commentisfree/2020/jun/17/abolish-police-sexual-assault-violence

50   Fiona Leverick, 'What do we know about rape myths and juror decision making?', *The International Journal of Evidence & Proof* (Sage, volume: 24 issue: 3, page(s): 255–79): https://journals.sagepub.com/doi/full/10.1177/1365712720923157

51   Ibid.

52   Alissa J. Rubin, '"Revolt" in France against sexual harassment hits cultural resistance"', *The New York Times* 19 November 2017: https://www.nytimes.com/2017/11/19/world/europe/france-sexual-harassment.html

53   Ibid.

54   Alexandra Topping, 'Almost all young women in the UK have been sexually harassed, survey finds', *The Guardian* 10 March 2021: https://www.theguardian.com/world/2021/mar/10/almost-all-young-women-in-the-uk-have-been-sexually-harassed-survey-finds

55   Elizabeth Schulte, 'The year of #MeToo', *International Socialist Review* Issue 108, 1 March 2018: https://isreview.org/issue/108/year-metoo

56   Cited ibid.

57   Caroline Criado-Perez cited in Alexandra Topping, 'Jane Austen Twitter row: two plead guilty to abusive tweets', *The Guardian* 7 January 2014: https://www.theguardian.com/society/2014/jan/07/jane-austen-banknote-abusive-tweets-criado-perez

58   Isabella Sorley cited in Alexandra Topping, 'Jane Austen Twitter row: two plead guilty to abusive tweets', *The Guardian* 7 January 2014: https://www.theguardian.com/society/2014/jan/07/jane-austen-banknote-abusive-tweets-criado-perez

59	Zoe Williams, 'Laura Bates on the men who hate women: "They canonise and revere and idolise murderers"', *The Guardian* 27 August 2020: https://www.theguardian.com/lifeandstyle/2020/aug/27/laura-bates-on-the-men-who-hate-women-idolise-murderers

60	Ibid.

61	Laura Bates cited in Zoe Williams, 'Laura Bates on the men who hate women: "They canonise and revere and idolise murderers"', *The Guardian* 27 August 2020: https://www.theguardian.com/lifeandstyle/2020/aug/27/laura-bates-on-the-men-who-hate-women-idolise-murderers

62	Caroline Criado Perez cited in Zoe Williams, 'Feminazi: the go-to term for trolls out to silence women', *The Guardian* 15 September 2015: https://www.theguardian.com/world/2015/sep/15/feminazi-go-to-term-for-trolls-out-to-silence-women-charlotte-proudman

63	Elizabeth Schulte, 'The year of #MeToo', *International Socialist Review* Issue 108, 1 March 2018: https://isreview.org/issue/108/year-metoo

Chapter 3

1	Reality Check Team, 'George Floyd: How are African-Americans treated under the law?', *BBC News* 21 April 2021: https://www.bbc.co.uk/news/world-us-canada-52877678

2	And this, by the way, isn't an exclusively 'white' instinct. People of colour too are often acculturated in the same direction, the cashier who alerted the police to George Floyd was a young man of colour.

3	Appian, *Roman History: The Civil Wars IV*. trans. Horace White (Harvard University Press, Cambridge: 1913), p. 134.

4	Vitruvius: The Ten Books on Architecture. Vitruvius. Morris Hicky Morgan. Cambridge: Harvard University Press. London: Humphrey Milford. Oxford University Press. 1914: http://www.perseus.tufts.edu/hopper/text?doc=urn:cts:latinLit:phi1056.phi001.perseus-eng1:6.1.1

5	Alexander Koch, Chris Brierly, Mark Maslin, and Simon Lewis, 'European colonization of the Americas killed 10 percent of world population and caused global cooling', *The Conversation* 21 January 2019: https://www.pri.org/stories/2019-01-31/european-colonization-americas-killed-10-percent-world-population-and-caused

6	Walter Rodney, *How Europe Underdeveloped Africa* (Verso, London: 2018), p. 110.

7	Ibid., p. 108.

8   Ibid., p. 108.

9   Bartolomé de Las Casas, *Historia Apologetica*, cited in Wagner & Parish (1967), pp. 203–4.

10 William Petty cited in Loren Goldner, 'Race and the enlightenment', *Race Traitor* August 1997: https://thecharnelhouse.org/2017/03/19/race-and-the-enlightenment/

11 C.L.R. James, *The Black Jacobins* (Penguin Books, London: 2001), p. 6.

12 Ibid., p. 7.

13 'Slave ships and the middle passage', *The Encyclopedia Virginia*, Virginia Humanities: https://encyclopediavirginia.org/entries/slave-ships-and-the-middle-passage/#:~:text=Background,-Tobacco%20Wrapper&text=Between%201500%20and%201866%2C%20Europeans,bodies%20thrown%20into%20the%20Atlantic.

14 David Olusoga, 'The toppling of Edward Colston's statue is not an attack on history. It is history', *The Guardian* 8 June 2020: https://www.theguardian.com/commentisfree/2020/jun/08/edward-colston-statue-history-slave-trader-bristol-protest

15 C.L.R. James, *The Black Jacobins* (Penguin Books, London: 2001), pp. 8–9.

16 Ibid., pp. 8–9.

17 Ibid., p. 10.

18 Historian and Anthropologist Guy E. Cameron, cited in Gillian Brockewell, 'Before 1619, there was 1526: The mystery of the first enslaved Africans in what became the United States', *The Washington Post* 7 September 2019: https://www.washingtonpost.com/history/2019/09/07/before-there-was-mystery-first-enslaved-africans-what-became-us/

19 Kenneth M. Bilby, *True-Born Maroons* (University Press of Florida, Gainesville: 2005), pp. 150–6.

20 C.L.R. James, *The Black Jacobins* (Penguin Books, London: 2001), p. xviii.

21 David F. Allmendinger Jr, *Nat Turner and the Rising in Southampton County* (Johns Hopkins University Press, Baltimore: 2014), pp. 21–2.

22 'Douglass Monthly' V (August 1863), p. 852.

23 Steven Hahn, 'The largest, most successful slave revolt in history?', *Slate* 13 October 2015: https://slate.com/human-interest/2015/10/why-historians-are-reluctant-to-call-the-american-civil-war-a-slave-rebellion.html

24 Ibid.

25 Eric Foner, 'Reconstruction' Encyclopaedia Britannica: https://www.britannica.com/event/Reconstruction-United-States-history/The-end-of-Reconstruction

26   There is a particularly vicious irony here in as much as the vast majority of rapes, historically speaking, were committed by white male slave owners against female Black slaves.

27   Richard Nixon cited in 'War on Drugs', *History* 17 December 2019: https://www.history.com/topics/crime/the-war-on-drugs

28   John Ehrlichman cited in Tom LoBianco, 'Report: Aide says Nixon's war on drugs targeted Blacks, hippies', *CNN* 24 March 2016: https://edition.cnn.com/2016/03/23/politics/john-ehrlichman-richard-nixon-drug-war-Blacks-hippie/index.html

29   James Cullen, 'The history of mass incarceration', *Brennan Centre for Justice* 20 July 2018: https://www.brennancenter.org/our-work/analysis-opinion/history-mass-incarceration

30   Hillary Clinton cited in Allison Graves, 'Did Hillary Clinton call African-American youth "superpredators?"', *PolitiFact* 28 August 2016: https://www.politifact.com/factchecks/2016/aug/28/reince-priebus/did-hillary-clinton-call-african-american-youth-su/

31   Thomas Frank, 'Bill Clinton's crime bill destroyed lives, and there's no point denying it', *The Guardian* 15 April 2016: https://www.theguardian.com/commentisfree/2016/apr/15/bill-clinton-crime-bill-hillary-Black-lives-thomas-frank

32   Ed Pilkington, 'Bill Clinton: mass incarceration on my watch "put too many people in prison"', *The Guardian* 28 April 2015: https://www.theguardian.com/us-news/2015/apr/28/bill-clinton-calls-for-end-mass-incarceration

33   Lauren-Brooke Eisen and Inimai Chettiar, '39% of prisoners should not be in prison', *Time Magazine* 9 December 2016: https://time.com/4596081/incarceration-report/

34   Nina Totenberg, 'High court rules Calif. must cut prison population', *N.P.R* 23 May 2011: https://www.npr.org/2011/05/23/136579580/california-is-ordered-to-cut-its-prison-population?t=1621508180660

35   German Lopez, 'Kamala Harris's controversial record on criminal justice, explained', *Vox* 12 August 2020: https://www.vox.com/future-perfect/2019/1/23/18184192/kamala-harris-president-campaign-criminal-justice-record

36   D.L. Davis, 'American Family CEO makes a point about Black male enslavement and today's incarceration,' *PolitiFact* 1 November 2019: https://www.politifact.com/factchecks/2019/nov/01/jack-salzwedel/american-family-ceo-makes-point-about-19th-century/

37   Stephen Miller, 'Black workers still earn less than their white counterparts', *S.H.R.M* 11 June 2020: https://www.shrm.org/resourcesandtools/hr-topics/compensation/pages/racial-wage-gaps-persistence-poses-challenge.aspx

38   John Eligon, 'Michael Brown spent last weeks grappling with problems and promise', *The New York Times* 24 August 2014: https://www.nytimes.com/2014/08/25/us/michael-brown-spent-last-weeks-grappling-with-lifes-mysteries.html?hp&action=

click&pgtype=Homepage&version=HpSumSmallMedia&module=second-column-region*ion=top-news&WT.nav=top-news&_r=0

39   Mike Pence cited in Nikki Carvajal, 'Asked repeatedly to say "Black Lives Matter,"
     Mike Pence says "all lives matter"', *CNN* 19 June 2020: https://edition.cnn.
     com/2020/06/19/politics/mike-pence-Black-lives-matter-all-lives-matter/index.html

40   Sarah A. Downey, 'This politically-correct witch-hunt is killing free speech, and we
     have to fight it', *Medium* June 2020: https://sarahadowney.medium.com/this-politically-
     correct-witch-hunt-is-killing-free-speech-and-we-have-to-fight-it-7ced038d33ae

41   Ibid.

42   Ibid.

43   Phillip Hammond, 'This is McCarthyism in BLM clothing', *Spiked* 30 June 2020:
     https://www.spiked-online.com/2020/06/30/this-is-mccarthyism-in-blm-clothing/

44   Evgeny Lebedev, 'I left the USSR in the 1980s. I've seen the perils of whitewashing
     history – even when it's ugly', *The Independent* 15 June 2020: https://www.
     independent.co.uk/voices/stalin-ussr-blm-uk-protests-winston-churchill-
     statue-a9565351.html

45   Justin Neufeld cited in Andrew Weichel, 'BC Liberal volunteer fired for comparing
     Black Lives Matter protesters to Nazis', *CTV News* 9 June 2020: BC Liberal volunteer
     fired for comparing Black Lives Matter protesters to Nazis.

46   One might argue that Derek Chauvin, the cop who murdered George Floyd, was
     convicted because of the Black Lives Matter protests, and the spotlight they held on
     the case which got Chauvin fired and the case brought to court. But while I think that
     is certainly true, it also bears remembering that Chauvin was convicted because of the
     video footage which showed him murdering George Floyd, footage which the twelve jury
     members saw and were moved by such that they felt compelled to return a 'guilty' verdict.

47   Michael Sainato, '"They set us up": US police arrested over 10,000 protesters, many
     non-violent', *The Guardian* 8 June 2020: https://www.theguardian.com/us-news/2020/
     jun/08/george-floyd-killing-police-arrest-non-violent-protesters

48   Sam Levin and Maanvi Singh, 'America's protest crackdown: five months after George
     Floyd, hundreds face trials and prison', *The Guardian* 27 October 2020: https://www.
     theguardian.com/us-news/2020/oct/27/americas-protest-crackdown-five-months-
     after-george-floyd-hundreds-face-trials-and-prison

49   Tucker Carlson cited in Ed Mazza, 'Tucker Carlson stuns Twitter users with
     "Most Racist" thing he's ever said', *The Huffington Post* 9 June 2020: https://www.
     huffingtonpost.co.uk/entry/tucker-carlson-coming-for-you_n_5edf056ac5b6948cbc5
     c8d0f?ri18n=true

50   Sarah A. Downey, 'This politically-correct witch-hunt is killing free speech, and we
     have to fight it', *Medium* June 2020: https://sarahadowney.medium.com/this-politically-
     correct-witch-hunt-is-killing-free-speech-and-we-have-to-fight-it-7ced038d33ae

51   For a more detailed critique of 'Intersectionality' see Tony McKenna, 'The broken mirror: intersectionality and the loss of the universal', *Open Democracy* 12 August 2019: https://www.opendemocracy.net/en/can-europe-make-it/broken-mirror-intersectionality-and-loss-universal/

52   Dana R. Fisher, 'The diversity of the recent Black Lives Matter protests is a good sign for racial equity', *Brookings* 8 June 2020: https://www.brookings.edu/blog/how-we-rise/2020/07/08/the-diversity-of-the-recent-Black-lives-matter-protests-is-a-good-sign-for-racial-equity/

53   Kim Parker, Juliana Menasce Horowitz, and Monica Anderson, 'Amid protests, majorities across racial and ethnic groups express support for the Black Lives Matter movement', *Pew Research Centre* 12 June 2020: https://www.pewresearch.org/social-trends/2020/06/12/amid-protests-majorities-across-racial-and-ethnic-groups-express-support-for-the-Black-lives-matter-movement/

54   Piers Morgan cited in Holly Fleet, 'Piers Morgan slams TV bosses over 'stupid' Fawlty Towers decision: 'Getting ridiculous', *The Daily Express* 12 June 2020: https://www.express.co.uk/celebrity-news/1294900/Piers-Morgan-Fawlty-Towers-episode-germans-dont-mention-the-war-removed-Twitter-news

55   Tom Slater, 'Binning Fawlty Towers does nothing to solve racism', *The Spectator* 12 June 2020: https://www.spectator.co.uk/article/binning-fawlty-towers-does-nothing-to-solve-racism

56   Brendan O'Neill, 'Now even Fawlty Towers is being erased', *Spiked* 12 June 2020: https://www.spiked-online.com/2020/06/12/now-even-fawlty-towers-is-being-erased/

57   Dr Katie Donington cited in Laura Jane Turner, 'What's happened to Little Britain and Fawlty Towers is long overdue', *Digital Spy* 17 June 2020: https://www.digitalspy.com/tv/a32891803/little-britain-fawlty-towers-racist/

58   David Olusoga, 'The toppling of Edward Colston's statue is not an attack on history. It is history', *The Guardian* 8 June 2020: https://www.theguardian.com/commentisfree/2020/jun/08/edward-colston-statue-history-slave-trader-bristol-protest

59   Tristan Cork, 'How the city failed to remove Edward Colston's statue for years', *The Bristol Post* 10 June 2020: https://www.bristolpost.co.uk/news/bristol-news/how-city-failed-remove-edward-4211771

Chapter 4

1   Amrit Dhillon, 'When "political correctness" goes too far: Oxford University's drive to abolish "she" and "he"' *The Times of India* 22 December 2016: https://timesofindia.indiatimes.com/blogs/toi-edit-page/when-political-correctness-goes-too-far-oxford-universitys-drive-to-abolish-she-and-he/

2   Ibid.

3   Ibid.

4   Marianna Spring and Alexandra Topping, 'Oxford student union denies telling students to use gender-neutral pronoun', *The Guardian* 13 December 2016: https://www.theguardian.com/education/2016/dec/13/oxford-student-union-denies-telling-students-to-use-gender-neutral-pronoun

5   Amrit Dhillon, 'When "political correctness" goes too far: Oxford University's drive to abolish "she" and "he"', *The Times of India* 22 December 2016: https://timesofindia.indiatimes.com/blogs/toi-edit-page/when-political-correctness-goes-too-far-oxford-universitys-drive-to-abolish-she-and-he/

6   Conor Payne, 'Transphobia and the left: bogus science and bogus marxism', *Socialist Alternative* 12 May 2020: https://www.socialistalternative.org/2020/05/12/transphobia-and-the-left-bogus-science-and-bogus-marxism/

7   Lizzie Dearden, 'Hate crimes rise 10 per cent amid surge in anti-gay and transgender attacks', *The Independent* 15 October 2019: https://www.independent.co.uk/news/uk/crime/hate-crimes-england-wales-lgbt-rise-anti-gay-transgender-attacks-a9156291.html

8   Derrick Clifton, 'At least 350 transgender people have been killed globally in 2020', *Them* 11 November 2020: https://www.them.us/story/at-least-350-transgender-people-killed-globally-in-2020

9   Christopher Carpenter and Gilbert Gonzales, 'Transgender americans are more likely to be unemployed and poor', *The Conversation* 13 February 2020: https://theconversation.com/transgender-americans-are-more-likely-to-be-unemployed-and-poor-127585

10   Chaka L. Bachmann and Becca Gooch, 'LGBT in Britain: Trans report', *YouGov, Stonewall* January 2018: https://www.stonewall.org.uk/system/files/lgbt_in_britain_-_trans_report_final.pdf

11   Joseph Rojas, Jr, 'Protecting the world's trans population requires political representation', *New Atlanticist* 23 March 2021: https://www.atlanticcouncil.org/blogs/new-atlanticist/protecting-the-worlds-trans-population-requires-political-representation/

12   J K Rowling, 'J.K. Rowling writes about her reasons for speaking out on sex and gender issues', *J K Rowling.com* 10 June 2020: https://www.jkrowling.com/opinions/j-k-rowling-writes-about-her-reasons-for-speaking-out-on-sex-and-gender-issues/

13   J K Rowling cited in Amber Milne and Rachel Savage, 'J. K. Rowling and trans women in single-sex spaces: what's the furore?', *Thompson-Reuters Foundation* 11 June 2020: https://news.trust.org/item/20200611202849-fvume/

14   Will Doran, '"There have not been any public safety issues" in cities that allow transgender people to use the bathroom of the gender they identify as', *PolitiFact*

1 April 2016: https://www.politifact.com/factchecks/2016/apr/01/chris-sgro/equality-nc-director-no-public-safety-risks-cities/

15   Julie Moreau, 'No link between trans-inclusive policies and bathroom safety, study finds', *ABC News* 19 September 2018: https://www.nbcnews.com/feature/nbc-out/no-link-between-trans-inclusive-policies-bathroom-safety-study-finds-n911106

16   Julie Birchill cited in Joe Morgan, 'Julie Birchill's anti-trans "dicks in chics" clothing' aticle sparks outrage', *Gay Star News* 13 January 2013: https://www.gaystarnews.com/article/julie-burchill%e2%80%99s-anti-trans-%e2%80%98dicks-chicks%e2%80%99-clothing%e2%80%99-article-sparks-outrage130113/

17   J.K. Rowling, 'J.K. Rowling writes about her reasons for speaking out on sex and gender issues', *J K Rowling.com* 10 June 2020: https://www.jkrowling.com/opinions/j-k-rowling-writes-about-her-reasons-for-speaking-out-on-sex-and-gender-issues/

18   Ibid.

19   'The tricky business of policing sex in public', *BBC News Magazine* 16 September 2014: https://www.bbc.co.uk/news/magazine-29205198

20   Gillian Frank cited in Sarah Frostenson and Zachary Crockett, 'It's not just transgender people: public restrooms have bred fear for centuries', *Vox* 27 May 2016: https://www.vox.com/2016/5/27/11792550/transgender-bathroom

21   'Report – Gendered Restrooms and Minority Stress', *UCLA Williams Institute* June 2013: https://williamsinstitute.law.ucla.edu/publications/gendered-restrooms-minority-stress/

22   Brynn Tannehill cited in Nico Lang, 'What it's like to use a public bathroom while trans', *Rolling Stone* 31 March 2016: https://www.rollingstone.com/culture/culture-news/what-its-like-to-use-a-public-bathroom-while-trans-65793/

23   National L.G.B.T Research Report, *Government Equalities Office* July 2018: https://assets.publishing.service.gov.uk/government/uploads/system/uploads/attachment_data/file/721704/LGBT-survey-research-report.pdf

24   Cited in Nick Duffy, 'Attempting to change how I felt only made me hide it': How conversion therapy impacts trans people', *inews* 31 March 2021: https://inews.co.uk/news/uk/conversion-therapy-trans-people-report-ozanne-foundation-stonewall-936746

25   George Galloway cited in Lev Taylor, 'Progressively speaking: The last thing we need is more division on LGBT education', *Jewish News* 9 July 2021: https://jewishnews.timesofisrael.com/progressively-speaking-last-thing-we-need-is-more-division-on-lgbt-education/

26   The National Archives, UK Public General Acts, 'Local Government Act 1988': https://www.legislation.gov.uk/ukpga/1988/9/introduction

27   Margaret Thatcher cited in Harvey Day, 'Section 28: what was it and how did it affect LGBT+ people?', *BBC II* 1 November 2019: https://www.bbc.co.uk/bbcthree/article/cacc0b40-c3a4-473b-86cc-11863c0b3f30

28 Anita Bryant cited in Owen Jones, 'Transphobia was always going to end up as crude, old-fashioned homophobia', *Owen Jones* 5 April 2021: https://owenjones84.medium.com/transphobia-was-always-going-to-end-up-as-crude-old-fashioned-homophobia-a98af68b3a73

29 Ruth Smith, 'Lucy Meadows was a transgender teacher who took her own life. her story must be remembered', *The Independent* 19 November 2017: https://www.independent.co.uk/news/long_reads/lucy-meadows-transgender-teacher-ruth-smith-media-press-daily-mail-lgbt-rights-a8063946.html

30 Ibid.

31 Lucy Meadows cited in Ruth Smith, 'Lucy Meadows was a transgender teacher who took her own life. Her story must be remembered', *The Independent* 19 November 2017: https://www.independent.co.uk/news/long_reads/lucy-meadows-transgender-teacher-ruth-smith-media-press-daily-mail-lgbt-rights-a8063946.html

32 Lucy Meadows cited in Jessica Cree, 'Tragic suicide note left by accrington transgender teacher Lucy Meadows', *Lancashire Telegraph* 29 May 2013: https://www.lancashiretelegraph.co.uk/news/10448625.tragic-suicide-note-left-accrington-transgender-teacher-lucy-meadows/

33 Lucy Meadows cited in Ruth Smith, 'Lucy Meadows was a transgender teacher who took her own life. Her story must be remembered', *The Independent* 19 November 2017: https://www.independent.co.uk/news/long_reads/lucy-meadows-transgender-teacher-ruth-smith-media-press-daily-mail-lgbt-rights-a8063946.html

34 Ruth Smith, 'Lucy Meadows was a transgender teacher who took her own life. Her story must be remembered', *The Independent* 19 November 2017: https://www.independent.co.uk/news/long_reads/lucy-meadows-transgender-teacher-ruth-smith-media-press-daily-mail-lgbt-rights-a8063946.html

35 Richard Littlejohn cited in Roy Gleenslade, 'Daily mail urged to fire Richard Littlejohn after death of Lucy Meadows', *The Guardian* 22 March 2013: https://www.theguardian.com/media/greenslade/2013/mar/22/richard-littlejohn-transgender

36 Michael Singleton cited in Helen Pidd, 'Lucy Meadows coroner tells press: "shame on you"', *The Guardian* 28 May 2013: https://www.theguardian.com/uk/2013/may/28/lucy-meadows-coroner-press-shame

37 Andrea Dworkin, *Intercourse* (The Free Press, New York: 1987), p. 87.

38 Ibid.

39 W. S. Scott (translator) 'The Trial of Joan of Arc Being the Verbatim Report of the Proceedings from the Orleans Manuscript' (Associated Booksellers, Connecticut: 1956), p. 169.

40 Andrea Dworkin, *Intercourse* (The Free Press, New York: 1987), p. 103.

41 Greg Jericho, 'Women continue to carry the load when it comes to unpaid work', *The Guardian* 22 February 2021: https://www.theguardian.com/business/

grogonomics/2021/feb/23/women-continue-to-carry-the-load-when-it-comes-to-unpaid-work

42   Gus Wezerek and Kristen R. Ghodsee, 'Women's unpaid labor is worth $10,900,000,000,000', *The New York Times* 5 March 2020: https://www.nytimes.com/interactive/2020/03/04/opinion/women-unpaid-labor.html

43   'Women shoulder the responsibility of "unpaid work"', *Office for National Statistics* 10 November 2016: https://www.ons.gov.uk/employmentandlabourmarket/peopleinwork/earningsandworkinghours/articles/womenshouldertheresponsibilityofunpaidwork/2016-11-10

44   Jasmine Andersson, 'Women's unpaid labour is worth £140bn to the UK economy, analysis finds', *i news* 4 March 2020: https://inews.co.uk/news/women-unpaid-labour-value-uk-economy-analysis-office-national-statistics-404287

45   Gus Wezerek and Kristen R. Ghodsee, 'Women's unpaid labor is worth $10,900,000,000,000', *The New York Times* 5 March 2020: https://www.nytimes.com/interactive/2020/03/04/opinion/women-unpaid-labor.html

46   Jules Joanne Gleeson, 'On the guardian's transphobic centrism', *New Socialist* 21 October 2018: https://newsocialist.org.uk/on-the-guardians-transphobic-centrism/

47   Germaine Greer cited in 'Germaine Greer: Transgender women are "not women"' *BBC News* 24 October 2015: https://www.bbc.co.uk/news/av/uk-34625512

48   Jessie Muldoon, 'A Marxist theory of women's oppression', *International Socialist Review* Issue #112, Spring 2019: https://isreview.org/issue/100/marxist-theory-womens-oppression

49   Amrit Dhillon, 'When "political correctness" goes too far: Oxford University's drive to abolish "she" and "he"', *The Times of India* 22 December 2016: https://timesofindia.indiatimes.com/blogs/toi-edit-page/when-political-correctness-goes-too-far-oxford-universitys-drive-to-abolish-she-and-he/

50   C. Sara, 'Protecting transgender people is not a political choice', *Medium* 9 February 2019: https://medium.com/@QSE/protecting-transgender-people-is-not-a-political-choice-c5c2187f3773

Chapter 5

1   Donald Trump cited in Tommy Beer, 'Trump attacks "Cancel Culture" – But tried recently to cancel these people', *Forbes* 6 September 2020: https://www.forbes.com/sites/tommybeer/2020/09/06/trump-attacks-cancel-culturebut-tried-recently-to-cancel-these-people/?sh=2fafebe74b2a

2   Ibid.

3   Ibid.

4   Ibid.

5   'How is the net worth of Joe Rogan $100 million?' *The Success Bug* 12 July 2021: https://thesuccessbug.com/joe-rogan-net-worth/

     https://www.theshovel.com.au/2021/05/18/white-men-arent-allowed-to-talk-anymore-joe-rogan/

6   Sam Shead, 'JK rowling criticizes "cancel culture" in open letter signed by 150 public figures', *CNBC* 8 July 2020: https://www.cnbc.com/2020/07/08/jk-rowling-cancel-culture.html

7   '#28 J.K. Rowling', *Forbes* 6 April 2020: https://www.forbes.com/profile/jk-rowling/?sh=13af52f23aeb

8   'Permanent suspension of @realDonaldTrump', *Twitter* 8 January 2021: https://blog.twitter.com/en_us/topics/company/2020/suspension

9   James Clayton, 'Trump launches new "communications" platform', *BBC News* 5 May 2021: https://www.bbc.co.uk/news/technology-56989500

10   'A letter on justice and open debate', *Harper's Magazine* 7 July 2020: https://harpers.org/a-letter-on-justice-and-open-debate/

11   Ibid.

12   Jessica Valenti, 'Cancel Culture' is how the powerful play victim', *Medium* 8 July 2020: https://gen.medium.com/cancel-culture-is-how-the-powerful-play-victim-e840fa55ad49

13   David Taylor, 'How one article capsized a New York literary institution', *The Guardian* 29 September 2018: https://www.theguardian.com/world/2018/sep/29/new-york-review-of-book-ian-buruma-jian-ghomeshi

14   Ruth Spencer cited in Ashifa Kassam, 'Jian Ghomeshi essay on sexual assault trial met with backlash', *The Guardian* 14 September 2018: https://www.theguardian.com/world/2018/sep/14/jian-ghomeshi-essay-new-york-review-of-books-trial-metoo

15   Jian Ghomeshi cited in Isaac Chotiner, 'Why did the New York review of books publish that Jian Ghomeshi essay?' *Slate* 14 September 2018: https://slate.com/news-and-politics/2018/09/jian-ghomeshi-new-york-review-of-books-essay.html

16   Ian Buruma cited in Isaac Chotiner, 'Why did the New York review of books publish that Jian Ghomeshi Essay?' *Slate* 14 September 2018: https://slate.com/news-and-politics/2018/09/jian-ghomeshi-new-york-review-of-books-essay.html

17   Michael Hobbes, 'Don't fall for the "Cancel Culture" scam', *The Huffington Post* 10 August 2020: https://www.huffingtonpost.co.uk/entry/cancel-culture-harpers-jk-rowling-scam_n_5f0887b4c5b67a80bc06c95e?ri18n=true

18   Ibid.

19   Jessica Valenti, 'Cancel culture' is how the powerful play victim', *Medium* 8 July 2020: https://gen.medium.com/cancel-culture-is-how-the-powerful-play-victim-e840fa55ad49

20   Jessica Valenti, 'Not all opinions matter', *Medium* 9 June 2020: https://gen.medium.com/not-all-opinions-matter-4f2605165dd0

21   Ibid.

22   Sean Coughlan and David Brown, 'Private school and Oxbridge "take top jobs"', *BBC News* 25 June 2019: https://www.bbc.co.uk/news/education-48745333

23   Dominic Ponsford, 'Four men own Britain's news media. Is that a problem for democracy?' *New Statesman* 12 February 2021: https://www.newstatesman.com/2021/02/four-men-own-britain-s-news-media-problem-democracy

24   Tom Symonds, 'Grenfell Tower inquiry: 9 things we now know about the cladding', *BBC News* 23 March 2017: https://www.bbc.co.uk/news/uk-56403431

25   Robert Booth and Calla Wahlquist, 'Grenfell Tower residents say managers "brushed away" fire safety concerns', *The Guardian* 14 June 2017: https://www.theguardian.com/uk-news/2017/jun/14/fire-safety-concerns-raised-by-grenfell-tower-residents-in-2012

26   Caelainn Barr, 'Wealth and poverty sit side by side in Grenfell Tower's borough', *The Guardian* 15 June 2017: https://www.theguardian.com/uk-news/2017/jun/15/wealth-and-poverty-sit-side-by-side-in-grenfell-towers-borough

27   John Snow cited in Graham Ruddick, 'Jon Snow: reporting on Grenfell made me feel on wrong side of social divide', *The Guardian* 23 August 2017: https://www.theguardian.com/media/2017/aug/23/jon-snow-grenfell-mactaggart-media-diversity

28   Ibid.

29   'Ten years on: The financial crisis in numbers', *This Week* 7 August 2017: https://www.theweek.co.uk/87574/ten-years-on-the-financial-crisis-in-numbers

30   William Keegan, 'This austerity U-turn by Ed Balls is a mistake', *The Guardian* 16 June 2013: https://www.theguardian.com/business/2013/jun/16/austerity-uturn-ed-balls-mistake

31   Theresa May cited in 'The Hostile environment explained', *The Joint Council for the Welfare of Immigrants*: https://www.jcwi.org.uk/the-hostile-environment-explained

32   Frances Perraudin, 'Diane Abbott: Labour's "controls on immigration" mugs are shameful', *The Guardian* 29 March 2015: https://www.theguardian.com/politics/2015/mar/29/diane-abbott-labour-immigration-controls-mugs-shameful

33   Jeremy Corbyn cited in Matt Dathan, 'Corbyn says immigration isn't a problem', *The Independent* 30 September 2015: https://www.independent.co.uk/news/uk/politics/corbyn-says-immigration-isn-t-problem-a6673231.html

34 Jeremy Corbyn, 'Jeremy Corbyn's full speech at the 2016 Labour Party conference', *New Statesman* 28 September 2016: https://www.newstatesman.com/politics/staggers/2016/09/jeremy-corbyns-full-speech-2016-labour-party-conference

35 Jessica Elgot, 'Labour signs up more than 180,000 supporters to vote in leadership contest', *The Guardian* 20 July 2016: https://www.theguardian.com/politics/2016/jul/20/labour-stops-crowd-funding-bid-to-help-supporters-pay-for-vote

36 Lesley Docksey, 'The British Chicken Coup: 172 Labour MPs against a pro-Corbyn Party', *Global Research* 6 July 2016: https://www.globalresearch.ca/the-british-chicken-coup-172-labour-mps-against-a-pro-corbyn-party/5534421

37 Matt Turner, 'BBC admit intentionally damaging Corbyn leadership with contrived live resignation', *Evolve Politics* 8 January 2016: https://evolvepolitics.com/bbc-admit-intentionally-damaging-corbyn-leadership-contrived-live-resignation/

38 Michael Cricked cited in Matt Turner, 'BBC admit intentionally damaging Corbyn leadership with contrived live resignation', *Evolve Politics* 8 January 2016: https://evolvepolitics.com/bbc-admit-intentionally-damaging-corbyn-leadership-contrived-live-resignation/

39 Richard Pendlebury, 'Jeremy Corbyn, the bomb-maker's friend: IRA terrorist gloried in the Hyde Park bombing – yet after he left jail, admirer Corbyn helped create a council job for him and he jumped a 12,000-strong queue for genteel Islington council flat', *The Daily Mail* 3 December 2019: https://www.dailymail.co.uk/news/article-7752923/Jeremy-Corbyn-bomb-makers-friend-IRA-terrorist-admirer-Corbyn.html

40 Daily Mail Reporter, 'Holding the wreath. Copying prayers: The pictures that make a mockery of Labour leader Jeremy Corbyn who says: "I was present, but I don't think I was involved"' *The Daily Mail* 14 August 2016: https://www.dailymail.co.uk/news/article-6057277/Jeremy-Corbyn-wreath-laying-Palestinian-Munich-massacre-terrorists-gravesite.html

41 Laura O'Callaghan, 'Outrage as Corbyn accused of failing to bow in respect to war dead at Remembrance ceremony', *The Daily Express* 11 November 2019: https://www.express.co.uk/news/politics/1202502/jeremy-corbyn-remembrance-sunday-cenotaph-service-labour-party-queen-latest

42 Mail on Sunday Reporter, 'Jeremy Corbyn is caught taking a nap on a train to Scotland as the rest of the country cheered on England against the All Blacks' *The Daily Mail* 26 October 2019: https://www.dailymail.co.uk/news/article-7617707/Jeremy-Corbyn-caught-taking-nap-train-rest-country-cheered-England.html

43 Chi Onwurah, 'In any other job, Jeremy Corbyn would have faced an industrial tribunal', *New Statesman* 22 August 2016: https://www.newstatesman.com/politics/staggers/2016/08/labour-mp-any-other-job-jeremy-corbyn-would-have-faced-industrial-tribunal

44 Elizabeth Day, 'Jeremy Corbyn's misogynist put-downs. Neglecting his wives while expecting them to do all the chores. How could any woman vote for this sorry excuse for a man?' *The Daily Mail* 9 February 2019: https://www.dailymail.co.uk/debate/article-6686927/ELIZABETH-DAY-woman-vote-sorry-excuse-man.html

45 Martin Amis, 'Amis on Corbyn: Undereducated, humourless, third rate', *The Times* 25 October 2015: https://www.thetimes.co.uk/article/amis-on-corbyn-undereducated-humourless-third-rate-dhvgj99fjxv

46 Jake Ryan, 'THE CORBYN FILES Former Soviet spy makes shock claims that 'Jeremy Corbyn was our asset … he had been recruited' and was 'a paid collaborator', *The Sun* 16 February 2018: https://www.thesun.co.uk/news/5597516/jeremy-corbyn-paid-communist-spy-czech-republic-labour/

47 The only mainstream paper whose editorial line supported Corbyn's Labour in this period – was *The Daily Mirror*. But they were the exception rather than the rule.

48 Helen Lewis, 'Why British Jews are worried by Jeremy Corbyn', *The Atlantic* 10 December 2019: https://www.theatlantic.com/international/archive/2019/12/british-jews-are-worried-jeremy-corbyn-and-labour-party/603259/

49 Glen Owen, 'Jeremy Corbyn is the biggest global threat to Jews, warns Simon Wiesenthal Centre – the world's leading Nazi-hunting organisation – as Boris Johnson urges voters to save Britain from a "nightmare"', *The Daily Mail* 7 December 2019: https://www.dailymail.co.uk/news/article-7767789/Jeremy-Corbyn-biggest-global-threat-Jews-warns-worlds-leading-Nazi-hunting-organisation.html

50 John Harris, 'The unanswered question: why do antisemites think Labour is the party for them?' *The Guardian* 4 March 2019: https://www.theguardian.com/commentisfree/2019/mar/04/labour-antisemitism-party-left-bigotry

51 Guido Fawkes cited in Eleanor Penny, 'Jewdas, Corbyn and the policing of Jewishness', *Red Pepper* 3 April 2019: https://www.redpepper.org.uk/jewdas-corbyn-and-the-policing-of-jewishness/

52 Leo Panitch, 'Historical record shows Jeremy Corbyn is a defender of Jews', *Toronto Star* 5 December 2019: https://www.thestar.com/opinion/contributors/2019/12/03/historical-record-shows-jeremy-corbyn-is-a-defender-of-jews.html

53 Cited in Leo Panitch, 'Historical record shows Jeremy Corbyn is a defender of Jews', *Toronto Star* 5 December 2019: https://www.thestar.com/opinion/contributors/2019/12/03/historical-record-shows-jeremy-corbyn-is-a-defender-of-jews.html

54 Greg Philo and Mike Berry, 'Bad news for labour: A response to Channel 4's "FactCheck"', *Pluto Press*: https://www.plutobooks.com/blog/bad-news-for-labour-channel-4-factcheck/

55 Harriet Agerholm, 'Jeremy Corbyn was just 2,227 votes away from chance to be Prime Minister', *The Independent* 9 June 2017: https://www.independent.co.uk/news/uk/politics/corbyn-election-results-votes-away-prime-minister-theresa-may-hung-parliament-a7782581.html

56   Jon Stone, 'Anti-Corbyn Labour officials worked to lose general election to oust
     leader, leaked dossier finds', *The Independent* 13 April 2020: https://www.independent.
     co.uk/news/uk/politics/labour-leak-report-corbyn-election-whatsapp-antisemitism-
     tories-yougov-poll-a9462456.html#r3z-addoor

57   Luke Harding, Jessica Elgot, and Andrew Sparrow, 'Accusations of lying pile up
     against Boris Johnson. Does it matter?' *The Guardian* 30 April 2021: https://www.
     theguardian.com/politics/2021/apr/30/accusations-of-lying-pile-up-against-boris-
     johnson-does-it-matter

58   Boris Johnson cited in Adam Bienkov, 'Boris Johnson called gay men "tank-topped
     bumboys" and black people "piccaninnies" with "watermelon smiles"', *The Insider*
     9 June 2020: https://www.businessinsider.com/boris-johnson-record-sexist-
     homophobic-and-racist-comments-bumboys-piccaninnies-2019-6?r=US&IR=T

59   Boris Johnson cited in Joshua Taylor, 'Boris Johnson called working class men "drunk,
     criminal and feckless"' *The Daily Mirror* 28 November 2019: https://www.mirror.
     co.uk/news/politics/boris-johnson-called-working-class-20981604

60   Boris Johnson cited in Rob Merick, 'Boris Johnson said children of poorer working
     mothers are more likely to "mug you on the street corner"', *The Independent* 4
     December 2019: https://www.independent.co.uk/news/uk/politics/boris-johnson-
     women-working-class-sexism-mug-general-election-tories-a9232896.html

61   Louis Doir, 'The truth about that awful alleged Boris Johnson quote on Hillsborough',
     The Independent 26 April 2016: https://www.indy100.com/people/the-truth-about-
     that-awful-boris-johnson-quote-on-hillsborough-7296241

62   Lizzie Deardon, 'Islamophobic incidents rose 375% after Boris Johnson compared
     Muslim women to "letterboxes", figures show', *The Independent* 2 September 2019:
     https://www.independent.co.uk/news/uk/home-news/boris-johnson-muslim-
     women-letterboxes-burqa-islamphobia-rise-a9088476.html

63   Boris Johnson cited in Jon Stone, 'Boris Johnson book depicts Jews as controlling
     the media', *The Independent* 9 December 2019: https://www.independent.co.uk/news/
     uk/politics/boris-johnson-book-jews-control-media-general-election-a9239346.
     html

64   Andrew Griffin, 'BBC admits it made "mistake" by editing Boris Johnson footage to
     remove audience laughing at him', *The Independent* 25 November 2019: https://www.
     independent.co.uk/news/uk/politics/boris-johnson-laughing-question-time-video-
     edited-general-election-a9217141.html

65   Peter Oborne and David Hearst, 'The killing of Jeremy Corbyn', *Middle East Eye*
     5 June 2020: https://www.middleeasteye.net/opinion/killing-jeremy-corbyn

66   Peter Oborne, 'British journalists have become part of Johnson's fake news
     machine', *Open Democracy* 22 April 2019: https://www.opendemocracy.net/en/
     opendemocracyuk/british-journalists-have-become-part-of-johnsons-fake-news-
     machine/

67 Dr Bart Cammaerts, Brooks DeCillia, João Carlos Magalhães and Dr Cesar Jimenez-Martinez, 'Journalistic Representations of Jeremy Corbyn in the British Press', *London School of Economics*: https://www.lse.ac.uk/media-and-communications/research/research-projects/representations-of-jeremy-corbyn

68 Dawn Foster cited in Lynsey Hanley, 'Remembering Dawn Foster', *Tribune* 20 July 2021: https://tribunemag.co.uk/2021/07/in-memory-of-dawn-foster

69 Lynsey Hanley, 'Remembering Dawn Foster', *Tribune* 20 July 2021: https://tribunemag.co.uk/2021/07/in-memory-of-dawn-foster

70 If one wanted other instances of genuine cancellation one might be tempted to look at what happens to whistle-blowers like Chelsea Manning or Edward Snowdon.

71 This is as true in the US as it is in the UK. Any cursory examination would reveal this; there are, for instance, perhaps six or seven senators in the US who might conceivably be described as being on the 'radical left' – the 'squad' composed of Alexandria Ocasio-Cortez of New York, Ilhan Omar of Minnesota, Ayanna Pressley of Massachusetts, and Rashida Tlaib of Michigan – along with Bernie Sanders, the Senator of Vermont. Now that's six or seven out of a Senate of one hundred members. Sanders and the 'squad', whatever their politics, have the ability to 'cancel' precisely no-one.

Chapter 6

1 Gillian Duffy cited in Matthew Weaver, 'The gordon brown and gillian duffy transcript', *The Guardian* 28 April 2010: https://www.theguardian.com/politics/2010/apr/28/gordon-brown-gillian-duffy-transcript

2 Gordon Brown cited in Matthew Weaver, 'The gordon brown and gillian duffy transcript', *The Guardian* 28 April 2010: https://www.theguardian.com/politics/2010/apr/28/gordon-brown-gillian-duffy-transcript

3 Jason Okundaye @jasebyjason Twitter 28 April 2020.

4 Nicholas Watt and Patrick Wintour, 'How immigration came to haunt Labour: the inside story', *The Guardian* 24 March 2015: https://www.theguardian.com/news/2015/mar/24/how-immigration-came-to-haunt-labour-inside-story

5 Robert Booth, 'Middle income earners behind rising racial tensions, research suggests', *The Guardian* 5 March 2019: https://www.theguardian.com/society/2019/mar/05/middle-income-earners-behind-rising-racial-tensions-research-suggests

6 Eric Kaufmann, 'Positive contact or "white flight"?: why whites in diverse places are more tolerant of immigration', *LSE Blog*: https://blogs.lse.ac.uk/politicsandpolicy/positive-contact-or-white-flight-why-whites-in-diverse-places-are-more-tolerant-of-immigration/

7   Ibid.

8   Robert Booth, 'Middle income earners behind rising racial tensions, research suggests', *The Guardian* 5 March 2019: https://www.theguardian.com/society/2019/mar/05/middle-income-earners-behind-rising-racial-tensions-research-suggests

9   'UEA research claims link between obesity and Brexit voters', *ITV News* 30 June 2016: https://www.itv.com/news/anglia/2016-06-30/uea-research-suggests-link-between-obesity-and-brexit-voters

10   Dorling, D. (2016) Brexit: the decision of a divided country, BMJ 2016; 354 DOI: http://dx.doi.org/10.1136/bmj.i3697 (Published 6 July 2016)

11   Lorenza Antonucci, Laszlo Horvath, and André Krouwel, 'Brexit was not the voice of the working class nor of the uneducated – it was of the squeezed middle', *LSE Blog* 13 October 2017: https://blogs.lse.ac.uk/politicsandpolicy/brexit-and-the-squeezed-middle/

12   S. Fenton, 'Resentment, class and social sentiments about the nation: The ethnic majority in England', *Ethnicities*, 12(4) (2012), 465–83. DOI: 10.1177/1468796812448023

13   Anna Edwards, 'Tearaway teenage mother who starred in Channel 4 documentary Skint was caught for headbutting girl, 10, after she recognised her from TV', *The Daily Mail* 23 August 2013: https://www.dailymail.co.uk/news/article-2400794/Tearaway-teenage-mother-starred-Channel-4-documentary-Skint-caught-headbutting-girl-10-recognised-TV.html

14   David Pilditch, 'Teenage mum to bring up triplets on the state', *The Express* 11 February 2009: https://www.express.co.uk/news/uk/84307/Teenage-mum-to-bring-up-triplets-on-the-state

15   David Maddox, 'What about white working class? Race disparity head says white privilege focus is damaging', *The Express* 30 May 2021: https://www.express.co.uk/news/uk/1442999/white-privilege-working-class-racism-tony-sewell

16   Ibid.

17   Ed Miliband, '"We will control immigration with fair rules" – Miliband announces Labour's second election pledge', *Labour List* 15 December 2014: https://labourlist.org/2014/12/we-will-control-immigration-with-fair-rules-miliband-announces-labours-second-election-pledge/

18   Roland Watson, 'Miliband seeks policies to appeal to white working class', *The Times* 4 October 2012: https://www.thetimes.co.uk/article/miliband-seeks-policies-to-appeal-to-white-working-class-m2w7sbq277v

19   Toby Helm, 'Labour will be tougher than Tories on benefits, promises new welfare chief', *The Observer* 12 October 2013: https://www.theguardian.com/politics/2013/oct/12/labour-benefits-tories-labour-rachel-reeves-welfare

20 Liz Truss, 'LIZ TRUSS: Equality should be for everyone' – not just for the woke warrior's favoured few', *The Daily Mail* 30 September 2020: https://www.dailymail.co.uk/news/article-9089985/LIZ-TRUSS-Equality-not-just-woke-warriors-favoured-few.html

21 Ibid.

22 Ibid.

23 Ibid.

24 Editorial, 'What have the immigrants ever done for us?' *The Economist* 8 November 2014: https://www.economist.com/britain/2014/11/08/what-have-the-immigrants-ever-done-for-us

25 Donald Trump cited in Veronica Stracqualursi, 'Trump re-ups "infestation" rhetoric in immigration debate', *CNN* 3 July 2018: https://edition.cnn.com/2018/07/03/politics/trump-ms13-illegal-immigration-rhetoric/index.html

26 Donald Trump cited in Amber Phillips, '"They're rapists." President Trump's campaign launch speech two years later, annotated', *The Washington Post* 16 June 2017: https://www.washingtonpost.com/news/the-fix/wp/2017/06/16/theyre-rapists-presidents-trump-campaign-launch-speech-two-years-later-annotated/

27 Donald Trump cited in Kevin Brueninger, 'Trump says more than 63,000 Americans were killed by illegal immigrants since 9/11. But the math doesn't add up', *CNBC* 26 June 2018: https://www.cnbc.com/2018/06/25/trump-says-63000-killed-by-illegal-aliens-the-math-doesnt-add-up.html

28 Laura Finley and Luigi Esposito, 'The immigrant as Bogeyman: Examining Donald Trump and the right's anti-immigrant, anti-PC rhetoric', *Humanity & Society*, 44(2) (2019), 016059761983262–. DOI: 10.1177/0160597619832627

29 Ibid.

30 Robert J Sampson, 'rethinking crime and immigration', *Contexts* 9 January 2008: https://contexts.org/articles/sampson/

31 Michele Lamont, Bo Yun Park, and Elena Ayala-Hurtado, 'What Trump's campaign speeches show about his lasting appeal to the white working class', *Harvard Business Review* 8 November 2017: https://hbr.org/2017/11/what-trumps-campaign-speeches-show-about-his-lasting-appeal-to-the-white-working-class

32 Donald Trump cited in Finley, Laura; Luigi Esposito. The immigrant as Bogeyman: Examining Donald Trump and the right's anti-immigrant, anti-PC rhetoric', *Humanity & Society*, 44(2) (2019), 016059761983262–. DOI: 10.1177/0160597619832627

33 Laura Finley and Luigi Esposito, 'The immigrant as Bogeyman: Examining Donald Trump and the right's anti-immigrant, anti-PC rhetoric', *Humanity & Society*, 44(2) (2019), 016059761983262–. DOI: 10.1177/0160597619832627

34 Maria E. Enchautegui, 'Immigrant and native workers compete for different low-skilled jobs', *Urban Institute* 13 October 2015: https://www.urban.org/urban-wire/immigrant-and-native-workers-compete-different-low-skilled-jobs

35 Ibid.

36 Ibid.

37 Stuart Anderson, 'If you want less outsourcing, then increase immigration', *Forbes* 10 June 2017: https://www.forbes.com/sites/stuartanderson/2017/06/10/if-you-want-less-outsourcing-then-increase-immigration/?sh=7cece9d34349

38 Angie Mohr, '4 ways outsourcing damages industry', *Investopia* 25 June 2019: https://www.investopedia.com/financial-edge/0312/4-ways-outsourcing-damages-industry.aspx

39 Robert E. Scott, 'We can reshore manufacturing jobs, but Trump hasn't done it', *Economic Policy Institute* 10 August 2021: https://www.epi.org/publication/reshoring-manufacturing-jobs/

40 Ibid.

41 Donald Trump cited in Finley, Laura; Luigi Esposito, The immigrant as Bogeyman: Examining Donald Trump and the right's anti-immigrant, anti-PC rhetoric. *Humanity & Society*, 44(2) (2019), 016059761983262–. DOI: 10.1177/01605976619832627

42 Donald Trump cited in Chris Cillizza, 'The dangerous consequences of Trump's all-out assault on "political correctness"', *CNN* 30 October 2018: https://edition.cnn.com/2018/10/30/politics/donald-trump-hate-speech-anti-semitism-steve-king-kevin-mccarthy/index.html

43 Chris Cillizza, 'The dangerous consequences of Trump's all-out assault on "political correctness"', *CNN* 30 October 2018: https://edition.cnn.com/2018/10/30/politics/donald-trump-hate-speech-anti-semitism-steve-king-kevin-mccarthy/index.html

44 Donald Trump cited in Amy Sherman, 'Donald Trump says Hillary Clinton wants to have open borders', *PoliFact* 19 October 2016: https://www.politifact.com/factchecks/2016/oct/20/donald-trump/donald-trump-says-hillary-clinton-wants-have-open-/

45 Jean Guerrero, '3 Million people were deported under Obama. What will Biden do about it?', *The New York Times* 23 January 2021: https://www.nytimes.com/2021/01/23/opinion/sunday/immigration-reform-biden.html

46 'Barack Obama deported more people in his first term than Trump', *Logically* 1 September 2020: https://www.logically.ai/factchecks/library/8930b4ea

47 Ibid.

48 James Kirchick, 'Op-Ed: What Trump supporters mean when they say they hate PC culture', *The LA Times* 6 September 2016: https://www.latimes.com/opinion/op-ed/la-oe-kirchick-trump-provocation-pc-20160906-snap-story.html

49 Finley, Laura; Luigi Esposito, The immigrant as Bogeyman: Examining Donald Trump and the right's anti-immigrant, anti-PC rhetoric', *Humanity & Society*, 44(2) (2019), 016059761983262–. DOI: 10.1177/0160597619832627

50 'Emergency Economic Stabilization Act of 2008', *Encyclopaedia Britannica*: https://www.britannica.com/topic/Emergency-Economic-Stabilization-Act-of-2008

51 Jason Margolis, 'Hillary Clinton's stand on NAFTA and the TPP: it's complicated, and evolving', *The World* 28 July 2016: https://www.pri.org/stories/2016-07-28/hillary-clinton-s-stand-nafta-and-tpp-it-s-complicated-and-evolving

52 Ibid.

53 Eugene Beaulieu and Dylan Klemen, 'You Say USMCA or T-MEC and I Say CUSMA: The New NAFTA-Let's Call the Whole Thing On.' The School of Public Policy Publications (2020)

54 Finley, Laura; Luigi Esposito, 'The immigrant as Bogeyman: Examining Donald Trump and the right's anti-immigrant, anti-PC rhetoric', *Humanity & Society*, 44(2) (2019), 016059761983262–. DOI: 10.1177/0160597619832627

55 Kevin Williamson cited in 'Donald Trump is making conservatives turn on the white working class', *Vox* 15 March 2016: https://www.vox.com/2016/3/15/11236618/trump-conservatives-working-class

56 Kevin D. Williamson, 'The Father-Führer', *National Review* 28 March 2016: https://www.nationalreview.com/magazine/2016/03/28/father-f-hrer/

57 '2008 United States presidential election' Wikipedia: https://en.wikipedia.org/wiki/2008_United_States_presidential_election

58 '2016 United States presidential election', Wikipedia: https://en.wikipedia.org/wiki/2016_United_States_presidential_election

59 '2008 United States presidential election' Wikipedia: https://en.wikipedia.org/wiki/2008_United_States_presidential_election

60 '2016 United States presidential election', Wikipedia: https://en.wikipedia.org/wiki/2016_United_States_presidential_election

61 'Obama's covert drone war in numbers: ten times more strikes than Bush' *The Bureau of Investigative Journalism* 17 January 2017: https://www.thebureauinvestigates.com/stories/2017-01-17/obamas-covert-drone-war-in-numbers-ten-times-more-strikes-than-bush

62 Nicholas Carnes and Noam Lupu, 'Why Trump's appeal is wider than you might think', *MSNBC* 8 April 2016: https://www.msnbc.com/msnbc/why-trumps-appeal-wider-you-might-think-msna829531

63 Nicholas Carnes and Noam Lupu, 'It's time to bust the myth: most Trump voters were not working class', *The Washington Post* 5 June 2017: https://www.washingtonpost.

com/news/monkey-cage/wp/2017/06/05/its-time-to-bust-the-myth-most-trump-voters-were-not-working-class/

64 Nicholas Carnes and Noam Lupu, 'Why Trump's appeal is wider than you might think' *MSNBC* 8 April 2016: https://www.msnbc.com/msnbc/why-trumps-appeal-wider-you-might-think-msna829531

65 Adam Serwer, 'The Capitol Rioters weren't "Low Class"', *The Atlantic* 12 January 2021: https://www.theatlantic.com/ideas/archive/2021/01/thoroughly-respectable-rioters/617644/

66 Ibid.

67 Ibid.

68 Toby Helm, 'Austerity to blame for 130,000 "preventable" UK deaths – report', *The Guardian* 1 June 2019: https://www.theguardian.com/politics/2019/jun/01/perfect-storm-austerity-behind-130000-deaths-uk-ippr-report

Conclusion

1 Aristotle, *Politics*, 1254b 16–21.

2 Manuel Doria, 'The unreasonable destructiveness of "political correctness" in philosophy', Advanced Studies Research Group MDPI 3 August 2017: file:///C:/Users/mike/Downloads/philosophies-02-00017-v3.pdf

3 Lawrence Summers cited in Suzanne Goldenberg, 'Why women are poor at science, by Harvard president', *The Guardian* 18 June 2005: https://www.theguardian.com/science/2005/jan/18/educationsgendergap.genderissues

4 Ibid.

5 'Larry Summers II on Conversations with Bill Kristol'. Conversations with Bill Kristol. org. Retrieved 8 November 2017: https://conversationswithbillkristol.org/video/larry-summers-ii/?start=15&end=1606

6 Jordan Peterson cited in Kelefa Sanneh, 'Jordan Peterson's gospel of masculinity', *The New Yorker* 26 February 2018: https://www.newyorker.com/magazine/2018/03/05/jordan-petersons-gospel-of-masculinity

7 Jordan Peterson cited in Leah Morris, 'Why Jordan Peterson Is Wrong about the Pay Gap', *Linkedin* 20 August 2020: https://www.linkedin.com/pulse/why-jordan-peterson-wrong-pay-gap-leah-morris

8 Slavoj Žižek, *Against the Double Blackmail: Refugees, Terror and Other Troubles with the Neighbours* (Allen Lane, UK: 2016), p. 98.

9   Slavoj Žižek, 'The Non-Existence of Norway – Slavoj Žižek on the Refugee Crisis',
     London Review of Books Vol. 37 No. 17 · 10 September 2015: https://www.lrb.co.uk/
     the-paper/v37/n17/slavoj-zizek/the-non-existence-of-norway

10   Slavoj Žižek cited in Annalisa Merelli, 'Marxist philosopher Slavoj Žižek explains
     why we shouldn't pity or romanticize refugees', *Quartz* 9 September 2016: https://
     qz.com/767751/marxist-philosopher-slavoj-zizek-on-europes-refugee-crisis-the-left-
     is-wrong-to-pity-and-romanticize-migrants/

11   Slavoj Žižek, 'The Big Think', *YouTube* 16 April 2016: https://www.youtube.com/
     watch?v=5dNbWGaaxWM

12   Martin Amis cited in Laura Clark and Tahira Yaqoob, 'Martin Amis launches fresh
     attack on Muslim faith saying Islamic states are "less evolved"', *Daily Mail* 18 October
     2007: https://www.dailymail.co.uk/news/article-488239/Martin-Amis-launches-fresh-
     attack-Muslim-faith-saying-Islamic-states-evolved.html

13   Martin Amis cited in Maev Kennedy, 'Enough, says Amis, in Eagleton feud',
     The Guardian 13 October 2007: https://www.theguardian.com/uk/2007/oct/13/
     highereducation.islam

14   Katie Hopkins cited in 'Katie Hopkins compares migrants to "cockroaches" and
     suggests using gunships to stop them crossing the Mediterranean', *ITV News*
     18 April 2015: https://www.itv.com/news/2015-04-18/katie-hopkins-compares-
     migrants-to-cockroaches-and-suggests-using-gunships-to-stop-them-crossing-the-
     mediterranean

15   Donald Trump cited in Ben Zimmer, 'What Trump talks about when he talks about
     infestations', *Politico Magazine* 29 July 2019: https://www.politico.com/magazine/
     story/2019/07/29/trump-baltimore-infest-tweet-cummings-racist-227485/

16   Donald Trump cited in Ben Zimmer, 'Why Donald Trump's racist language isn't
     debatable', *The Atlantic* 18 July 2019: https://www.theatlantic.com/entertainment/
     archive/2019/07/donald-trump-racist-tweets-to-congresswomen/594295/

17   Jamil Smith, Twitter 19 June 2019: https://twitter.com/jamilsmith/
     status/1009093067171745792

18   Friedrich Neitzsche cited in Ishay Landa, *Fascism and the Masses: The Revolt against
     the Last Humans, 1848–1945* (Routledge, New York and London: 2018), p. 92.

19   Jordan Peterson, 'Inequality and hierarchy give life its purpose', *Big Think YouTube*
     5 April 2018: https://www.youtube.com/watch?v=lF-bXNQ4wzs

20   Sophia Hatzisavvidou, 'Truth-tellers: creating Britain's anti-austerity campaign', *LSE
     Blog* 18 January 2018: https://blogs.lse.ac.uk/politicsandpolicy/truth-tellers-creating-
     britains-anti-austerity-campaign/

21   David Cameron, 'David Cameron: the age of austerity', Conservative Party Speeches,
     SayIt 26 April 2009: https://conservative-speeches.sayit.mysociety.org/speech/601367

22 Margaret Thatcher cited in Stephen Colgrave, 'Thatcher's household fallacy led to Austerity and killed thousands – What was the point of it?' *Byline Times* 19 November 2019: https://bylinetimes.com/2019/11/19/thatchers-household-fallacy-led-to-austerity-and-killed-thousands-what-was-the-point-of-it/

23 Frank Van Lerven, Andrew Jackson, 'A government is not a household', *New Economics Foundation* 26 October 2018: https://neweconomics.org/2018/10/a-government-is-not-ahousehold.

24 Nigel Farage cited in Cyrus Engineer, 'Farage hits back – "Getting immigration right isn't racist, it is COMMON SENSE"', *The Express* 11 July 2016: https://www.express.co.uk/news/uk/688020/nigel-farage-immigration-racist-lbc

25 Editorial, 'What have the immigrants ever done for us?', *The Economist* 8 November 2014: https://www.economist.com/britain/2014/11/08/what-have-the-immigrants-ever-done-forus

26 Katherine Timpf, 'University researchers: we have to accept people who "Identify as real vampires"', *National Review* 13 July 2015: https://www.nationalreview.com/2015/07/vampires-identify-study-discrimination/

27 Katherine Timpf, 'Professor: small chairs in preschools are sexist, "Problematic," and "Disempowering"', *National Review* 21 January 2013: https://www.nationalreview.com/2018/01/preschoolers-small-chairs-sexist-problematic-disempowering/

28 Leo Mckinstry, 'A to Z of politically correct madness: the Left's "Thought Police" continues to censor language as "manfully" is labelled sexist', *The Daily Mail* 18 October 2017: https://www.dailymail.co.uk/news/article-5094791/A-Z-politically-correct-madness.html

29 Priya Sridhar, 'SDG&E worker fired over alleged racist gesture says he was cracking knuckles', *NBC San Diego* 15 June 2020: https://www.nbcsandiego.com/news/local/sdge-worker-fired-over-alleged-racist-gesture-says-he-was-cracking-knuckles/2347414/

30 Leila Fadel, 'After being called out for racism, what comes next?' *Code Switch* 28 July 2020: https://www.npr.org/sections/codeswitch/2020/07/28/891829285/after-being-called-out-for-racism-what-comes-next

31 Jordan Peterson, 'Joe Rogan – Jordan Peterson: why identity politics lead to totalitarian oppression', Joe Rogan YouTube, 30 November 2018: https://www.youtube.com/watch?v=OtFFlDMnaJs

32 Stephen Fry, *Political Correctness Gone Mad?* (Oneworld, London: 2020), p. 26.

33 Ibid.

34 Shamira Ibrahim cited in Aja Romano, 'The second wave of "cancel culture"', *Vox* 5 May 2021: https://www.vox.com/22384308/cancel-culture-free-speech-accountability-debate

35 Michael Hobbes, 'Don't fall for the "Cancel Culture" scam', *The Huffington Post*
    10 August 2020: https://www.huffingtonpost.co.uk/entry/cancel-culture-harpers-jk-
    rowling-scam_n_5f0887b4c5b67a80bc06c95e?ri18n=true

36 Ibid.

37 'Nigel Farage attacked over Romanians "slur"', *BBC News* 18 May 2014: https://www.
    bbc.co.uk/news/uk-27459923

38 Jordan Peterson, 'Inequality and hierarchy give life its purpose', *Big Think YouTube*
    5 April 2018: https://www.youtube.com/watch?v=lF-bXNQ4wzs

Bibliography

David F. Allmendinger Jr, *Nat Turner and the Rising in Southampton County* (Johns Hopkins University Press, Baltimore: 2014).

Lorenza Antonucci, Laszlo Horvath and André Krouwel, 'Brexit was not the voice of the working class nor of the uneducated – it was of the squeezed middle', *LSE Blog* 13 October 2017: https://blogs.lse.ac.uk/politicsandpolicy/brexit-and-the-squeezed-middle/

Kenneth M. Bilby, *True-Born Maroons* (University Press of Florida, Gainesville: 2005).

Robert Booth, 'Middle income earners behind rising racial tensions, research suggests', *The Guardian* 5 March 2019: https://www.theguardian.com/society/2019/mar/05/middle-income-earners-behind-rising-racial-tensions-research-suggests

Chris Cillizza, 'The dangerous consequences of Trump's all-out assault on "political correctness"', *CNN* 30 October 2018: https://edition.cnn.com/2018/10/30/politics/donald-trump-hate-speech-anti-semitism-steve-king-kevin-mccarthy/index.html

James Cullen, 'The history of mass incarceration', *Brennan Centre for Justice* 20 July 2018: https://www.brennancenter.org/our-work/analysis-opinion/history-mass-incarceration

Andrea Dworkin, *Intercourse* (The Free Press, New York: 1987).

Editorial, 'What have the immigrants ever done for us?', *The Economist* 8 November 2014: https://www.economist.com/britain/2014/11/08/what-have-the-immigrants-ever-done-forus

Frantz Fanon, *The Wretched of the Earth* (Penguin Classics, New York: 2001).

Shon Faye, *The Transgender Issue: An Argument for Justice* (Penguin, UK: 2021).

Laura Finley and Luigi Esposito. The Immigrant as Bogeyman: Examining Donald Trump and the Right's Anti-immigrant, Anti-PC Rhetoric. *Humanity & Society*, 44:2 (2019), 016059761983262–. DOI: 10.1177/0160597619832627.

Jules Joanne Gleeson, 'On the Guardian's transphobic centrism', *New Socialist* 21 October 2018: https://newsocialist.org.uk/on-the-guardians-transphobic-centrism/

Loren Goldner, 'Race and the enlightenment', *Race Traitor* August 1997: https://thecharnelhouse.org/2017/03/19/race-and-the-enlightenment/

Priyamvada Gopal, *Insurgent Empire: Anticolonial Resistance and British Dissent* (Verso, London: 2019).

Steven Hahn, 'The largest, most successful slave revolt in history?', *Slate* 13 October 2015: https://slate.com/human-interest/2015/10/why-historians-are-reluctant-to-call-the-american-civil-war-a-slave-rebellion.html

Michael Hobbes, 'Don't fall For The "cancel culture" scam', *The Huffington Post* 10 August 2020: https://www.huffingtonpost.co.uk/entry/cancel-culture-harpers-jk-rowling-scam_n_5f0887b4c5b67a80bc06c95e?ri18n=true

C. L. R. James, *The Black Jacobins* (Penguin Books, London: 2001).

Owen Jones, 'It's socialism for the rich and capitalism for the rest of us in Britain', *The Guardian* 29 August 2014: https://www.theguardian.com/books/2014/aug/29/socialism-for-the-rich

Owen Jones, 'Benefits street: A healthy media would stand up to the powerful and wealthy. Ours targets the poor and voiceless', *The Independent* 8 January 2014: https://www.independent.co.uk/voices/comment/benefits-street-healthy-media-would-stand-powerful-and-wealthy-ours-targets-poor-and-voiceless-9046773.html

Alexander Koch, Chris Brierly, Mark Maslin and Simon Lewis, 'European colonization of the Americas killed 10 percent of world population and caused global cooling', *The Conversation* 21 January 2019: https://www.pri.org/stories/2019-01-31/european-colonization-americas-killed-10-percent-world-population-and-caused

Ishay Landa, *The Apprentice's Sorcerer: Liberal Tradition and Fascism* (Haymarket Books, Chicago: 2012).

Ishay Landa, *Fascism and the Masses: The Revolt against the Last Humans* 1848–1945 (Routledge, New York and London: 2018).

Tony McKenna, 'Method in the madness: Three moments in Nietzsche's philosophy – An exposition', *Critique*, 41:3 (2013), 391–409. DOI: 10.1080/03017605.2013.851938.

Tony McKenna, 'Here be monsters: Trump's "white working class"', *Al Jazeera* 17 January 2018: https://www.aljazeera.com/opinions/2018/1/17/here-be-monsters-trumps-white-working-class

Tony McKenna, *Angels and Demons: A Radical Anthology of Political Lives* (Zero Books, Winchester UK: 2019).

Tony McKenna, 'The Jeremy Kyle factor', *Counterpunch* 28 May 2019: https://www.counterpunch.org/2019/05/28/the-jeremy-kyle-factor/

Tony McKenna, 'The broken mirror: Intersectionality and the loss of the universal', *Open Democracy* 12 August 2019: https://www.opendemocracy.net/en/can-europe-make-it/broken-mirror-intersectionality-and-loss-universal/

Annalisa Merelli, '"Lone wolf" vs "terrorist": the vocabulary of mass shootings', *Quartz* 2 October 2017: https://qz.com/1092042/las-vegas-shooting-terrorist-vs-lone-wolf/

Peter Oborne and David Hearst, 'The killing of Jeremy Corbyn', *Middle East Eye* 5 June 2020: https://www.middleeasteye.net/opinion/killing-jeremy-corbyn

David Olusoga, 'The toppling of Edward Colston's statue is not an attack on history. It is history', *The Guardian* 8 June 2020: https://www.theguardian.com/commentisfree/2020/jun/08/edward-colston-statue-history-slave-trader-bristol-protest

David Olusoga, Black and British: A forgotten history (Picador, London: 2021).

Leo Panitch, 'Historical record shows Jeremy Corbyn is a defender of Jews', *Toronto Star* 5 December 2019: https://www.thestar.com/opinion/contributors/2019/12/03/historical-record-shows-jeremy-corbyn-is-a-defender-of-jews.html

Walter Rodney, *How Europe Underdeveloped Africa* (Verso, London: 2018).

Elizabeth Schulte, 'The year of #MeToo', *International Socialist Review*, Issue 108, 1 March 2018: https://isreview.org/issue/108/year-metoo

Adam Serwer, 'The capitol Rioters weren't "low class"', *The Atlantic* 12 January 2021: https://www.theatlantic.com/ideas/archive/2021/01/thoroughly-respectable-rioters/617644/

Joan Smith, *Misogynies* (The Westbourne Press, London: 2013).

Katie Terezakis, 'The Revival of Romantic Anti-Capitalism on the Right: A Synopsis Informed by Agnes Heller's Philosophy', *Critical Horizons*, 21:4 (2020), 291–302. DOI: 10.1080/14409917.2020.1835038.

Leon Trotsky, *Fascism: What It Is, How to Fight It: A Compilation* (Martino Fine Books, Connecticut: 2011).

Jessica Valenti, 'Cancel culture' is how the powerful play victim', *Medium* 8 July 2020: https://gen.medium.com/cancel-culture-is-how-the-powerful-play-victim-e840fa55ad49

Zoe Williams, 'Feminazi: The go-to term for trolls out to silence women', *The Guardian* 15 September 2015: https://www.theguardian.com/world/2015/sep/15/feminazi-go-to-term-for-trolls-out-to-silence-women-charlotte-proudman